Paul Verlaine

Paul Verlaine

A Bilingual Selection of His Verse

Translated by
Samuel N. Rosenberg

Edited by
Nicolas Valazza

THE PENNSYLVANIA STATE UNIVERSITY PRESS | UNIVERSITY PARK, PENNSYLVANIA

Frontispiece: Félix Vallotton, *À Paul Verlaine*, 1891. Photo: Bibliothèque nationale de France.

Library of Congress Cataloging-in-Publication Data

Names: Verlaine, Paul, 1844–1896, author. | Rosenberg, Samuel N., translator. | Valazza, Nicolas, editor.
Title: Paul Verlaine : a bilingual selection of his verse / translated by Samuel N. Rosenberg ; edited by Nicolas Valazza.
Description: University Park, Pennsylvania : The Pennsylvania State University Press, [2019] | Includes bibliographical references and index. | Poems in French with English translations on facing pages.
Summary: "An anthology of works by nineteenth-century French poet Paul Verlaine, presenting both the French texts and new translations and setting the poems in the context of Verlaine's troubled life and his literary development"—Provided by publisher.
Identifiers: LCCN 2019028833 | ISBN 9780271084930 (cloth)
Subjects: LCSH: Verlaine, Paul, 1844–1896—Translations into English. | LCGFT: Poetry.
Classification: LCC PQ2463.A2 2019 | DDC 841/.8—dc23
LC record available at https://lccn.loc.gov/2019028833

Many variations appear in the published French texts of Verlaine's poetry. The French versions included in this volume have been selected and verified by Nicolas Valazza.

Translations and Translator's Note copyright 2019 by Samuel N. Rosenberg. Some translations were previously published in *Metamorphoses*. The Translator's Note began as a presentation to a Translation Seminar at the Indiana University Lilly Library.

Annotations and other editorial apparatus copyright 2019 by Nicolas Valazza.

Contents

Illustrations

Preface

Among the most important French poets of the last decades of the nineteenth century, Paul Verlaine (1844–1896) is considered, along with Charles Baudelaire, Arthur Rimbaud, and Stéphane Mallarmé, one of the founders of modernist poetics in France. Nowadays, Verlaine's poetry is widely read and studied in secondary schools and universities around the world. This has not always been the case: as a matter of fact, Verlaine did not achieve his canonical status until well into the twentieth century, for during his lifetime his poetry was read and praised only by a few peers, who, in his later years, came to consider him a master. What we now consider masterpieces of French poetry, such as Verlaine's *Poèmes saturniens* [Saturnine Poems] (1866), *Romances sans paroles* [Songs Without Words] (1874), and *Sagesse* [Wisdom] (1880), were published in no more than a few hundred copies that went unsold for many years, while the books of poets who are now almost forgotten, such as François Coppée and Eugène Manuel, were selling tens of thousands of copies in the same period.

The fact is that, contrary to Coppée's and Manuel's naturalist works, the poetry of Verlaine was hardly understood by his contemporary readers. Several early critics lamented that they could not puzzle out what the poet was trying to convey in his verse. Jules Lemaître, for example, maintained that "there is nothing to understand" in Verlaine's poetry, and that his verse is made of "series of words such as one forms in dreams [. . .]. When, by chance, one still remembers them on waking, nothing . . . , the idea faded away."[1] Lemaître had a point, though, when he observed the "vagueness" of this verse, composed mainly of "impressionist notations." Verlaine had himself enjoined the poet, in his "Art poétique" [Art of Poetry] (1874), to "choose all words with some disregard; / No better choice than a somewhat blurred song / That treats clear and not-clear as but one." In *Les Poètes maudits* [The

Accursed Poets] (1884), Verlaine referred to himself with anagrammatic self-indulgence as "Pauvre Lelian" [Poor Lelian], and grouped himself with other poets considered by critics at the time to be "les incompris" [the misunderstood]: Arthur Rimbaud, Stéphane Mallarmé, and a few others.[2] The kind of poetry that was then deemed almost unreadable and, indeed, a symptom of literary *decadence* was in fact a remarkable source of poetic renewal, based on the ambiguity of words, the musicality of phrases, the indistinctness of poetic images, the indefiniteness of sentiments, and the opacity of symbols, which would culminate in the Symbolist movement in the 1890s.

Why translate the poetry of Verlaine in the twenty-first century? In 1999 two significant translations of Verlaine's verse were published, by Norman R. Shapiro and Martin Sorrell, in collections of 101 and 170 poems, respectively.[3] That in and of itself attests to the sustained interest in Verlaine for Anglophone readers. Twenty years later, the present edition is now the largest translated collection of Verlaine's œuvre in English, comprising 192 of his poems, many of which have never been translated before. In his Translator's Note that follows, Samuel N. Rosenberg discusses the formal considerations that guided him in selecting and translating these poems. In this introduction we will offer a few scholarly and thematic considerations that justify the endeavor of translating anew a wide and representative selection of Verlaine's poems.

Verlaine studies have, indeed, made great progress in the last two decades, particularly since the rediscovery in 2004 of the manuscript of *Cellulairement* [Cellularly], the collection of verse that the poet composed in prison, between 1873 and 1875, and that was never published during his lifetime. The reappearance of this collection some 130 years after its writing has thus prompted scholars to reinterpret several key poems in Verlaine's work, such as "Sur les eaux" [Upon the Waters] and "Art poétique" [Art of Poetry], that were previously extracted from their original context (see the notes on these poems). Because the selection of poems in the present volume is arranged in the chronological and thematic order of their composition rather than by their date of publication, often many years later, this edition makes a point of presenting Verlaine's work in the context of the various stages of his life, an approach not taken in other translations.

Many of the poems presented here have not appeared in previous translated editions, presumably because they were not deemed representative of Verlaine as a *decadent* or *symbolist* poet, that is, a poet detached from current historical and political events, who self-sufficiently cultivates his poetry according to the principle of *l'art pour l'art* [art for art's sake]. Thus, we include the long insurrectionary poem "Les Vaincus" [The Vanquished], which was written during Verlaine's socialist fervor at the end of the 1860s. It describes the revolutionary ideal of his youth, something he later renounced, along with his rejection of the very possibility of social poetry, except perhaps in one of the very last poems he wrote before he died: "Mort!" [Dead!].

It is notable that a substantial portion of Verlaine's poetic corpus contains erotic or even *pornographic* texts (in the etymological sense of writings on prostitution). This libertine component of the poetry of Verlaine has generally been relegated to the *curiosa* and the addenda to the poet's so-called "complete works," if not excluded altogether, as is the case in most anthologies. We see no reason *not* to include such a significant aspect of Verlaine's poetics in a translated edition highly representative of his works—all the more because the sexuality and gender roles that the poet displays in his licentious verses strongly challenge the heteronormativity that characterizes traditional lyric poetry. The selection of poems we include from the lesbian collection *Les Amies* [Girlfriends] and the gay collection *Hombres* [Men], translated here for the first time in a comprehensive anthology, are therefore likely to be of great interest not only to general readers and literary scholars, but also to students and scholars in the growing field of queer studies.

Lastly, this volume features a couple of collaborative poems from the *Album zutique* [Damn Album], a handwritten notebook containing satirical poems and caricatures composed by a group of transgressive poets in 1871–72 that appear in translation nowhere else: "La Mort des cochons" [The Death of Pigs], which Verlaine wrote with poet Léon Valade, is a scatological parody of Baudelaire's "La Mort des amants" [The Death of Lovers]; and the "Sonnet du trou du cul" [Sonnet on the Asshole], the only poem known to be cowritten by Verlaine and Rimbaud (his lover at the time), is a homoerotic parody of Albert Mérat's collection of sonnets *L'Idole* [The Idol].

Verlaine's poetic output was markedly autobiographical. We shall see in the poems that follow the profound impact that his personal experience had on his œuvre: his marriage to Mathilde Mauté de Fleurville, his subsequent affairs with Rimbaud and several other male and female lovers, his conversion to Catholicism, and the tumultuous political events of the time (more biographical details are provided in the chronology, the part introductions, and the notes). Poems represented in Part I, "The Parnassian Years," relate to the launch of Verlaine's literary career within the circle of young poets called "les Parnassiens," who were influenced by Leconte de Lisle's neoclassical and anti-romantic poetics, as well as Théophile Gautier's theory of *l'art pour l'art*. These young poets, led by Catulle Mendès and Louis-Xavier de Ricard, assembled around the collective volume *Le Parnasse contemporain* [Contemporary Parnassus] in 1866.[4] Verlaine's first personal collections are from this period: *Poèmes saturniens* [Saturnine Poems] (1866), *Les Amies* [Girlfriends] (1868), *Fêtes galantes* [Gallant Festivities] (1869), and *La Bonne Chanson* [The Good Song] (1870). However, the Franco-Prussian War from July 1870 to January 1871 and the Paris Commune from March to May 1871 led to a significant setback in Verlaine's career. Since the poet had taken the side of the insurrectionary *Communards* against the Versailles government, he was effectively banished from the Parnassian circle in the aftermath of the bloody repression of the Commune at the end of May. All established publishers, in the following ten years, refused to publish Verlaine's verse. The poet sought refuge then in underground literary circles, such as the Cercle des poètes zutiques [Circle of Damn Poets!], which produced the above-mentioned *Album zutique*.

Yet it was the meeting with Arthur Rimbaud, a sixteen-year-old poet, ten years his junior, on September 10, 1871, that came to have the greatest impact on Verlaine's life and works. Poems included in Part 2, "Under the Spell of Rimbaud," reflect this. The disruptive effects of that love relationship with Rimbaud on Verlaine's marriage and, more generally, on his existence have already been extensively recounted in numerous books (see the Selected Bibliography), as well as at least two films: *A Season in Hell* by Nelo Risi in 1971 and *Total Eclipse* by Agnieszka Holland in 1995, featuring David Thewlis as Verlaine and Leonardo DiCaprio as Rimbaud. But what is of interest here is the influence that this relationship had on Verlaine's poetry. The tumultuous encounter with Rimbaud is indeed at the source of some of the most beautiful poems by Verlaine, for example the "Ariettes oubliées" [Forgotten Ariettas], written in 1872 and included in the collection *Romances sans paroles* in 1874. These poems eminently convey the poet's ambivalent and elusive feelings, torn as he is between love for his neglected wife and passionate devotion to his young lover. But the persons involved in this triangular relationship are never mentioned in the poems; it is rather the feelings themselves that become the lyrical subjects of the verse, as in the third "arietta": "The pain in my heart / Is like rain in the city. / What languor is this / That envelops my heart?" We know that this relationship found its dramatic ending in one of the most famous "affairs" in literary history, with Verlaine firing two revolver shots at Rimbaud in Brussels on July 10, 1873, resulting in a hand injury for the victim and imprisonment for the shooter.

During the year and a half that Verlaine spent in prison in Belgium, first in Brussels and then in Mons, which came to an end on January 16, 1875, he did not stop writing poetry, and this is the basis for Part 3 of our edition, "From Prison to Conversion." In fact, several key poems by Verlaine, such as "Le ciel est, par-dessus le toit" ["The sky is, above the rooftop"] and "Art poétique" were written during that very detention. Certain of these poems were meant to be published in a collection of verse entirely composed in prison titled *Cellulairement*

[Cellularly]. However, released, Verlaine thought it preferable to erase all evidence of his imprisonment and to disseminate the poems through later volumes, namely *Sagesse* (1880), *Jadis et Naguère* [Long Ago and Yesterday] (1884), and *Parallèlement* [In Parallel] (1889). Besides, while in prison Verlaine converted to Catholicism, and the final sonnets of *Cellulairement* are accounts of this conversion, as are most poems of *Sagesse*—for example, the verse in *terza rima* "Ô mon Dieu, vous m'avez blessé d'amour" ["O my God, you have wounded me with love"]. From then on, Verlaine's publications would split into religious and secular—even licentious—collections, as he would explain in *Les Poètes maudits*: "[Pauvre Lelian's] work beginning in 1880 bifurcates into two very distinct paths [. . .]—books in which Catholicism unfolds its logic and its charms, its blandishments and its terrors; and other, purely worldly books: sensual with a distressing good humor and full of pride in life." Verlaine tries to justify this discrepancy in his poetic works with reasons that appear dubious from a Catholic standpoint: "I believe, and I sin in thought as by action; I believe, and I repent by thought while waiting for better things. Or rather, I believe, and am a good Christian in that moment; I believe, and am a bad Christian in the next. Memory, hope and the invocation of a sin delight me with or without remorse, sometimes under the same form and furnished with all the consequences of Sin; more often, both the flesh and blood are strong—natural and animal, like memories, hopes and invocations of the first excellent free-thinker."[5]

The rehabilitation of Verlaine in the literary field did not occur until the mid-1880s, when small literary magazines, such as *Paris moderne* and *La Nouvelle Rive Gauche*, started to publish and review his poems, most of which had been written ten years earlier, such as "Art poétique." Indeed, several poetry collections that Verlaine published later in his life, from *Jadis et Naguère* to the unfinished *Livre posthume* [The Posthumous Book], through *Parallèlement*, are heterogeneous collections of poems, often composed much earlier. These collections do not therefore appear as such in the present edition, lest they disturb its thematic and chronological coherence.

It is in the 1880s, tied in particular with the publication of the novel *À rebours* [Against the Grain] (1884) by Joris-Karl Huysmans, that the somewhat uncritical label of "decadent poet" was applied to Verlaine and has remained with him to the present day. The poet certainly did little to distance himself from this label, which helped to popularize his poetry among young poets and to promote him as the master of the Decadent movement led by Anatole Baju, the founder of the magazine *Le Décadent* in 1886. For example, in the poem "Langueur" [Languor] (1883), the poet proclaims: "Je suis l'Empire à la fin de la décadence" [I am the Empire as Decadence ends]. Verlaine was nevertheless unwilling to be associated with any literary school, as he told Jules Huret, who asked him, in 1891, why he had accepted the epithet "decadent": "They threw this epithet at us like an insult; I picked it up like a war-cry; but it meant nothing special, as far as I know. Is the twilight of a beautiful day not worth every dawn? Decadent, basically, did not mean anything at all."[6] We are not completely in disagreement with the poet on this last point.

Despite publishing several collections of verse in the late 1880s and early 1890s (presented here in Part 4, "The Last Years"), and though he achieved a certain critical—if not public—recognition, Verlaine lived in poverty and sickness during his last years, dividing his time between cafés and hospitals,[7] while he was working on *Amour* [Love] (1888), *Parallèlement* [In Parallel] (1889), *Dédicaces* [Dedications] (1890), *Femmes* [Women] (1890), *Bonheur* [Happiness] (1891), *Chansons pour Elle* [Songs for Her] (1891), *Liturgies intimes* [Intimate Liturgies] (1892), *Odes en son honneur* [Odes in Her Honor] (1893), *Élégies* (1893), *Dans les limbes* [In Limbo] (1894), *Épigrammes* (1894), *Chair* [Flesh] (1896), and *Invectives* (1896). Until his death on January 8, 1896, he took part in the animated bohemian lifestyle peculiar to *fin-de-siècle* Paris by frequenting cabarets like Le Chat noir in Montmartre, where he met a multitude of writers, artists, and composers, such as Claude Debussy.

Verlaine is a poet much favored by musicians. It is no doubt impossible to list all the composers and singers who have set his verse to music, from Debussy, who composed melodies for about twenty poems by Verlaine, starting with the "Ariettes oubliées" in 1888, to Jean-Marc Versini.[8] But of particular relevance, in addition to Debussy, are the names of Charles Bordes, Gabriel Fauré, Reynaldo Hahn, Ernest Chausson, and, among twentieth-century popular singers, Georges Brassens, Léo Ferré, and Charles Trenet.[9] One of Verlaine's most famous lines, from the opening of "Art poétique," announces the poet's intention to place musicality at the very heart of his work: "De la musique avant toute chose" [Music before all else]. Many titles of his early poems and collections are directly borrowed from music: "En sourdine" [Muted], *La Bonne Chanson*, "Ariettes oubliées," *Romances sans paroles*—this latter paradoxical title referring to Felix Mendelssohn's *Lieder ohne Worte* [Songs Without Words], which, contrary to Verlaine's, do not contain lyrics and are therefore not sung. Moreover, the *vers impairs* (lines with an odd number of syllables), which are characteristic of popular songs, as well as the striking rhythms that distinguish most of Verlaine's poems, make them particularly suitable to musical settings—to such an extent that many critics have claimed that Verlaine's verse tends to dissolve its meaning in the abstraction of music, although this is inaccurate in many ways.[10] The assimilation of poetry to music is certainly a dream that haunted many poets in addition to Verlaine at the end of the nineteenth century, such as René Ghil with his "verbal instrumentation," or the Mallarmé of "Music and Letters"; but this dream has often led commentators to take a critical shortcut by viewing as identification what is merely analogy or emulation.

That said, the poetry of Verlaine is first and foremost written: before being adapted to music, it is the offspring of the multisecular tradition of French metrical poetry, with its strict prosodic rules. Verlaine, along with Rimbaud, greatly contributed to the loosening of those rules. He is notable for writing unconventional lines of eleven or even thirteen syllables (see, for example, the "Sonnet boiteux" [Limping Sonnet]), thus breaking the 6+6 law of the alexandrine meter, or for not strictly adhering to the rules of rhyming (replacing, for example, rhymes with assonances, or using exclusively feminine rhymes in his lesbian sonnets). The choice made by Samuel N. Rosenberg not to impose a metrical and rhyming system on his translations, but rather to echo the phonetic and rhythmic aspects of Verlaine's verse in order to convey its euphonic qualities, is therefore particularly effective and consistent with the poet's own practice. Contrary to Rimbaud, however, Verlaine had never intended to rid his work of metrical structures and, as a matter of fact, he strongly rejected the very concept of *vers libre* [free verse] as it was practiced, beginning in the mid-1880s, by such poets as Marie Krysińska, Jules Laforgue, and Gustave Kahn. Concerning the *vers libre*, Verlaine states unequivocally in his interview with Jules Huret that "this is no longer verse, it is prose—sometimes it is just gibberish."[II]

Whether it is a question of vers-librism, musicalism, instrumentism, Symbolism, or decadentism, we maintain that it is preferable to refrain from categorizing the poetry of Verlaine according to *fin-de-siècle* literary trends. What ranks his verse among the highest expressions of modernist poetry is precisely the fact that it goes beyond the framework that one tries to apply to it. Verlaine is then the quintessential poet of ambiguous meanings, ambivalent feelings, as well as duplicity of character.

—NICOLAS VALAZZA

Translator's Note

De la musique avant toute chose
Music before everything else

That statement, perhaps the best-known single line in Verlaine, opens the poem "Art poétique" with its announcement of the poet's intention to place musicality, the very sound of lyric poetry, at the heart of his work. But the line is also a prescription for poets in general—and it must be taken as an injunction to anyone translating Verlaine's poetry. It has certainly been a guiding principle of this translation—though never to the exclusion of the poet's serious grappling with social, spiritual, even political realities. Verlaine was a poet of music; he was also a poet of meaningful reflection. Superb craft, for him, worked ever in support of feeling and thought.

The musicality of rhyme is an obvious feature of Verlaine's work, all of which is rhymed. My first formal consideration had therefore to be the use or non-use of rhyme in translation. To rhyme or not to rhyme was the basic, unavoidable question, a question particularly pressing in English, whose morphology does not lend itself to rhyming from French as would the grammatical forms of another Romance language.

While readily accepting Verlaine's injunction to give fundamental importance to musicality—and while recognizing that that feature is often taken to mean rhyme first of all—I realized that, generally speaking, the search for rhyme in English could too easily denature and distort the text. This is an especially consequential challenge in the case of stanzas comprising very short lines, which offer little opportunity for variation in word arrangements. An insistence on rhyme could produce lexical choices and syntactic configurations that would be regrettably divergent from the original text.

Such difference for the sake of rhyme could be excessive, marking an essential infidelity to the poet's work—and no translator wants to be guilty of disregarding the all-important principle of fidelity to the original text!

An important aspect of that fidelity, in my judgment, was the need to respect the autonomy of the individual lines—that is, the need to follow the sequence of the poet's ideas and images, instead of recasting the stanzas globally and thereby disrupting the movement of his thought.

In accordance with that respect, I had to accept the notion that, more often than not, it would be necessary to forgo rhyme in my English versions.

There are in fact, many prosodic techniques that may be used to express musicality other than uninterrupted rhyming.

I have occasionally used a pattern of partial rhyming, as in the scheme AXYA, where the first and last words rhyme with each other, while the middle lines show no rhyme with first and last or with each other. See, for example, the poem "Seascape" in *Poèmes saturniens* (Part I, p. 19).

While rhyme achieves its euphony through the recurrence of the final vowel of a word and the consonant that follows, *assonance* achieves a similar end through repetition of the final vowel alone, as in the poem "Green" (Part 2, p. 115), which makes use of both rhyme and assonance with no distinction between the two, as formulated in the scheme AXYA.

Note that "rhyme" and "assonance," as used so far, refer to recurrences taking place at the end of lines of verse. Both devices, however, may occur within lines, or even across subsequent lines, and, in fact, such *internal rhymes* and *internal assonances* contribute mightily to the musicality of Verlaine's poetry. I have made abundant use of such internal echoes in my translations. In English as in French, they constitute a significant part of the complex homophony characteristic of this work.

No less relevant to musicality, even though less visible, are *oblique echoes*. In the poem "Seascape" cited above, for example, "maddening" is an indirect phonetic reminder of "menacing," just as "fearsome" echoes "far," reinforcing the musicality of the passage.

For a translated text that exemplifies the use of several homophonic techniques, consider the sonnet "Anguish" (Part 1, p. 15). In this text, *alliteration*, the recurrence of word-initial consonants, is a particularly prominent factor of musicality, occurring with nasals and sibilants as well as other sounds, and interwoven with instances of *internal assonance* and the line-to-line fluidity of *enjambment*.

Let us look for a moment at the rather late sonnet "The catalogue arrives" (Part 4, p. 319). It is striking to see how the sheer musicality, the glowing lyricism, of the earlier works is now considerably reduced and, in particular, how the poet's earlier taste for occasional enjambment has now developed into a veritable fragmentation of the discourse—but still within the confines of traditional meter and rhyming. Notably, along with enjambment—which makes one line flow into the next—this composition introduces the opposite technique of breaking the line of verse, thereby ending the statement before the end of the line. The stanzas are thus linked by enjambment, but at the same time broken into abnormal segments.

As suggested by my final example, an important aspect of Verlaine's musicality is his treatment of *rhythm*.

The challenge for the translator is to find an equivalent in accordance with the normal English principle of accentual rhythm—that is, patterns of variation between stressed and unstressed units—as opposed to the French principle of meter defined by the number of syllables in the line of verse and by their subgrouping(s).

Where French counts syllables within a numerically fixed frame, English measures stresses, or beats, separated by one or more unstressed syllables. After some number of syllables, French, too, shows stress variation within a given line of verse, but such variation is not a defining feature of French prosody.

There are basically two ways in which French can escape the constraint of a syllable-based line: by *enjambment* and by its apparent opposite, which may be called *fragmentation* or, as in French, *discordance*.

Enjambment involves bringing a grammatically cohesive phrase to its conclusion only in the line following its opening. The phrase is said to contain a run-on line. Verlaine used this procedure frequently in his poetry, and it contributes greatly to the impression of a smooth musical flow from one line to the next. Much less frequently did he make use of *fragmentation*, which entails bringing a grammatically cohesive statement to a full stop *before* the end of a syllabically complete line. My final example, the sonnet "The catalogue arrives," shows a number of instances of this breaking up of the verse line.

My approach to rhythm in translation is clearly fluid, with the accentual patterns varying liberally from poem to poem and even line to line, without undue regard to metrical regularity. I do what, to my ear, the sense of a given line requires for the achievement of a pleasing acoustical flow. Uppermost in my mind is always Verlaine's injunction to give musicality its place of privilege.

Much could be said about *lexical* challenges facing a translator of Verlaine—that is, finding the right translation for a given word or phrase.

A very few examples will suffice for this Translator's Note:

1. The problem of rendering a technical term, such as "petit bleu" (see "The catalogue arrives"). A "télégramme" is no longer an ordinary tool of written communication, but it is still sufficiently understood to require no explanation; the same is true of the English cognate "telegram." The "petit bleu," on the other hand, a blue form used for many decades in Paris post offices for rapid delivery of small messages within the city, had no equivalent in English; nor did it remain a viable means of communication long enough to justify its use in French today; in English it is now best replaced by a contextually appropriate word meaning "message."

2. The challenge of a common French term often used in English, but with a different sense, such as "agonie/agony" (see "The sound of the horn . . . ," Part 2, p. 125). While the French term evokes

the actual pangs of death, the English word refers only to intense suffering.

3. A play on words, such as "maire et père de famille" (see "Monsieur Prudhomme," Part 1, p. 24). The challenge here is to find a device for conveying in a single utterance the distinct meanings of "maire" and its homophone "mère."[1]

Finally, a word about an issue that faces any translator assembling an anthology. What to include and what not? Nicolas Valazza, in his preface, treats this question—from the points of view of thematic interest and the development of Verlaine's poetic and life experience over time—as an important part of the rationale for a new translation. I add that certain material was excluded from the start on formal grounds. The corpus contains a small amount of dramatic material. I decided not to translate it. Likewise, I decided to exclude lengthy narrative, contemplative, or expository compositions that fell outside the realm of what we normally call lyric poetry. The focus of this volume of translations, I decided, would be predominantly poetry composed in traditional short forms, such as sonnets, ballades, sets of quatrains and the like. Such pieces do, after all, constitute the bulk of Verlaine's output and best exemplify his lyricism. I also opted for relatively few compositions heavily marked by allusions to particular persons and events that seemed of questionable interest or significance for modern anglophone readers.

Here, at the end, I must add a word of thanks to Nicolas Valazza for his masterful contribution to our shared volume—and more than a word of deepest devotion to my incomparable Jeff for his inspiring presence and arduous work throughout this endeavor.

—SAMUEL N. ROSENBERG

Chronology

1844 Birth of Paul-Marie Verlaine on March 30 in Metz, in the northeastern region of Lorraine. His father, Nicolas-Auguste, is a captain in the army and his mother, Élisa, comes from a prosperous farming family.

1851 The Verlaine family moves to Paris, in the right-bank neighborhood of Batignolles.

1858 While in high school, Verlaine sends to Victor Hugo, on December 12, "La Mort" [Death], his earliest known poem.

1862 He obtains his bachelor of letters degree and enrolls in law school, which he neglects in favor of spending time in cafés.

1863 He meets several poets of the postromantic generation: Théodore de Banville, Auguste de Villiers de L'Isle-Adam, François Coppée, José-Maria de Heredia, and Louis-Xavier de Ricard, who includes in his *Revue du progrès* the first poem published by Verlaine, under the pseudonym "Pablo": the sonnet "Monsieur Prudhomme" [Mister Prude].

1865 In November and December, Verlaine publishes a critical essay on Charles Baudelaire in the pre-Parnassian journal L'Art.

1866 On April 28, seven poems by Verlaine appear in the collective volume *Le Parnasse contemporain*. Verlaine's first personal book of verse, *Poèmes saturniens* [Saturnine Poems], is published in November.

1867 Verlaine meets Victor Hugo in Brussels in August. He attends the funeral of Baudelaire on September 2. In December, the collection of lesbian sonnets *Les Amies* [Girlfriends] is clandestinely published in Brussels.

1869 Publication of the volume *Fêtes galantes* [Gallant Festivities] in March. In the summer, Verlaine meets Mathilde Mauté de Fleurville, to whom he proposes marriage in October and sends the engagement poems of *La Bonne Chanson* [The Good Song].

1870 The volume *La Bonne Chanson* is printed, but not released until 1872, after the end of the Franco-Prussian War. Paul and Mathilde are married on August 11. September 4 marks the end of the Second Empire and the proclamation of the Third Republic.

1871 Proclamation, on March 18, of the Paris Commune, which Verlaine supports and which is suppressed in blood on May 28. On September 10, Verlaine welcomes Rimbaud to Paris. On October 30, Verlaine's only child, Georges, is born.

1872 On July 7 Verlaine abandons his wife and runs off to Belgium with Rimbaud; in September they go to London. Composition of *Romances sans paroles*.

1873 On July 10, in Brussels, Verlaine fires two revolver shots at Rimbaud, wounding his wrist. Verlaine is arrested and a day later incarcerated in Belgium, where he will remain imprisoned until January 1875.

1874 Publication of *Romances sans paroles* in March. In May, Verlaine is informed of the judgment of separation from his wife and child, which leads to his conversion to Catholicism.

1875 On January 16, soon after his release from prison, Verlaine sees Rimbaud, perhaps for the last time, in Stuttgart. He plans to publish *Cellulairement*. In March, Verlaine moves to England, where he teaches French in Lincolnshire until 1877.

1877 Verlaine is back in France in October. He is appointed professor in Rethel (Ardennes), where he meets Lucien Létinois, one of his students.

1879 He moves to England with Létinois.

1880 Back in France, Verlaine and Létinois buy a farm in Juniville (Ardennes) in March. In December, publication of *Sagesse* [Wisdom], dated 1881.

1882 After ten years, Verlaine is back in Paris, where a few of his poems are published in the journal *Paris moderne*, including "Art poétique" [Art of Poetry] in November.

1883 Death of Lucien Létinois on April 7.

1884 Publication of the critical anthology *Les Poètes maudits* [The Accursed Poets] in March and the collection of verse *Jadis et Naguère* [Long Ago and Yesterday] in November.

1885 In March, Verlaine is imprisoned for trying to kill his mother. He is released a month later.

1886 Death of Verlaine's mother on January 21. In July, the poet is hospitalized for leg ulcers. In November, publication of the autobiographical volume *Mémoires d'un veuf* [Memoirs of a Widower].

1887 Ill and wretched, Verlaine spends part of the year at the hospital. In September he meets Philomène Boudin, who will become his lover.

1888 Verlaine's poetry gains some critical recognition thanks to an essay by Jules Lemaître published in the *Revue bleue* on January 7. Publication of *Amour* [Love] in March and the second edition of *Les Poètes maudits*, including the autobiographical chapter "Pauvre Lelian," in August.

1889 Publication of *Parallèlement* [In Parallel] in June. Verlaine is hospitalized again in July.

1890 The poet spends half of the year in the hospital. In December, publication of *Dédicaces* [Dedications] and the erotic collection *Femmes* [Women], dated 1891.

1891 Publication of the Catholic collection *Bonheur* [Happiness] in May, the autobiographical volume *Mes Hôpitaux* [My Hospitals] in November, and the love collection *Chansons pour Elle* [Songs for Her], partly inspired by Eugénie Krantz, who will become Verlaine's last lover.

1892 Publication of *Liturgies intimes* [Intimate Liturgies] in March. The manuscript of the erotic collection *Hombres* is completed but will not be published until 1904. In November, Verlaine gives a series of lectures in Holland.

1893 Series of lectures in Belgium from February to March. Publication of the collections *Élégies* [Elegies] and *Odes en son honneur* [Odes in Her Honor] in May, as well as of the autobiographical volume *Mes Prisons* [My Prisons] in June. Series of lectures in England (London, Oxford, and Manchester) from November to December.

1894 Publication of the collection *Dans les limbes* [In Limbo] in May. In August, Verlaine is elected "Prince of Poets" after the death of Leconte de Lisle the previous month. Publication of the collection *Épigrammes* [Epigrams] in December.

1895 Publication of the autobiographical volume *Confessions* in May. In September, Verlaine moves in with Eugénie Krantz in the rue Descartes.

1896 Verlaine dies of a pulmonary congestion on January 8. Publication of the collections *Chair* [Flesh] and *Invectives* [Invective] in February and in December, respectively.

The Parnassian Years

"La Mort" [Death], the first poem known to have been written by Verlaine, dates from 1858, when the poet was a fourteen-year-old high school student at the Lycée Bonaparte in Paris. No other poem can be traced to that earliest period. In 1863, enrolled in law school but spending most of his time in the cafés of the Latin Quarter, Verlaine met the poets Théodore de Banville, Villiers de L'Isle Adam, François Coppée, José Maria de Heredia, and Louis-Xavier de Ricard, who would be part of the first Parnassian circle, characterized by a rejection of romantic sentimentality and the return to neoclassical and formalist poetics. The poems composed by Verlaine in the 1860s, including those featured in the collective volume *Le Parnasse contemporain* and the personal collection *Poèmes saturniens* [Saturnine Poems], both published in 1866, are markedly inspired by the masters of Parnassus: Baudelaire, Gautier, Banville, and Leconte de Lisle. But in spite of the Parnassian and postromantic doctrine of *impassibility*, reasserted by Verlaine in the "Epilogue," the *Poèmes saturniens* already show a wide range of sentiments, often vague and unconventional, but generally dominated by melancholia—an array of sentiments that would come to distinguish the poet's mature works. This is also true of Verlaine's second volume of verse, *Les Amies* [Girlfriends], published clandestinely under the pseudonym Pablo de Herlagnez in 1868 and comprising six lesbian sonnets, as is true of his third collection of verse, *Fêtes galantes* [Gallant Festivities], published the following year. The latter title refers to the Rococo genre of painting notably practiced by Antoine Watteau in the eighteenth century, which presents courtship scenes in idealized and mythological landscapes, such as those in *The Embarkation for Cythera* (1717). Yet Verlaine's collection focuses rather on the melancholy that hides behind the comic masks, and thus on the underside of the *Fêtes galantes*. At the end of June 1869, Verlaine met Mathilde Mauté de Fleurville, who a few months later agreed to marry him. Out of their engagement came the poems of *La Bonne Chanson* [The Good Song], an anticipatory epithalamium consisting of twenty-one poems, all dedicated to Mathilde and completed in June 1870, two months before the marriage, on August 11.

First Poems

La Mort—À Victor Hugo

Tel qu'un moissonneur, dont l'aveugle faucille
Abat le frais bleuet, comme le dur chardon,
Tel qu'un plomb cruel qui, dans sa course, brille,
Siffle, et, fendant les airs, vous frappe sans pardon;

Telle l'affreuse mort sur un dragon se montre,
Passant comme un tonnerre au milieu des humains,
Renversant, foudroyant tout ce qu'elle rencontre
Et tenant une faulx dans ses livides mains.

Riche, vieux, jeune, pauvre, à son lugubre empire
Tout le monde obéit; dans le cœur des mortels
Le monstre plonge, hélas! ses ongles de vampire!
Il s'acharne aux enfants, tout comme aux criminels:

Aigle fier et serein, quand du haut de ton aire
Tu vois sur l'univers planer ce noir vautour,
Le mépris (n'est-ce pas, plutôt que la colère)
Magnanime génie, dans ton cœur, a son tour?

Mais, tout en dédaignant la mort et ses alarmes,
Hugo, tu t'apitoies sur les tristes vaincus;
Tu sais, quand il le faut, répandre quelques larmes,
Quelques larmes d'amour pour ceux qui ne sont plus.

.

First Poems

Death—To Victor Hugo

Just like a reaper, whose sightless sickle
Cuts down the cornflower along with the thistle,
Just like a cruel lead that in bright shining flight
Whistles through the air and strikes with no pardon—

Just so, frightful death shows itself on its dragon,
Flashing like lightning through a crowd of us humans,
Throwing over, crushing down whatever it meets
And wielding a scythe in its ice-blue hands.

Rich and old, young and poor, every soul is subjected
To its lugubrious command; deep into mortal hearts
The monster then sinks, alas, its vampirical nails,
Without pity for the child, just as there's none for the vile.

Eagle proud and serene, when from your aerie on high
You see that dark vulture gliding over the globe,
Does not scorn (rather than wrath, don't you think?)
Take its turn, magnanimous force, in your heart?

But, although disdainful of death and its many alarms,
Hugo, you take pity on those sadly vanquished;
You know, when it's called for, how to shed a few tears,
Tears of love for those who have come to their end.

À Don Quichotte

Ô don Quichotte, vieux paladin, grand Bohème
En vain la foule absurde et vile rit de toi;
Ta mort fut un martyre et ta vie un poème,
Et les moulins à vent avaient tort, ô mon roi!

Va toujours, va toujours, protégé par ta foi,
Monté sur ton coursier fantastique que j'aime.
Glaneur sublime, va!—les oublis de la loi
Sont plus nombreux, plus grands qu'au temps jadis lui-même.

Hurrah! nous te suivons, nous, les petits saints
Aux cheveux de folie et de verveine ceints.
Conduis-nous à l'assaut des hautes fantaisies,

Et bientôt, en dépit de toute trahison
Flottera l'étendard ailé des Poësies
Sur le crâne chenu de l'inepte raison!

Les Dieux

Vaincus, mais non domptés, exilés, mais vivants,
Et malgré les édits de l'Homme et ses menaces,
Ils n'ont point abdiqué, crispant leurs mains tenaces
Sur des tronçons de sceptre, et rôdent dans les vents.

Les nuages coureurs aux caprices mouvants
Sont la poudre des pieds de ces spectres rapaces
Et la foudre hurlant à travers les espaces
N'est qu'un écho lointain de leurs durs olifants.

Ils sonnent la révolte à leur tour contre l'Homme,
Leur vainqueur stupéfait encore et mal remis
D'un tel combat avec de pareils ennemis.

To Don Quixote

O Don Quixote, knight errant and old paladin,
In vain does the foolish, base crowd laugh at you;
You died as a martyr, and your life was a poem,
And the windmills were wrong, O my king!

Go ahead, keep advancing, protected by faith,
Astride your fantastic good steed that I love!
Gleaner sublime, go ahead! The law is forgetful
More often, more broadly, than in past time was the case.

Bravo! we're right here behind you, we little saints,
Tousled hair wreathed in madness and myrtle,
Lead us on to attack those fantastical demons,

And soon, in despite of whatever treason,
The high wingèd banner of Poesy shall flutter
Above the old head of incompetent reason.

The Gods

Beaten, but undefeated, exiled, but alive,
Wearied, but not silenced, by edicts of Man,
They have not abdicated, but stubbornly gripping
Old scepters, they prowl about in the wind.

The clouds running past in whimsical movement
Are the dust kicked up by these ravening specters,
And thunder howling through wide-open spaces
Is but an echo far off of their harsh hunting horns.

They're sounding in turn their revolt against Man,
Still dumfounded by success and barely recovered
From his fight against foes of such sorts.

Du Coran, des Védas et du Deutéronome,
De tous les dogmes, pleins de rage, tous les dieux
Sont sortis en campagne: Alerte! et veillons mieux.

La Pucelle

Quand déjà pétillait et flambait le bûcher,
Jeanne qu'assourdissait le chant brutal des prêtres,
Sous tous ces yeux dardés de toutes les fenêtres
Sentit frémir sa chair et son âme broncher.

Et semblable aux agneaux que revend au boucher
Le pâtour qui s'en va sifflant des airs champêtres,
Elle considéra les choses et les êtres
Et trouva son seigneur bien ingrat et léger.

"C'est mal, gentil Bâtard, doux Charles, bon Xaintrailles,
De laisser les Anglais faire ces funérailles
À qui leur fit lever le siège d'Orléans."

Et la Lorraine, au seul penser de cette injure,
Tandis que l'étreignait la mort des mécréants,
Las! pleura comme eût fait une autre créature.

L'Enterrement

Je ne sais rien de gai comme un enterrement!
Le fossoyeur qui chante et sa pioche qui brille,
La cloche, au loin, dans l'air, lançant sa svelte trille,
Le prêtre, en blanc surplis, qui prie allègrement,

L'enfant de chœur avec sa voix fraîche de fille,
Et quand, au fond du trou, bien chaud, douillettement,

The gods of Deuteronomy, the Koran and Vedas,
The gods of those dogmas, filled now with rage,
Have emerged to do battle: Watch out! Careful now!

Maid Joan

As the flames at the stake crackled and rose,
Joan, ears assailed by the priests' ruthless chant
And watched by all eyes peering from windows,
Felt her flesh shudder and her soul flinch.

She was a lamb now led to the slaughter,
Her shepherd gone home with a song on his lips;
She remembered events and thought about persons
And considered her lord ungrateful and fickle.

"It's not right, dear Bastard, Charles, and John Poton,
To let the English stage this defaming cremation
Of the maid of Orleans who made them abandon their siege."

And Lorraine, at the mere thought of that offense,
While embracing the death of foes of belief,
Wept, alas, as would any creature have wept.

The Burial

There's no fun like the fun of a funeral!
The gravedigger's humming a tune, his spade clean to go;
The bell tower sends its soft trills through the air;
The priest, in white surplice, blithely murmurs his prayers;

The choirboy sings in his fresh-voiced soprano;
And when, into the warm and welcoming hole

S'installe le cercueil, le mol éboulement
De la terre, édredon du défunt, heureux drille,

Tout cela me paraît charmant, en vérité!
Et puis, tout rondelets sous leur frac écourté,
Les croque-morts au nez rougi par les pourboires,

Et puis les beaux discours concis, mais pleins de sens,
Et puis, cœurs élargis, fronts où flotte une gloire,
    Les héritiers resplendissants!

The coffin is carefully lowered, soft clods of earth
Will pillow the jovial fellow who's passed—

That strikes me as all very charming, indeed!
And then, overly plump in coats sizes too tight,
The mortician's assistants weep themselves silly for tips.

Then come fine speeches oh, so earnest, but brief,
And then, with hearts full of pride and faces aglow,
        Behold the dutiful heirs!

From *Poèmes saturniens* [Saturnine Poems]

Melancholia I—Résignation

Tout enfant, j'allais rêvant Ko-Hinnor,
Somptuosité persane et papale,
Héliogabale et Sardanapale!

Mon désir créait sous des toits en or,
Parmi les parfums, au son des musiques,
Des harems sans fin, paradis physiques!

Aujourd'hui, plus calme et moins ardent,
Mais sachant la vie et qu'il faut qu'on plie,
J'ai dû refréner ma belle folie,
Sans me résigner par trop cependant.

Soit! le grandiose échappe à ma dent,
Mais, fi de l'aimable et fi de la lie!
Et je hais toujours la femme jolie,
La rime assonante et l'ami prudent.

Melancholia VI—Mon Rêve familier

Je fais souvent ce rêve étrange et pénétrant
D'une femme inconnue, et que j'aime, et qui m'aime
Et qui n'est, chaque fois, ni tout à fait la même
Ni tout à fait une autre, et m'aime et me comprend.

Car elle me comprend, et mon cœur, transparent
Pour elle seule, hélas! cesse d'être un problème

From *Poèmes saturniens* [Saturnine Poems]

Melancholia I—Resignation

As a child, I was dreaming of Koh-i-Noor,
The sumptuous splendors of Persia and pope,
Heliogabálus and Sardanapálus!

My desire created, under roofs of pure gold,
Amid the perfumes and lulled by soft music,
Numberless harems and paradisaical pleasures.

Today, more composed and less fervent,
Knowing something of life and the need to hold back,
I have had to restrain my extravagant dreams—
Though without ever yielding completely.

All right! I've let go of such grandiose longings.
Really, what do I care if things are lovely or ugly!
Pretty women I've detested I detest even now,
Just as I do limping rhyme and friends who are wimps.

Melancholia VI—My Familiar Dream

Often I have this strange and penetrating dream of a
Woman unknown, whom I love and who loves me;
She is different every time, never quite the same,
Never wholly changed; she loves and understands me.

She understands me, and my heart—which only she,
Alas, can see—ceases to present a problem; she alone

Pour elle seule, et les moiteurs de mon front blême,
Elle seule les sait rafraîchir, en pleurant.

Est-elle brune, blonde ou rousse?—Je l'ignore.
Son nom? Je me souviens qu'il est doux et sonore
Comme ceux des aimés que la Vie exila.

Son regard est pareil au regard des statues,
Et, pour sa voix, lointaine et calme, et grave, elle a
L'inflexion des voix chères qui se sont tues.

Melancholia VIII—L'Angoisse

Nature, rien de toi ne m'émeut, ni les champs
Nourriciers, ni l'écho vermeil des pastorales
Siciliennes, ni les pompes aurorales,
Ni la solennité dolente des couchants.

Je ris de l'Art, je ris de l'Homme aussi, des chants,
Des vers, des temples grecs et des tours en spirales
Qu'étirent dans le ciel vide des cathédrales,
Et je vois du même œil les bons et les méchants.

Je ne crois pas en Dieu, j'abjure et je renie
Toute pensée, et quant à la vieille ironie,
L'Amour, je voudrais bien qu'on ne m'en parlât plus.

Lasse de vivre, ayant peur de mourir, pareille
Au brick perdu jouet du flux et du reflux,
Mon âme pour d'affreux naufrages appareille.

Can see the beads of worry on my ashen forehead;
She alone can cool them—with her tears.

The color of her hair? I can't say if brown, blond, or red.
Her name? I recall it's sweet and gentle to the ear,
Like the names of dear persons exiled from this life.

Her gaze is like the gaze of a statue,
And her voice, far-off, calm and grave,
Echoes voices once loved, but now at rest.

Melancholia VIII—Anguish

Nature, nothing in you is moving to me,
Neither fruit-laden fields nor silvery echoes of
Sicilian pastoral scenes nor the splendors of dawn
Nor the somber reserve of the sun as it sets.

I laugh at Art, at Humanity too, at music no less,
At verse and Greek temples and the spiraling towers
That cathedrals stretch up to a heaven that's empty,
And my eye sees no gap between good men and bad.

I believe not in God; I renounce and reject
All reflection; and as for that ironical staple
Called Love, I'd prefer it be mentioned no more.

Tired of living but fearful of dying, much like
A lost boat tossed here and there on the waves,
My soul is on course for a frightening wreck.

Eaux-fortes II—Cauchemar

J'ai vu passer dans mon rêve
—Tel l'ouragan sur la grève,—
D'une main tenant un glaive
Et de l'autre un sablier,
    Ce cavalier

Des ballades d'Allemagne
Qu'à travers ville et campagne,
Et du fleuve à la montagne,
Et des forêts au vallon,
    Un étalon

Rouge-flamme et noir d'ébène,
Sans bride, ni mors, ni rêne,
Ni hop! ni cravache, entraîne
Parmi des râlements sourds
    Toujours! toujours!

Un grand feutre à longue plume
Ombrait son œil qui s'allume
Et s'éteint. Tel, dans la brume,
Éclate et meurt l'éclair bleu
    D'une arme à feu.

Comme l'aile d'une orfraie
Qu'un subit orage effraie,
Par l'air que la neige raie,
Son manteau se soulevant
    Claquait au vent,

Et montrait d'un air de gloire
Un torse d'ombre et d'ivoire,

Etchings II—Nightmare

I saw gallop past in a dream,
—Like a hurricane on shore—
Holding a sword in one hand
And an hourglass in the other,
    The horseman

Of those German ballads
Whom through countryside and town,
From riverside to mountainside,
From forests down to valley floor
    A stallion

Flame-red and black as ebony,
With no bridle, bit, nor rein,
No jump! no whip, still pulls along
With deep-throat muffled rattling
    Ever forward!

A great felt long-plumed hat
Covered one eye, shining now,
Then shut. In the mist, like that,
A blue flash bursts, then dies away:
    A firearm!

Like the wing of an erne
Suddenly frightened by a storm
Streaking through air filled with snow,
His cloak shot up 'round his neck
    And flapped about

And showed as if with pride
A chest of ivory and umber,

Tandis que dans la nuit noire
Luisaient en des cris stridents
 Trente-deux dents.

Eaux-fortes III—Marine

L'océan sonore
Palpite sous l'œil
De la lune en deuil
Et palpite encore,

Tandis qu'un éclair
Brutal et sinistre
Fend le ciel de bistre
D'un long zigzag clair,

Et que chaque lame
En bonds convulsifs
Le long des récifs
Va, vient, luit et clame,

Et qu'au firmament,
Où l'ouragan erre,
Rugit le tonnerre
Formidablement.

Paysages tristes I—Soleils couchants

Une aube affaiblie
Verse par les champs
La mélancolie
Des soleils couchants.
La mélancolie
Berce de doux chants

While in the black of night
There glowed 'mid strident cries
    Two-and-thirty teeth.

Etchings III—Seascape

The sonorous ocean
Throbs under the eye
Of the mourning moon
In unending motion,

While lightning bolts slash
Their menacing way
Through dark-colored skies
In a zigzag flash,

And every wave,
In maddening leaps,
Alongside the rocks
Recedes toward its grave,

And while far up high,
Where the storm-clouds swirl,
Thunder rolls and roars
With fearsome dark might.

Dreary Landscapes I—Setting Suns

A pallid dawn
Covers the fields
With the melancholy
Of setting suns.
Melancholy lulls
My heart with soft songs

Mon cœur qui s'oublie
Aux soleils couchants.

Et d'étranges rêves,
Comme des soleils
Couchants sur les grèves,
Fantômes vermeils,
Défilent sans trêve,
Défilent, pareils
À de grands soleils
Couchants sur les grèves.

Paysages tristes II—Crépuscule du soir mystique

Le Souvenir avec le Crépuscule
Rougeoie et tremble à l'ardent horizon
De l'Espérance en flamme qui recule
Et s'agrandit ainsi qu'une cloison
Mystérieuse où mainte floraison
—Dahlia, lys, tulipe et renoncule—
S'élance autour d'un treillis, et circule
Parmi la maladive exhalaison
De parfums lourds et chauds, dont le poison
—Dahlia, lys, tulipe et renoncule—
Noyant mes sens, mon âme et ma raison,
Mêle, dans une immense pâmoison
Le Souvenir avec le Crépuscule.

Paysages tristes III—Promenade sentimentale

Le couchant dardait ses rayons suprêmes
Et le vent berçait les nénuphars blêmes;
Les grands nénuphars, entre les roseaux
Tristement luisaient sur les calmes eaux.
Moi j'errais tout seul, promenant ma plaie

As it drifts off
With setting suns.
Strange dreams appear,
Like suns now setting
On the sands of the shore;
Red phantoms they are,
Steadily streaming,
Streaming just like
The suns I see setting
On the sands of the shore.

Dreary Landscapes II—Mystical Twilight

Memory, like the twilight sun,
Turns tremulous red in the burning sky
Of hope on fire; it backs away and then
Grows large, as on a widening mystical
Wall, where flowers abound and flourish
—Dahlia, lily, buttercup, and tulip—
And wrap around a trellis and move about
Amid the sickly exhalations
Of heavy scents that, noxious with decay
—Dahlia, lily, buttercup, and tulip—
Upsetting all my senses, soul, and reason,
Conjoin, in one all-embracing swoon,
Memory and the twilight sun.

Dreary Landscapes III—Sentimental Stroll

The setting sun cast its last rays
And breeze cradled the pale water-lilies,
Whose broad spread 'midst the reeds
Shimmered sadly on the still waters.
I, wand'ring alone, was walking my pain

Au long de l'étang, parmi la saulaie
Où la brume vague évoquait un grand
Fantôme laiteux se désespérant
Et pleurant avec la voix des sarcelles
Qui se rappelaient en battant des ailes
Parmi la saulaie où j'errais tout seul
Promenant ma plaie; et l'épais linceul
Des ténèbres vint noyer les suprêmes
Rayons du couchant dans ces ondes blêmes
Et les nénuphars, parmi les roseaux,
Les grands nénuphars sur les calmes eaux.

Paysages tristes V—Chanson d'automne

Les sanglots longs
Des violons
    De l'automne
Blessent mon cœur
D'une langueur
    Monotone.

Tout suffocant
Et blême, quand
    Sonne l'heure,
Je me souviens
Des jours anciens
    Et je pleure;

Et je m'en vais
Au vent mauvais
    Qui m'emporte
Deçà, delà,
Pareil à la
    Feuille morte.

Alongside the pond, surrounded by willows,
Where a thin mist brought to mind a great
Milk-white ghost in hapless lament,
Voicing the tears of the ducks in the pond,
Calling one to another with fluttering wings
'Midst the willows where, wand'ring alone,
I was walking my pain. Then the thick shroud
Of night descended to drown the last rays
Of sunlight going down over the pale ripplings
And water-lilies spread through the reeds,
The broad water-lilies shimmering still.

Dreary Landscapes V—Autumn Song

The long slow sobs
Of violins
    In autumn
Wound my heart
With the monotony
    Of languor.

Now smothering
And pale, when
    Strikes the hour,
I remember
Bygone times
    And I cry.

I drift away
On a troubling wind
    That bears me
Here and there,
As if I were
    A shriveled leaf.

Caprices V—Monsieur Prudhomme

Il est grave: il est maire et père de famille.
Son faux col engloutit son oreille. Ses yeux
Dans un rêve sans fin flottent insoucieux,
Et le printemps en fleurs sur ses pantoufles brille.

Que lui fait l'astre d'or, que lui fait la charmille
Où l'oiseau chante à l'ombre, et que lui font les cieux,
Et les prés verts et les gazons silencieux?
Monsieur Prudhomme songe à marier sa fille

Avec monsieur Machin, un jeune homme cossu.
Il est juste-milieu, botaniste et pansu.
Quant aux faiseurs de vers, ces vauriens, ces maroufles,

Ces fainéants barbus, mal peignés, il les a
Plus en horreur que son éternel coryza,
Et le printemps en fleurs brille sur ses pantoufles.

Initium

Les violons mêlaient leur rire au chant des flûtes
Et le bal tournoyait quand je la vis passer
Avec ses cheveux blonds jouant sur les volutes
De son oreille où mon Désir comme un baiser
S'élançait et voulait lui parler, sans oser.

Cependant elle allait, et la mazurque lente
La portait dans son rythme indolent comme un vers,
—Rime mélodieuse, image étincelante,—
Et son âme d'enfant rayonnait à travers
La sensuelle ampleur de ses yeux gris et verts.

Caprices V—Mister Prude

Grave as they come, mother-mayor and family man.
A stiff collar stands up to his ears. His eyes wander
About in an endless insouciant dream, and
The flowers of spring on his slippers are bright.

What to him is the golden star or the arbor
Whose bird sings at night? What to him are the skies
Or green fields and broad stretches of grass?
Mister Prudhomme's concern is to marry his daughter

To Mister Who-is-it, a young man of promise—
Just the right class, plant man and big-bellied.
As for those rimesters of jingles and ditties,

Those ill-kempt, unshaven do-nothings, he holds
Them in greater contempt than unending sniffles,
And the flowers of spring brighten his slippers.

Initium

The violins' laughter rippled through the song of the flutes
And the dance was whirling about, when I saw her pass by
With her blond tresses brushed into curls
Over ears where my Desire, as if with a kiss,
Reached out, wanting to speak—but not daring.

She, though, went on, and the mazurka slowed down
To bear her along in a rhythm as relaxed as in verse
—A melodious piece and a sparkling bright image—
And her soul, like a child's, shone through
The sensual embrace of her grey and green eyes.

Et depuis, ma Pensée—immobile—contemple
Sa Splendeur évoquée, en adoration,
Et dans son Souvenir, ainsi que dans un temple,
Mon Amour entre, plein de superstition.

Et je crois que voici venir la Passion.

Nevermore

Allons, mon pauvre cœur, allons, *mon vieux complice*,
Redresse et peins à neuf tous tes arcs triomphaux;
Brûle un encens ranci sur tes autels d'or faux;
Sème de fleurs les bords béants du précipice;
Allons, mon pauvre cœur, allons, *mon vieux complice*!

Pousse à Dieu ton cantique, ô chantre rajeuni;
Entonne, orgue enroué, des *Te Deum* splendides;
Vieillard prématuré, mets du fard sur tes rides;
Couvre-toi de tapis mordorés, mur jauni;
Pousse à Dieu ton cantique, ô chantre rajeuni.

Sonnez, grelots; sonnez, clochettes; sonnez, cloches!
Car mon rêve impossible a pris corps, et je l'ai
Entre mes bras pressé; le Bonheur, cet ailé
Voyageur qui de l'Homme évite les approches,
—Sonnez, grelots; sonnez, clochettes; sonnez, cloches!

Le Bonheur a marché côte à côte avec moi;
Mais la FATALITÉ ne connaît point de trêve:
Le ver est dans le fruit, le réveil dans le rêve,
Et le remords est dans l'amour: telle est la loi.
—Le Bonheur a marché côte à côte avec moi.

And my Mind, since that time, is fixedly awed
By her Splendor, adoring and still;
Into my Memory of her, as though into a temple,
My Love finds its way, with superstitious intent.

And I believe that what I behold is true Passion.

Nevermore

Let's go, my poor heart—let's go, my old partner!
Restore and repaint all your arches of triumph;
Burn rancid incense on false altars of gold;
Strew flowers around the mouth of the gulf;
Let's go, my poor heart—let's go, my old partner!

Lift your voice up to God, you, youth once again;
Intone, with that husky old organ, magnificent hymns;
Man too old for your time, hide all your wrinkles;
Cover yourself, yellowed wall, with new carpets;
Lift your voice up to God, you, youth once again!

Ring out, you bells! big bells and little, now ring!
Now is made real my impossible dream:
Happiness held truly tight in my arms: winged
Traveler known to avoid Man's approach.
Ring out, you bells! big bells and little, now ring!

Happiness walked with me, side by side;
Fatality, though, knows no truce;
The worm is in the fruit as night follows day
And regret comes with love. Is it not true?
Happiness walked with me, side by side.

Épilogue

I

Le soleil, moins ardent, luit clair au ciel moins dense.
Balancés par un vent automnal et berceur,
Les rosiers du jardin s'inclinent en cadence.
L'atmosphère ambiante a des baisers de sœur.

La Nature a quitté pour cette fois son trône
De splendeur, d'ironie et de sérénité:
Clémente, elle descend, par l'ampleur de l'air jaune,
Vers l'homme, son sujet pervers et révolté.

Du pan de son manteau, que l'abîme constelle,
Elle daigne essuyer les moiteurs de nos fronts,
Et son âme éternelle et sa forme immortelle
Donnent calme et vigueur à nos cœurs mous et prompts.

Le frais balancement des ramures chenues,
L'horizon élargi plein de vagues chansons,
Tout, jusqu'au vol joyeux des oiseaux et des nues,
Tout aujourd'hui console et délivre.—Pensons.

II

Donc, c'en est fait. Ce livre est clos. Chères Idées
Qui rayiez mon ciel gris de vos ailes de feu
Dont le vent caressait mes tempes obsédées,
Vous pouvez revoler devers l'Infini bleu!

Et toi, Vers qui tintait, et toi, Rime sonore,
Et vous, Rhythmes chanteurs, et vous, délicieux
Ressouvenirs, et vous, Rêves, et vous encore,
Images qu'évoquaient mes désirs anxieux,

Epilogue

I

The sun burns less bright in a clear sky less clouded.
Brushed by a wind autumnal and soothing,
The garden's rose bushes gently sway back and forth.
The whole atmosphere breathes innocent kisses.

Nature has stepped down for once from her throne
Of splendor, of all that's serene, that's ironic—
Steps tenderly through the expanse of bright sunlit air
To reach man, her subject perverse and rebellious.

With a corner of her abyssally star-studded cloak,
She deigns to wipe away the sweat of our brows,
And her everlasting soul and her deathless appearance
Bring vigor and calm to our hearts soft and ready.

The brisk rustling of now-leafless branches,
The broadened horizon full of nebulous songs,
Everything, birds happy in flight, clouds fleeting by,
Everything now consoles and now frees us. Let's think.

II

So, that's it! This book is now closed. Dear Ideas
That brightened my grey sky with your fiery wings
As the wind was caressing my preoccupied mind,
You can fly back now to the Infinite blue!

And you, humming Verses, and you, sonorous Rhyme,
And you, singing Rhythms, and you, welcome thoughts
Of old Recollections, and you, Dreams, and you too,
Images brought to mind by my anxious desires,

Il faut nous séparer. Jusqu'aux jours plus propices
Où nous réunira l'Art, notre maître, adieu,
Adieu, doux compagnons, adieu, charmants complices!
Vous pouvez revoler devers l'Infini bleu.

Aussi bien, nous avons fourni notre carrière
Et le jeune étalon de notre bon plaisir,
Tout affolé qu'il est de sa course première,
A besoin d'un peu d'ombre et de quelque loisir.

—Car toujours nous t'avons fixée, ô Poésie,
Notre astre unique et notre unique passion,
T'ayant seule pour guide et compagne choisie,
Mère, et nous méfiant de l'Inspiration.

III
Ah! l'Inspiration superbe et souveraine,
L'Égérie aux regards lumineux et profonds,
Le Genium commode et l'Erato soudaine,
L'Ange des vieux tableaux avec des ors au fond,

La Muse, dont la voix est puissante sans doute,
Puisqu'elle fait d'un coup dans les premiers cerveaux,
Comme ces pissenlits dont s'émaille la route,
Pousser tout un jardin de poëmes nouveaux,

La Colombe, le Saint-Esprit, le saint Délire,
Les Troubles opportuns, les Transports complaisants,
Gabriel et son luth, Apollon et sa lyre,
Ah! l'Inspiration, on l'invoque à seize ans!

Ce qu'il nous faut à nous, les Suprêmes Poëtes
Qui vénérons les Dieux et qui n'y croyons pas,

The time for parting has come. Until happier days, then,
Farewell! Farewell till we're brought back together by Art,
Our master. Farewell, good companions and winsome allies!
You can fly back now to the Infinite blue!

Besides, we've achieved the goal we had set,
But the young stallion that performed as we wanted
Was unnerved and excited by his very first race
And now needs cool shade and time for some rest.

—For we have always seen in you, Poetry,
Our lode star and our sole occupation,
The only leader we have and our consort of choice,
Mother, in fact, and a brake on Inspiration.

III
Ah, Inspiration arrogant and almighty,
Egeria whose insight is clear and profound,
Genius speaking with ease and Erato rising,
Angel of old gold-enclosed paintings,

Muse whose voice carries undoubted power,
Since she allows, with one note to a welcoming mind,
The quick growth, like wild grass on the road,
Of a whole living garden of poems that are new,

The Dove, Holy Spirit, and divine sacred Frenzy,
Timeless confusions and obliging new raptures,
Gabriel with his lute and Apollo with his lyre—
Ah, Inspiration, so right when you're sixteen years old!

What we need, we the Greatest of Poets,
Who worship the Gods without ever believing,

À nous dont nul rayon n'auréola les têtes,
Dont nulle Béatrix n'a dirigé les pas,

À nous qui ciselons les mots comme des coupes
Et qui faisons des vers émus très froidement,
À nous qu'on ne voit point les soirs aller par groupes
Harmonieux au bord des *lacs* et nous pâmant,

Ce qu'il nous faut, à nous, c'est, aux lueurs des lampes,
La science conquise et le sommeil dompté,
C'est le front dans les mains du vieux Faust des estampes,
C'est l'Obstination et c'est la Volonté!

C'est la Volonté sainte, absolue, éternelle,
Cramponnée au projet comme un noble condor
Aux flancs fumants de peur d'un buffle, et d'un coup d'aile
Emportant son trophée à travers les cieux d'or!

Ce qu'il nous faut à nous, c'est l'étude sans trêve,
C'est l'effort inouï, le combat nonpareil,
C'est la nuit, l'âpre nuit du travail, d'où se lève
Lentement, lentement, l'Œuvre, ainsi qu'un soleil!

Libre à nos Inspirés, cœurs qu'une œillade enflamme,
D'abandonner leur être aux vents comme un bouleau;
Pauvres gens! l'Art n'est pas d'éparpiller son âme:
Est-elle en marbre, ou non, la Vénus de Milo?

Nous donc, sculptons avec le ciseau des Pensées
Le bloc vierge du Beau, Paros immaculé,
Et faisons-en surgir sous nos mains empressées
Quelque pure statue au péplos étoilé,

We who have lived with no halo to crown our heads,
For whom no Beatrice has come to guide our steps,

We who chisel our words as if they were goblets
And coldly create emotion-filled verses,
We who won't spend our evenings in harmonious
Groups wrapt in the trap of lake banks,

What we need, really do, in the glimmer of lamps,
Is the conquest of knowledge and the taming of sleep.
It is Faust in old prints, hands pressed to his brow;
It is Obstinacy and the force of the Will!

It is holy Will, absolute and eternal,
Clinging tight to its project like a glorious condor
To the steaming remains of a terrified beast and with a sweep
Of its wing, flying off with its prize across golden skies!

What we need, really do, is unending study;
It is an unheard-of effort, an unparalleled fight;
It's the night, the harsh night of labor, whence slowly
Rises, ever so slowly! the Work, along with the sun!

They are free, the Inspired, hearts aroused by a glance,
To rustle at will in the wind like the leaves of a tree;
Poor fellows! Art doesn't lie in scattering bits of your soul:
Is she, yes or no, made of marble, the Venus de Milo?

We, then, sculpt with the chisel of Thought
The untouched block of the Beautiful, pure Paros,
And under our diligent hands there then can arise
A spotless new figure in a peplos covered with stars,

Afin qu'un jour, frappant de rayons gris et roses
Le chef-d'œuvre serein, comme un nouveau Memnon,
L'Aube-Postérité, fille des Temps moroses,
Fasse dans l'air futur retentir notre nom!

So that one day, bathed in grey and rose light,
The serene masterwork, our successor to Memnon,
Posterity's Dawn, daughter of grim and dark Times,
May make future air resound with our name!

From *Les Amies* [Girlfriends]

I—Sur le balcon

Toutes deux regardaient s'enfuir les hirondelles:
L'une pâle aux cheveux de jais, et l'autre blonde
Et rose, et leurs peignoirs légers de vieille blonde
Vaguement serpentaient, nuages, autour d'elles.

Et toutes deux, avec des langueurs d'asphodèles,
Tandis qu'au ciel montait la lune molle et ronde,
Savouraient à longs traits l'émotion profonde
Du soir, et le bonheur triste des cœurs fidèles.

Telles, leurs bras pressant, moites, leurs tailles souples,
Couple étrange qui prend pitié des autres couples,
Telles, sur le balcon, rêvaient les jeunes femmes.

Derrière elles, au fond du retrait riche et sombre,
Emphatique comme un trône de mélodrames
Et plein d'odeurs, le Lit, défait, s'ouvrait dans l'ombre.

II—Pensionnaires

L'une avait quinze ans, l'autre en avait seize;
Toutes deux dormaient dans la même chambre.
C'était par un soir très lourd de septembre:
Frêles, des yeux bleus, des rougeurs de fraise.

Chacune a quitté, pour se mettre à l'aise,
La fine chemise au frais parfum d'ambre.

From *Les Amies* [Girlfriends]

I—On the Balcony

The two women were watching as the swallows flew off;
One was pale with hair of jet black and the other was fair
With pinkish complexion, and their peignoirs of old lace
Lazily billowed, white and cloud-like, around them.

And both, with the languorous stirring of opening petals,
While in the sky the moon slowly rose soft and round,
Savored long draughts of the evening's deep feeling
And the sad sense of pleasure of all-trusting hearts.

Like that, with arms warmly pressing their willowy waists,
The unusual couple, young women with pity for more
Usual pairs, remained on their balcony, dreaming.

Behind them, in the plush darkness of their special retreat,
As if it were set with the grandness of a theatrical stage,
The perfumed, unmade bed opened into the shadows.

II—Schoolgirls

One was fifteen, the other sixteen;
The two of them shared the same room.
It was September, an evening sultry and warm—
Delicate girls, red-cheeked and eyes blue.

To feel more at ease, each had removed
Her sheer cotton chemise, fragrant with amber.

La plus jeune étend les bras, et se cambre,
Et sa sœur, les mains sur ses seins, la baise,

Puis tombe à genoux, puis devient farouche
Et tumultueuse et folle, et sa bouche
Plonge sous l'or blond, dans les ombres grises;

Et l'enfant, pendant ce temps-là, recense
Sur ses doigts mignons des valses promises,
Et, rose, sourit avec innocence.

VI—Sappho

Furieuse, les yeux caves et les seins roides,
Sappho, que la langueur de son désir irrite,
Comme une louve court le long des grèves froides,

Elle songe à Phaon, oublieuse du Rite,
Et, voyant à ce point ses larmes dédaignées,
Arrache ses cheveux immenses par poignées;

Puis elle évoque, en des remords sans accalmies,
Ces temps où rayonnait, pure, la jeune gloire
De ses amours chantés en vers que la mémoire
De l'âme va redire aux vierges endormies:

Et voilà qu'elle abat ses paupières blêmies
Et saute dans la mer où l'appelle la Moire,—
Tandis qu'au ciel éclate, incendiant l'eau noire,
La pâle Séléné qui venge les Amies.

The younger, arms out, arched her back,
As her sister, hands on breast, bent to kiss her,

Then fell to her knees and grew wild
With excitement, and mad, as her mouth
Dove past blond gold toward shadowy depths;

Meanwhile, the child was just counting
On delicate fingers all the dances to come,
And she smiled the innocent smile of a rose.

VI—Sappho

Furious, hollow-eyed and stiff-nippled,
Sappho, impelled by exhausting desire,
Runs like a wolf along frozen stretches of shore.

Dreaming of Phaon, casting Rite now aside,
And seeing her tears unavailing,
She tears out her hair in measureless handfuls.

Then she recalls, with no soothing regret,
Days when the pure youthful glory of love
Shone in verses she sang and that memory
Now in the soul will recite to virgins asleep.

Now she shuts livid-lidded eyes tight
And leaps, as Fate summons, into the sea;
Overhead there appears, torching the darkness,
Selene, blue-pale, avenger of Lovers.

From *Fêtes galantes* [Gallant Festivities]

Clair de lune

Votre âme est un paysage choisi
Que vont charmant masques et bergamasques
Jouant du luth et dansant et quasi
Tristes sous leurs déguisements fantasques.

Tout en chantant sur le mode mineur
L'amour vainqueur et la vie opportune,
Ils n'ont pas l'air de croire à leur bonheur
Et leur chanson se mêle au clair de lune,

Au calme clair de lune triste et beau,
Qui fait rêver les oiseaux dans les arbres
Et sangloter d'extase les jets d'eau,
Les grands jets d'eau sveltes parmi les marbres.

À la promenade

Le ciel si pâle et les arbres si grêles
Semblent sourire à nos costumes clairs
Qui vont flottant légers, avec des airs
De nonchalance et des mouvements d'ailes.

Et le vent doux ride l'humble bassin,
Et la lueur du soleil qu'atténue
L'ombre des bas tilleuls de l'avenue
Nous parvient bleue et mourante à dessein.

From *Fêtes galantes* [Gallant Festivities]

Moonlight

Your soul is a landscape of choice
Where masks and bergamasks go casting their spells,
Playing the lute and dancing and yet seeming
Sad in their fanciful garb and disguises.

As they go singing in their minor key
Of conquering love and life full of promise,
They haven't the look of believing their words,
And their song now blends with the light of the moon—

With the calm moonlight, beautiful and sad,
That brings dreams to birds in the trees
And tears of release to the fountains,
The tall slender fountains 'mid figures of marble.

As We Stroll

The sky so pale and the trees so spare
Seem to smile at our bright attire,
Costumes floating lightly, with an air
Of nonchalance and winglike grace.

A soft breeze ripples across the humble pond,
And sun-glow, filtered through the shade
Of low-trimmed lindens lining the path,
Reaches us as blue and meant to die away.

Trompeurs exquis et coquettes charmantes,
Cœurs tendres, mais affranchis du serment,
Nous devisons délicieusement,
Et les amants lutinent les amantes,

De qui la main imperceptible sait
Parfois donner un soufflet, qu'on échange
Contre un baiser sur l'extrême phalange
Du petit doigt, et comme la chose est

Immensément excessive et farouche,
On est puni par un regard très sec,
Lequel contraste, au demeurant, avec
La moue assez clémente de la bouche.

Les Ingénus

Les hauts talons luttaient avec les longues jupes,
En sorte que, selon le terrain et le vent,
Parfois luisaient des bas de jambes, trop souvent
Interceptés!—et nous aimions ce jeu de dupes.

Parfois aussi le dard d'un insecte jaloux
Inquiétait le col des belles sous les branches,
Et c'étaient des éclairs soudains de nuques blanches,
Et ce régal comblait nos jeunes yeux de fous.

Le soir tombait, un soir équivoque d'automne:
Les belles, se pendant rêveuses à nos bras,
Dirent alors des mots si spécieux, tout bas,
Que notre âme, depuis ce temps, tremble et s'étonne.

Exquisite rakes and charming coquettes,
All tender hearts with no ties to an oath,
We prattle on with endless delight,
As would-be lovers clown around with their belles,

And when there comes a hidden hand
Administering a slap in quick response
To a kiss bestowed upon a little
Finger tip, and as the act is taken to be

Too terribly, boldly audacious,
It's punished by a sharp, reproving look,
A glance fast belied, though,
By a pout coyly saying all's well.

The Artless

High heels and long skirts were struggling together,
So that, depending on wind and terrain,
Ankles darted out on occasion, then too often
Dashed back!—and we adored that fools' game.

Sometimes as well, the sting of a jealous insect
Under the trees would loosen a feminine collar
And release sudden flashes of flesh at the neck,
Regaling the eyes of the young dolts that we were.

Evening would fall, an equivocal evening of autumn:
The ladies, hanging dreamily draped on our arms,
Then uttered words so suggestively whispered
That our souls ever since have quivered in wonder.

Les Coquillages

Chaque coquillage incrusté
Dans la grotte où nous nous aimâmes
A sa particularité.

L'un a la pourpre de nos âmes
Dérobée au sang de nos cœurs
Quand je brûle et que tu t'enflammes;

Cet autre affecte tes langueurs
Et tes pâleurs alors que, lasse,
Tu m'en veux de mes yeux moqueurs;

Celui-ci contrefait la grâce
De ton oreille, et celui-là
Ta nuque rose, courte et grasse;

Mais un, entre autres, me troubla.

Le Faune

Un vieux faune de terre cuite
Rit au centre des boulingrins,
Présageant sans doute une suite
Mauvaise à ces instants sereins

Qui m'ont conduit et t'ont conduite,
—Mélancoliques pèlerins,—
Jusqu'à cette heure dont la fuite
Tournoie au son des tambourins.

Seashells

Every incrusted shell
In the grotto of our love
Has a meaning of its own.

One shows the scarlet of our souls
Pulled from the blood in our hearts
When I burn and you turn to flame;

This other assumes your languorous look
And your pallor whenever fatigue
Makes you chafe at the jeers in my eyes.

Here is one that captures the grace
Of your ear, while the one over there
Shows the blush of your nape.

There is one, though, I found most confounding.

The Faun

An old faun of terra cotta
Sits laughing on the green,
Hinting perhaps at a sorrowful
End to these moments serene

That have led you as they have me,
Melancholy wayfarers both,
Up to this hour, whose passing
Resounds with the tambourins' beat.

Mandoline

Les donneurs de sérénades
Et les belles écouteuses
Échangent des propos fades
Sous les ramures chanteuses.

C'est Tircis et c'est Aminte,
Et c'est l'éternel Clitandre,
Et c'est Damis qui pour mainte
Cruelle fait maint vers tendre.

Leurs courtes vestes de soie,
Leurs longues robes à queue,
Leur élégance, leur joie
Et leurs molles ombres bleues

Tourbillonnent dans l'extase
D'une lune rose et grise,
Et la mandoline jase
Parmi les frissons de brise.

À Clymène

Mystiques barcarolles,
Romances sans paroles,
Chère, puisque tes yeux,
        Couleur des cieux,

Puisque ta voix, étrange
Vision qui dérange
Et trouble l'horizon
        De ma raison,

Mandolin

They who strum their serenades
And they who deign to listen
Exchange flat pleasantries
Under the thrumming leaves.

Tircis it is, and Aminta
And the inescapable Clitander
And it's Damis, who sings
Sweet songs to heartless maidens.

Their short silk vests,
Their long tailed robes,
Their elegance, their pleasure
And their soft blue silhouettes

Whirl and spin in ecstasy
Under a pale pink moon,
And the mandolin still
Murmurs in the evening chill.

To Clymene

Barcaroles barely heard,
Songs without words,
Love, since your eyes,
    The color of skies—

Since your voice, strange
Mirage disarranging
And clouding horizons,
    The lines of my mind—

Puisque l'arôme insigne
De ta pâleur de cygne,
Et puisque la candeur
    De ton odeur,

Ah! puisque tout ton être,
Musique qui pénètre,
Nimbes d'anges défunts,
    Tons et parfums,

A, sur d'almes cadences,
En ses correspondances
Induit mon cœur subtil,
    Ainsi soit-il!

En sourdine

Calmes dans le demi-jour
Que les branches hautes font,
Pénétrons bien notre amour
De ce silence profond.

Fondons nos âmes, nos cœurs
Et nos sens extasiés,
Parmi les vagues langueurs
Des pins et des arbousiers.

Ferme tes yeux à demi,
Croise tes bras sur ton sein,
Et de ton cœur endormi
Chasse à jamais tout dessein.

Laissons-nous persuader
Au souffle berceur et doux

Since the peerless aroma
Of your pallor like swans',
And since the innocent
    White of your scent—

Ah! since the whole of your being,
With music that moves one,
Haloes of angels long gone,
    Tones and sweet balm—

Has let alien rhythms,
In concurring accord,
Beguile my fine heart—
    Oh, let it be so!

Muted

Calm now in the shaded light
That the highest boughs create,
Let us imbue our love
With this deep, unstirring hush.

Let us blend our souls, our hearts,
Enraptured senses all,
With the languid whispers
Of evergreens and pines.

Keep your eyes almost closed;
Rest your arms on your breast;
And from your sleepy heart
Drive away calculation.

Let us quietly be lulled
By the gentle, soothing breath

Qui vient à tes pieds rider
Les ondes du gazon roux.

Et quand, solennel, le soir
Des chênes noirs tombera,
Voix de notre désespoir,
Le rossignol chantera.

Colloque sentimental

Dans le vieux parc solitaire et glacé,
Deux formes ont tout à l'heure passé.

Leurs yeux sont morts et leurs lèvres sont molles,
Et l'on entend à peine leurs paroles.

Dans le vieux parc solitaire et glacé,
Deux spectres ont évoqué le passé.

—Te souvient-il de notre extase ancienne?
—Pourquoi voulez-vous donc qu'il m'en souvienne?

—Ton cœur bat-il toujours à mon seul nom?
Toujours vois-tu mon âme en rêve?—Non.

—Ah! les beaux jours de bonheur indicible
Où nous joignions nos bouches!—C'est possible.

—Qu'il était bleu, le ciel, et grand, l'espoir!
—L'espoir a fui, vaincu, vers le ciel noir.

Tels ils marchaient dans les avoines folles,
Et la nuit seule entendit leurs paroles.

That softly blows past your legs
And ripples a path through the russet grass.

And when, in solemn steps,
Evening descends from the tall black oaks,
Then, giving voice to despair,
The nightingale will sing.

Lovers' Conversation

In the old park unattended and cold,
Two figures strolled by just a moment ago.

Their eyes are unsmiling, their lips barely moving,
It's hard to hear clearly the words that they're using.

In the old park unattended and cold,
Two specters were speaking of time long ago.

—Do you remember what rapture we felt?
—Should I remember those feelings long spent?

—Does your heart still leap at the sound of my name?
What of my soul in your dreams?—Not the same . . .

—Ah, those fine days of inexpressible bliss,
When our lips came together!—Lost in the mist . . .

—The sky was so blue, with great hope in my heart!
—Hope's beaten and gone, and the sky's very dark.

And so they walked through the fields of wild oats,
And only the night heard the words that they spoke.

Poems Contemporaneous with *Poèmes saturniens*, *Les Amies*, and *Fêtes galantes*

Circonspection

Donne ta main, retiens ton souffle, asseyons-nous
Sous cet arbre géant où vient mourir la brise
En soupirs inégaux sous la ramure grise
Que caresse le clair de lune blême et doux.

Immobiles, baissons nos yeux vers nos genoux.
Ne pensons pas, rêvons. Laissons faire à leur guise
Le bonheur qui s'enfuit et l'amour qui s'épuise,
Et nos cheveux frôlés par l'aile des hiboux.

Oublions d'espérer. Discrète et contenue,
Que l'âme de chacun de nous deux continue
Ce calme et cette mort sereine du soleil.

Restons silencieux parmi la paix nocturne:
Il n'est pas bon d'aller troubler dans son sommeil
La nature, ce dieu féroce et taciturne.

Allégorie I

Un très vieux temple antique s'écroulant
Sur le sommet indécis d'un mont jaune,
Ainsi qu'un roi déchu, pleurant son trône,
Se mire, pâle, au tain d'un fleuve lent.

Poems Contemporaneous with *Poèmes saturniens*, *Les Amies*, and *Fêtes galantes*

Circumspection

Give me your hand, hold your breath, let us sit down
Under this towering tree, where the breeze dies away
With irregular sighs through now-darkening branches
Embraced by the softness of moonlight's pale touch.

Let us remain unmoving and still, eyes looking down,
Not thinking, just dreaming. Let us not interfere
As happiness flees and love hastens away
And the wings of the owls brush past our hair.

Let us forget expectation. Subdued and reserved,
Let both our souls, yours and mine, hum an echo
Of the serene and calm death of the sun.

Let us resolve to be mute in this peace of the night:
It is not right, it is not wise, to trouble the sleep
Of nature's fierce, silent god and his might.

Allegory I

An old temple, ancient and crumbling
Sitting in a haze atop an ocherous height,
Like a downfallen king bewailing his throne,
Regards its reflection in the slow current below.

Grâce endormie et regard somnolent,
Une naïade âgée, auprès d'un aulne,
Avec un brin de saule agace un faune
Qui lui sourit, bucolique et galant.

Sujet naïf et fade qui m'attristes,
Dis, quel poète entre tous les artistes,
Quel ouvrier morose t'opéra,

Tapisserie usée et surannée,
Banale comme un décor d'opéra,
Factice, hélas! comme ma destinée?

Intérieur

À grands plis sombres une ample tapisserie
De haute lice, avec emphase descendrait
Le long des quatre murs immenses d'un retrait
Mystérieux où l'ombre au luxe se marie.

Les meubles vieux, d'étoffe éclatante flétrie,
Le lit entr'aperçu vague comme un regret,
Tout aurait l'attitude et l'âge du secret,
Et l'esprit se perdrait en quelque allégorie.

Ni livres, ni tableaux, ni fleurs, ni clavecins;
Seule, à travers les fonds obscurs, sur des coussins,
Une apparition bleue et blanche de femme

Tristement sourirait—inquiétant témoin—
Au lent écho d'un chant lointain d'épithalame,
Dans une obsession de musc et de benjoin.

Drowsily graceful and with somnolent eyes,
An elderly naiad, beside an alder at rest,
Teases a faun with the twig of a willow
And he smiles back with a willing reply.

Tell me, you artless and dull, dispiriting thing,
What poet, of all the artists we've known,
What sorrowful worker, thought of you to create,

Tapestry threadbare and outmoded,
Common and trite as a theatrical set,
Artificial, alas . . . is this not my own fate?

Interior

In great somber folds, the generous spread
Of a high-warp hanging seems to course boldly down
The four immense walls of a bay, a mysterious place
Where dark shadow meets wealth in an easy embrace.

Movables covered once in brightness now faded,
The merely glimpsed bed, suggesting regret—
All seem to bespeak some lost secret and age,
Allegorical spirit not of this, but an earlier, stage.

No books there, no pictures or flowers or music;
Alone, through the gloom, surrounded by pillows,
A woman's pale image takes shape in the dusk;

Sadly she smiles, a disquieting listener
To the faraway echo of a slow wedding hymn,
Rapt in a sinister mist of laurel and musk.

Allégorie II

Despotique, pesant, incolore, l'Été,
Comme un roi fainéant présidant un supplice,
S'étire par l'ardeur blanche du ciel complice
Et bâille. L'homme dort loin du travail quitté.

L'alouette au matin, lasse, n'a pas chanté,
Pas un nuage, pas un souffle, rien qui plisse
Ou ride cet azur implacablement lisse
Où le silence bout dans l'immobilité.

L'âpre engourdissement a gagné les cigales
Et sur leur lit étroit de pierres inégales
Les ruisseaux à moitié taris ne sautent plus.

Une rotation incessante de moires
Lumineuses étend ses flux et ses reflux . . .
Des guêpes, çà et là, volent, jaunes et noires.

Les Vaincus

I

La Vie est triomphante et l'Idéal est mort,
Et voilà que, criant sa joie au vent qui passe,
Le cheval enivré du vainqueur broie et mord
Nos frères, qui du moins tombèrent avec grâce.

Et nous que la déroute a fait survivre, hélas!
Les pieds meurtris, les yeux troublés, la tête lourde,
Saignants, veules, fangeux, déshonorés et las,
Nous allons, étouffant mal une plainte sourde,

Allegory II

Despotic and heavy, colorless Summer,
Like a slothful tyrant witnessing torture,
Stretches in the heat of a complaisant sky
And yawns. He slumbers now far from his labor.

The lark in the morning, too weary to sing . . .
Not a cloud, not a breath, not a thing to bestir
Or disturb the smooth, implacable blue
That lets stillness seethe, while nothing is moved.

Harsh torpor has silenced all the cicadas
And, in its bed lined with misshapen stones,
The stream, run half dry, gushes no more.

Incessant shimmering whirls send flashes
Of light across bounding and rebounding planes . . .
Wasps, here and there, fly in yellow and black.

The Vanquished

I

Life is triumphant and the Ideal is dead,
And there goes, neighing his joy to the passing wind,
The victor's drunk horse, crushing and nipping
Our brothers, who at least fell with grace.

And we, alas, who've survived that terrible rout,
With bruised feet, clouded eyes, bewildered and
Bleeding, feeble, muddied, dishonored and weary,
We move along, barely stifling a soundless lament—

Nous allons, au hasard du soir et du chemin,
Comme les meurtriers et comme les infâmes,
Veufs, orphelins, sans toit, ni fils, ni lendemain,
Aux lueurs des forêts familières en flamme!

Ah! puisque notre sort est bien complet, qu'enfin
L'espoir est aboli, la défaite certaine,
Et que l'effort le plus énorme serait vain,
Et puisque c'en est fait, même de notre haine,

Nous n'avons plus, à l'heure où tombera la nuit,
Abjurant tout risible espoir de funérailles,
Qu'à nous laisser mourir obscurément, sans bruit,
Comme il sied aux vaincus des suprêmes batailles.

II

Une faible lueur palpite à l'horizon
Et le vent glacial qui s'élève redresse
Les feuillages des bois et les fleurs du gazon;
C'est l'aube! tout renaît sous sa froide caresse.

De fauve l'Orient devient rose, et l'argent
Des astres va bleuir dans l'azur qui se dore;
Le coq chante, veilleur exact et diligent;
L'alouette a volé, stridente: c'est l'aurore!

Éclatant, le soleil surgit: c'est le matin!
Amis, c'est le matin splendide dont la joie
Heurte ainsi notre lourd sommeil, et le festin
Horrible des oiseaux et des bêtes de proie.

Ô prodige! en nos cœurs le frisson radieux
Met à travers l'éclat subit de nos cuirasses,

Move along, as the darkening road allows us,
As if we were killers or unspeakable brutes,
We, wifeless or orphaned, homeless or childless,
Move with no future through forests on fire!

No, since our fate is now known, since in the end
No hope is left and there's only certain defeat,
And the most arduous effort would be unavailing,
And since it's all said and done, even our hate,

There is nothing more we can do, as night falls,
Than forsake any laughable hope of funeral games
And let ourselves die in the dark nameless silence
So right for the vanquished in the greatest of battles.

II

Feeble light glimmers on the horizon
And a glacial wind rising stirs the leaves
In the branches and blooms of the field;
Break of day! and all is reborn in its frigid embrace.

Tawny hues in the East turn to rose, and silvery
Stars pale to blue in the goldening azure;
The cock crows, that exact and diligent watchman;
The lark's taken wing with a cry. This is dawn!

The sun bursts through the sky. This is morning!
Friends, it's the splendid morning of joy, joy that
Pulls us from sleep and proclaims the first feast
Of the terrible birds and the beasts that go preying.

O wonder! The shimmering thrill in our hearts
Throws the flashing outbreak of our armor,

Avec un violent désir de mourir mieux,
La colère et l'orgueil anciens des bonnes races.

Allons, debout! allons, allons! debout, debout!
Assez comme cela de hontes et de trêves!
Au combat, au combat! car notre sang qui bout
A besoin de fumer sur la pointe des glaives!

III

Les vaincus se sont dit dans la nuit de leurs geôles:
Ils nous ont enchaînés, mais nous vivons encor.
Tandis que les carcans font ployer nos épaules,
Dans nos veines le sang circule, bon trésor.

Dans nos têtes nos yeux rapides avec ordre
Veillent, fins espions, et derrière nos fronts
Notre cervelle pense, et s'il faut tordre ou mordre,
Nos mâchoires seront dures et nos bras prompts.

Légers, ils n'ont pas vu d'abord la faute immense
Qu'ils faisaient, et ces fous qui s'en repentiront
Nous ont jeté le lâche affront de la clémence.
Bon! la clémence nous vengera de l'affront.

Ils nous ont enchaînés! Mais les chaînes sont faites
Pour tomber sous la lime obscure et pour frapper
Les gardes qu'on désarme, et les vainqueurs en fêtes
Laissent aux évadés le temps de s'échapper.

Et de nouveau bataille! Et victoire peut-être,
Mais bataille terrible et triomphe inclément,
Et comme cette fois le Droit sera le maître,
Cette fois-là sera la dernière, vraiment!

With its violent desire for a worthy way to die,
Against the ancient arrogance and wrath of our betters.

Forward now, arise! Arise and move ahead!
We've had enough of disgrace and concessions!
It's time to fight, to fight! Our blood is at the boil
And needs to let off steam with swords pointed!

III
The vanquished said in the dark depths of their jails:
They've restrained us with chains, but still we're alive.
While shackles weigh us down at our shoulders,
The flow of good blood in our veins never stops.

The eyes in our heads, with alertness and order,
Watch like spies and take notes, and the brains
Back of our brows go on thinking; we're ready to twist
And ready to bite: our jaws are tight; our arms are strong.

Thoughtless, they first missed the great mistake
They were making, and the fools will regret it.
Clemency's the insult they threw us, the cowards!
Well, clemency will avenge their affront!

They put us into chains! But these chains are made
For secretly filing away and then striking the guards
We've disarmed! Victors will be so distracted by drink
They won't have time or the eyes to see us escape.

So back to the battle! Perhaps even to win,
But bloody, this fight, with no mercy in triumph!
And since this time what's Right will prevail,
This fight will be final, the last, unsurpassed!

IV

Car les morts, en dépit des vieux rêves mystiques,
Sont bien morts, quand le fer a bien fait son devoir
Et les temps ne sont plus des fantômes épiques
Chevauchant des chevaux spectres sous le ciel noir.

La jument de Roland et Roland sont des mythes
Dont le sens nous échappe et réclame un effort
Qui perdrait notre temps, et si vous vous promîtes
D'être épargnés par nous vous vous trompâtes fort.

Vous mourrez de nos mains, sachez-le, si la chance
Est pour nous. Vous mourrez, suppliants, de nos mains.
La justice le veut d'abord, puis la vengeance,
Puis le besoin pressant d'opportuns lendemains.

Et la terre, depuis longtemps aride et maigre,
Pendant longtemps boira joyeuse votre sang
Dont la lourde vapeur savoureusement aigre
Montera vers la nue et rougira son flanc,

Et les chiens et les loups et les oiseaux de proie
Feront vos membres nets et fouilleront vos troncs,
Et nous rirons, sans rien qui trouble notre joie,
Car les morts sont bien morts et nous vous l'apprendrons.

IV

The dead, you see, despite old mystical dreams,
Are truly dead, once the blade has done all its work,
And these are no more the days of epical ghosts
Riding specters of steeds under cover of night.

Roland's mare and Roland himself are old myths
Whose sense, to be clear, would require an effort,
A waste of our time. No. If you ever expected
We'd spare you, you were woefully wrong!

You may be sure you'll die at our hands, if luck
Is but with us. You will plead but shall die at our hands.
Justice is the first to demand it, then vengeance,
Then the powerful need for timely tomorrows.

And the earth, for so long arid and fruitless,
Shall come to be watered with the joy of your blood,
Whose heavy steam, deliciously bitter,
Will rise toward the skies and redden its passage.

And the dogs and the wolves and the birds of prey
Shall strip your limbs clean and scour your flesh,
While we, with no check on our pleasure, will laugh,
For the dead, they are dead, and you'll hear it from us.

From *La Bonne Chanson* [The Good Song]

IV

Puisque l'aube grandit, puisque voici l'aurore,
Puisque, après m'avoir fui longtemps, l'espoir veut bien
Revoler devers moi qui l'appelle et l'implore,
Puisque tout ce bonheur veut bien être le mien,

C'en est fait à présent des funestes pensées,
C'en est fait des mauvais rêves, ah! c'en est fait
Surtout de l'ironie et des lèvres pincées
Et des mots où l'esprit sans âme triomphait.

Arrière aussi les poings crispés et la colère
À propos des méchants et des sots rencontrés;
Arrière la rancune abominable! arrière
L'oubli qu'on cherche en des breuvages exécrés!

Car je veux, maintenant qu'un être de lumière
A dans ma nuit profonde émis cette clarté
D'une amour à la fois immortelle et première,
De par la grâce, le sourire et la bonté,

Je veux, guidé par vous, beaux yeux aux flammes douces,
Par toi conduit, ô main où tremblera ma main,
Marcher droit, que ce soit par des sentiers de mousses
Ou que rocs et cailloux encombrent le chemin;

Oui, je veux marcher droit et calme dans la Vie,
Vers le but où le sort dirigera mes pas,

From *La Bonne Chanson* [The Good Song]

IV

Now that dawn's breaking, now that daylight is here,
Now that, after long being gone, hope is inclined
To fly back toward me as I plead and implore,
Now that such joy is inclined to be mine,

There is no further question of direful thoughts,
There are no further nightmares—there's an end,
Above all, to ironic and pinch-lipped remarks
Whose high wit came stripped of all soul.

Gone as well are the fists clenched in anger
At the wicked and the fools you've encountered;
Gone, too, that terrible rancor! also gone is
Oblivion sought in abominable brews!

For I want, now that a Being of light
Has brought into my night truly radiant
Love as immortally bright as it was at the start,
Filled with goodness and grace and a smile—

I want, guided by you, eyes softly blazing,
Led by your hand holding my trembling hand,
To walk straight ahead, whether on grass
Or stumbling along on stone-covered paths;

Yes, I want to walk straight ahead in this Life,
Toward the goal that fate will dictate,

Sans violence, sans remords et sans envie:
Ce sera le devoir heureux aux gais combats.

Et comme, pour bercer les lenteurs de la route,
Je chanterai des airs ingénus, je me dis
Qu'elle m'écoutera sans déplaisir sans doute;
Et vraiment je ne veux pas d'autre Paradis.

V

Avant que tu ne t'en ailles,
Pâle étoile du matin,
    —Mille cailles
Chantent, chantent dans le thym.—

Tourne devers le poète,
Dont les yeux sont pleins d'amour,
    —L'alouette
Monte au ciel avec le jour.—

Tourne ton regard que noie
L'aurore dans son azur;
    —Quelle joie
Parmi les champs de blé mûr!—

Puis fais luire ma pensée
Là-bas,—bien loin, oh! bien loin!
    —La rosée
Gaîment brille sur le foin.—

Dans le doux rêve où s'agite
Ma mie endormie encore . . .
    —Vite, vite,
Car voici le soleil d'or.—

Free of violent force, of remorse, and of envy:
A felicitous duty with cheerful contention.

Then, to lull the slow laps of the journey,
I shall sing little innocent airs, telling myself
That she'll listen with no disapproval or doubt;
And truly I want no Heaven but this.

V

Before you fade from view,
Pale morning star,
　　—A thousand quail
Sing forth in field and glade.—

Look first toward the poet,
His eyes athirst for love,
　　—The meadow-lark
Flies up as daylight breaks.—

Look far from morning light
And azure-drowning dawn,
　　—What great delight
In fields of ripening grain!—

Then let my thoughts shine bright
Far from here—oh, far!
　　—Dew-drops sparkle
Gaily through the hay.—

Sweet dream wherein my love
Is tossed while sleeping still . . .
　　—Quickly, now!
Look here—the golden sun!

VI

La lune blanche
Luit dans les bois;
De chaque branche
Part une voix
Sous la ramée . . .

Ô bien-aimée.

L'étang reflète,
Profond miroir,
La silhouette
Du saule noir
Où le vent pleure . . .

Rêvons, c'est l'heure.

Un vaste et tendre
Apaisement
Semble descendre
Du firmament
Que l'astre irise . . .

C'est l'heure exquise.

VII

Le paysage dans le cadre des portières
Court furieusement, et des plaines entières
Avec de l'eau, des blés, des arbres et du ciel
Vont s'engouffrant parmi le tourbillon cruel
Où tombent les poteaux minces du télégraphe
Dont les fils ont l'allure étrange d'un paraphe.

VI

The moon at night
Shines through the woods;
From every limb
A murmured sigh,
A clear white voice . . .

O love, my joy.

The pool reflects,
In soundless depth,
The silhouette
Of shadowed willows
Bewept by wind . . .

Let's dream: begin.

A vast and tender
Silent calm
Glows iridescent
In its descent
From heaven's stars . . .

Begin, still charm.

VII

The landscape revealed from the train carriage windows
Dashes furiously by, and whole stretches
Of lakes, fields of grain, trees, and sky overhead
Go plunging ahead in a whirlwind of harshness
Where the wires of tall, slender telegraph poles
Strangely look like signatures strung with a flourish.

Une odeur de charbon qui brûle et d'eau qui bout,
Tout le bruit que feraient mille chaînes au bout
Desquelles hurleraient mille géants qu'on fouette;
Et tout à coup des cris prolongés de chouette.

—Que me fait tout cela, puisque j'ai dans les yeux
La blanche vision qui fait mon cœur joyeux,
Puisque la douce voix pour moi murmure encore,
Puisque le Nom si beau, si noble et si sonore
Se mêle, pur pivot de tout ce tournoiement
Au rythme du wagon brutal, suavement?

VIII

Une Sainte en son auréole,
Une Châtelaine en sa tour,
Tout ce que contient la parole
Humaine de grâce et d'amour;

La note d'or que fait entendre
Un cor dans le lointain des bois,
Mariée à la fierté tendre
Des nobles Dames d'autrefois;

Avec cela le charme insigne
D'un frais sourire triomphant
Eclos dans des candeurs de cygne
Et des rougeurs de femme-enfant;

Des aspects nacrés, blancs et roses,
Un doux accord patricien:
Je vois, j'entends toutes ces choses
Dans son nom Carlovingien.

An odor of burning coal and of water that's boiling,
All the noise a thousand chains would make, while
Hauling along a thousand howling whipped giants;
Then, all of a sudden, screeching like that of an owl . . .

But what's all that to me, since my eyes let me see
The splendid white vision that brings joy to my heart,
Since that soft voice still murmurs for me,
Since that beautiful Name, so resounding and noble,
Blends, a pure pivot of all this wheeling ahead,
With the train's heartless rhythm, so smoothly?

VIII

A Saint in her halo
A Chatelaine in her tower,
Everything human speech
Means by grace and by love—

The golden note that a horn
Sounds far off in the forest,
Wedded to the delicate pride
Of noble Ladies of old—

Along with the memorable charm
Of a bright, winning smile
Breaking through a field of swan white
And the blush of a wife-like child—

Ivory tones, both white and rose,
In a gentle, patrician accord:
I see and I hear all such things
In her Carolingian name.

XIII

Hier, on parlait de choses et d'autres,
Et mes yeux allaient recherchant les vôtres;

Et votre regard recherchait le mien
Tandis que courait toujours l'entretien.

Sous le sens banal des phrases pesées
Mon amour errait après vos pensées;

Et quand vous parliez, à dessein distrait,
Je prêtais l'oreille à votre secret:

Car la voix, ainsi que les yeux de Celle
Qui vous fait joyeux et triste, décèle,

Malgré tout effort morose et rieur,
Et met au plein jour l'être intérieur.

Or, hier je suis parti plein d'ivresse:
Est-ce un espoir vain que mon cœur caresse,

Un vain espoir, faux et doux compagnon?
Oh! non! n'est-ce pas? n'est-ce pas que non?

XIV

Le foyer, la lueur étroite de la lampe;
La rêverie avec le doigt contre la tempe
Et les yeux se perdant parmi les yeux aimés;
L'heure du thé fumant et des livres fermés;
La douceur de sentir la fin de la soirée;
La fatigue charmante et l'attente adorée

XIII

Yesterday as we spoke of one thing and another,
My eyes were in search of a meeting with yours;

And your glance never stopped seeking mine
Through the time we went on discoursing of things.

Just under the surface of meaningless chatter,
My love was casting about for your thoughts;

And as you were speaking, by design eyes averted,
I was trying to hear what you thought was a secret:

For the voice, like the eyes, of the One you see,
Who gives you joy and sadness as well, reveals

—Despite every effort whether sullen or cheerful—
And brings out into light the being within.

Yesterday, may I say? I came home all excited:
Was it a hope vainly lodged in my heart?

A vain hope, a falsely sweet friendly thought?
No! that can't be! . . . surely, can't be for nought!

XIV

Lamplight rings the hearth;
A pensive pose and quiet revery
Lets loving eyes engage belovèd eyes;
It's time for tea and rest from books,
Time to feel the cozy evening's end,
The weary charm of warm anticipation,

De l'ombre nuptiale et de la douce nuit,
Oh! tout cela, mon rêve attendri le poursuit
Sans relâche, à travers toutes remises vaines,
Impatient des mois, furieux des semaines!

XV

J'ai presque peur, en vérité,
Tant je sens ma vie enlacée
À la radieuse pensée
Qui m'a pris l'âme l'autre été,

Tant votre image, à jamais chère,
Habite en ce cœur tout à vous,
Mon cœur uniquement jaloux
De vous aimer et de vous plaire;

Et je tremble, pardonnez-moi
D'aussi franchement vous le dire,
À penser qu'un mot, un sourire
De vous est désormais ma loi,

Et qu'il vous suffirait d'un geste,
D'une parole ou d'un clin d'œil,
Pour mettre tout mon être en deuil
De son illusion céleste.

Mais plutôt je ne veux vous voir,
L'avenir dût-il m'être sombre
Et fécond en peines sans nombre,
Qu'à travers un immense espoir,

Plongé dans ce bonheur suprême
De me dire encore et toujours,

And the marital embrace of tender night.
Oh, all of that my gentle dream pursues
Without a pause, past vain postponements,
Raging against the weeks and months!

XV

I'm almost fearful, truth to tell,
So tightly bound is now my life
To the vibrant image
That seized my heart this summer last.

So fully does your visage live
Henceforth within my faithful heart,
This heart uniquely bent
On loving and on pleasing you;

I tremble—will you please forgive
This frank and forthright statement now?—
To see your smile, your word
Is nothing less than my command,

And understand your merest move
Or whispered frown might well suffice
    To throw a shroud
Around a heaven-sent illusion.

My wish is rather, though, to see you,
However dark the future may be
    And filled with fears,
Through an endless, vast expanse of hope,

Immersed in this, the highest bliss—
The knowledge now and evermore,

En dépit des mornes retours,
Que je vous aime, que je t'aime!

XVII

N'est-ce pas? en dépit des sots et des méchants
Qui ne manqueront pas d'envier notre joie,
Nous serons fiers parfois et toujours indulgents.

N'est-ce pas? nous irons, gais et lents, dans la voie
Modeste que nous montre en souriant l'Espoir,
Peu soucieux qu'on nous ignore ou qu'on nous voie.

Isolés dans l'amour ainsi qu'en un bois noir,
Nos deux cœurs, exhalant leur tendresse paisible,
Seront deux rossignols qui chantent dans le soir.

Quant au Monde, qu'il soit envers nous irascible
Ou doux, que nous feront ses gestes? Il peut bien,
S'il veut, nous caresser ou nous prendre pour cible.

Unis par le plus fort et le plus cher lien,
Et d'ailleurs, possédant l'armure adamantine,
Nous sourirons à tous et n'aurons peur de rien.

Sans nous préoccuper de ce que nous destine
Le Sort, nous marcherons pourtant du même pas,
Et la main dans la main, avec l'âme enfantine

De ceux qui s'aiment sans mélange, n'est-ce pas?

Despite whatever trials,
That you are my love, *et je t'aime!*

XVII

Isn't it true? despite all the fools and the spiteful
Who won't fail to envy our joy,
We'll be sometimes reserved and always indulgent.

Isn't it true? with cheer and with purpose we'll
Follow a modest path as directed by Hope,
Not caring if we're seen or we're not.

Alone in our love as if deep in a forest,
Our hearts breathe the soft calm that they feel—
Two nightingales they, singing airs in the dark.

As for the World, what's the difference to us
If it's testy or gentle? Let it do as it likes—
Hold us dear or take us for targets.

Conjoined by the strongest, most precious of ties,
And possessing, besides, a diamond-like shield,
We can smile to observers and have nothing to fear.

Undisturbed by whatever Fate has in store,
We'll move forward together step by step
Hand in hand, with the innocent soul

Of young lovers without any doubts, isn't it true?

XVIII

Nous sommes en des temps infâmes
Où le mariage des âmes
Doit sceller l'union des cœurs;
À cette heure d'affreux orages
Ce n'est pas trop de deux courages
Pour vivre sous de tels vainqueurs.

En face de ce que l'on ose
Il nous siérait, sur toute chose,
De nous dresser, couple ravi
Dans l'extase austère du juste,
En proclamant, d'un geste auguste
Notre amour fier, comme un défi.

Mais quel besoin de te le dire?
Toi la bonté, toi le sourire,
N'es-tu pas le conseil aussi,
Le bon conseil loyal et brave,
Enfant rieuse au penser grave,
À qui tout mon cœur dit: merci!

XX

J'allais par des chemins perfides,
Douloureusement incertain.
Vos chères mains furent mes guides.

Si pâle à l'horizon lointain
Luisait un faible espoir d'aurore;
Votre regard fut le matin.

Nul bruit, sinon son pas sonore,
N'encourageait le voyageur.

XVIII

We have come to unspeakable times,
When the marriage of souls
Must seal the union of hearts;
In this hour of frightening storms,
It takes the stout courage of two
To endure the rule of such victors.

Seeing what one dares sometimes to do,
It would above all behoove us
To rise as a couple enraptured
By the customs austere of the just
And proclaim, with a gesture august,
The love that is ours, proud and defiant.

But what need to say this to you—
You, goodness itself, you, all my cheer?
Are you not counsel as well,
Counsel that's good, loyal and brave,
O merry young lady sober and grave,
To whom my whole heart offers thanks?

XX

I was going along perfidious paths,
Unsure of my goal and in pain;
Your hands came along to show me the way.

So pale on the distant horizon
There glimmered a faint hope of dawn;
Your glance is what brought me the morning.

No sound beyond my sonorous steps
Could I hear to hearten my spirit;

Votre voix me dit: "Marche encore!"

Mon cœur craintif, mon sombre cœur
Pleurait, seul, sur la triste voie;
L'amour, délicieux vainqueur,

Nous a réunis dans la joie.

XXI

L'hiver a cessé: la lumière est tiède
Et danse, du sol au firmament clair.
Il faut que le cœur le plus triste cède
À l'immense joie éparse dans l'air.

Même ce Paris maussade et malade
Semble faire accueil aux jeunes soleils
Et comme pour une immense accolade
Tend les mille bras de ses toits vermeils.

J'ai depuis un an le printemps dans l'âme
Et le vert retour du doux floréal,
Ainsi qu'une flamme entoure une flamme,
Met de l'idéal sur mon idéal.

Le ciel bleu prolonge, exhausse et couronne
L'immuable azur où rit mon amour.
La saison est belle et ma part est bonne
Et tous mes espoirs ont enfin leur tour.

Que vienne l'été! que viennent encore
L'automne et l'hiver! Et chaque saison
Me sera charmante, ô Toi que décore
Cette fantaisie et cette raison!

Your voice called out: "Keep on ahead!"

My timid heart, my somber heart,
Was in tears and alone on its dismal road;
Love, that ravishing master,

Brought us together in joy!

XXI

Winter has passed; sunshine is warm
And dances from ground to bright sky.
Even the saddest of hearts has to yield
To the fullness of joy everywhere.

Even this Paris dreary and drab
Seems to greet all its new sun
With the vast, all-embracing acclaim
Of thousands of colorful rooftops.

For a year now I have felt in my soul
The bright green return and softness of spring;
Just as a flame becomes one with another,
Two ideals grow from the one I have known.

Blue sky now lengthens and raises and crowns
The immutable azure wherein my love smiles;
The season is good and my part in it true,
And all of my hopes can now be allowed.

Let summer now come! Let autumn return,
Like winter and all other seasons! Every one
Will enchant me, O You who gave birth
To my dreams and these wonder-filled words!

Under the Spell of Rimbaud

In September 1871, Verlaine received a letter from a sixteen-year-old budding poet, Arthur Rimbaud, accompanied by several poems, including "Les Effarés" [The bewildered ones] and "Les Premières Communions" [First communions]. Struck by the "extreme originality" and the "frightening beauty" of these poems, Verlaine urged this young provincial poet from the northern town of Charleville, in the Ardennes, to move to Paris: "Come, dear great soul, we call to you, we're waiting for you!" Upon his arrival in Paris on September 10, Rimbaud joined Verlaine in his parents-in-law's house and, in no time, the poet's life was turned upside down: Verlaine and Rimbaud began an alcohol-fueled, tumultuous romance that disrupted the elder poet's marriage and caused a scandal in Parisian literary circles. In July 1872 Verlaine, forsaking his wife and eight-month-old son, fled with Rimbaud to Belgium, later to London. This dramatic turn in the poet's life had a profound effect on his work: Verlaine came to abandon the conventional sentimentality that marked the nuptial poetry of *La Bonne Chanson* [The Good Song] in favor of a radical poetics deeply influenced by Rimbaud. This new poetic style is notably characterized by indeterminacy of meaning, as exemplified in the series of "Ariettes oubliées" [Forgotten Ariettas] in the collection *Romances sans paroles* [Songs Without Words], published in 1874, as well as by emotional ambivalence, often implying homoerotic themes, as in the inverted sonnet "Le Bon Disciple" [The Good Disciple], or even by obscenity, as shown in his contributions to the *Album zutique* (1871–72).

The liaison between the two poets, however, had a catastrophic outcome, with Verlaine firing a revolver at Rimbaud in Brussels on July 10, 1873. The two shots wounded his companion's wrist and led to Verlaine's imprisonment in Belgium until January 1875. In the end, the relationship between Verlaine and Rimbaud remains one of the most remarkable and fruitful events in French literary history, for it had a lasting impact not only on Verlaine's work, but also on French modernist poetry in general.

First Encounters

Le Bon Disciple

Je suis élu, je suis damné!
Un grand souffle inconnu m'entoure.
Ô terreur! *Parce, Domine!*

Quel Ange dur ainsi me bourre
Entre les épaules tandis
Que je m'envole aux Paradis?

Fièvre adorablement maligne,
Bon délire, benoît effroi,
Je suis martyr et je suis roi,
Faucon je plane et je meurs cygne!

Toi le Jaloux qui m'as fait signe,
[Or] me voici, voici tout moi!
Vers toi je rampe encore indigne!
—Monte sur mes reins, et trépigne!

MAI 72.

Vers pour être calomnié

Ce soir je m'étais penché sur ton sommeil.
Tout ton corps dormait chaste sur l'humble lit,
Et j'ai vu, comme un qui s'applique et qui lit,
Ah! j'ai vu que tout est vain sous le soleil!

First Encounters

The Good Disciple

I am blessed! I am damned!
I am caught in a whirlwind unknown!
Oh, terror! *Spare me, O Lord!*

What hard Angel fills me like this
Between my two cheeks
As Paradise beckons me come?

It's a fever of wicked excitement,
Kind frenzy and gentle new fright!
I'm a martyr! I'm a king!
I glide like a falcon and die like a swan!

O jealous You, who called me to come,
Well, here I am, here I am, all of me!
I crawl to your side, unworthy as ever!
—Straddle my back and prance as you like!

MAY 72.

Libelous Lines

This night, I'd bent over your figure at sleep.
Your body lay chastely in place on our bed,
And I saw, as a man intent on his reading,
Oh, I saw that all's vain here under the sun!

Qu'on vive, ô quelle délicate merveille,
Tant notre appareil est une fleur qui plie!
Ô pensée aboutissant à la folie!
Va, pauvre, dors! moi, l'effroi pour toi m'éveille.

Ah! misère de t'aimer, mon frêle amour
Qui vas respirant comme on expire un jour!
Ô regard fermé que la mort fera tel!

Ô bouche qui ris en songe sur ma bouche,
En attendant l'autre rire plus farouche!
Vite, éveille-toi. Dis, l'âme est immortelle?

Le Poète et la Muse

La Chambre, as-tu gardé leurs spectres ridicules,
Ô pleine de jour sale et de bruits d'araignées?
La Chambre, as-tu gardé leurs formes désignées
Par ces crasses au mur et par quelles virgules?

Ah fi! Pourtant, chambre en garni qui te recules
En ce sec jeu d'optique aux mines renfrognées
Du souvenir de trop de choses destinées,
Comme ils ont donc regret aux nuits, aux nuits d'Hercules!

Qu'on l'entende comme on voudra, ce n'est pas ça:
Vous ne comprenez rien aux choses, bonnes gens.
Je vous dis que ce n'est pas ce que l'on pensa.

Seule, ô chambre qui fuis en cônes affligeants,
Seule, tu sais! mais sans doute combien de nuits
De noce auront déviginé leurs nuits, depuis!

That we're alive is a delicate wonder,
So ready is our being to wilt like a flower!
Oh, such a thought could lead us to madness!
Go on, love, sleep! Fear for you keeps me sleepless.

Oh, the woe of this love, my frail love!
Your breath seems the breath of a man at his end—
Oh, eyes closed as they'll be when you're dead . . .

O lips! you touch my lips with a smile while sleeping,
As if awaiting a later, more passionate laughter!
Quickly now, wake! Can the soul be immortal?

Poet and Muse

O Room, have you retained their ridiculous shades,
You, filled with dim light and the scratchings of spiders?
O Room, have you retained the impress of their shapes
On the filth of the wall, with its spots and its stains?

Oh, shame! Still, tawdry room, you back away,
In this sharp optical game with scowling black looks,
From recalling too many of those long-destined things,
How they miss—oh, they miss!—those Hercúlean nights!

Read it however you like, you'll never be right;
You understand not a whit about things, you good people.
I tell you it's not what came into your mind.

O solitary room, so distant now in your pathetic long shadow,
Oh, solitary, yes! but how many nights since that time
Their nuptial-night deflowerings have happened anew!

Explication

Je vous dis que ce n'est pas ce que l'on pensa.

(P. V.).

Le bonheur de saigner sur le cœur d'un ami,
Le besoin de pleurer bien longtemps sur son sein,
Le désir de parler à lui, bas à demi,
Le rêve de rester ensemble sans dessein!

Le malheur d'avoir tant de belles ennemies,
La satiété d'être une machine obscène,
L'horreur des cris impurs de toutes ces lamies,
Le cauchemar d'une incessante mise en scène!

Mourir pour sa Patrie ou pour son Dieu, gaîment,
Ou pour l'autre, en ses bras, en baisant chastement
La main qui ne trahit, la bouche qui ne ment!

Vivre loin des devoirs et des saintes tourmentes
Pour les seins clairs et pour les yeux luisants d'amantes,
Et pour le . . . reste! vers telles morts infamantes!

Explanation

I tell you it's not what you thought.

(P. V.).

The good fortune of bleeding on the heart of a friend,
The need to weep at length on his breast,
The desire to speak in low tones and half words,
The dream of being together without any stress!

The misfortune of having inimical girlfriends,
The exhaustion of being an obscene drilling machine,
The horror of all of those blood-suckers' cries,
The nightmare of facing scene after scene!

Cheerfully dying for Nation or God
Or the friend in one's arms, chastely kissing
The hand that is steady, the lips that speak true.

Living without the commitments and God-awful storms
Brought on by breasts and sultry bright eyes and, yes,
All the rest that precedes those base little deaths!

From *Album zutique*

La Mort des cochons

Nous reniflerons dans les pissotières
Nous gougnotterons loin des lavabos
Et nous lécherons les eaux ménagères
Au risque d'avoir des procès-verbaux.

Foulant à l'envi les pudeurs dernières
Nous pomperons les vieillards les moins beaux
Et fourrant nos nez au sein des derrières
Nous humerons la candeur des bobos.

Un soir plein de foutre et de cosmétique
Nous irons dans un lupanar antique
Tirer quelques coups longs et soucieux

Et la maquerelle entrouvrant les portes
Viendra balayer,—ange chassieux—
Les spermes éteints et les règles mortes.

L. V.—P. V.

From *Album zutique*

The Death of Pigs

We will do heavy sniffing around pissotieres;
We will do cunnilingus far from the stalls;
We will slurp greasy waste from the drains in the house,
Although it may mean a ticket or brawl.

Stamping out bit by bit vestigial shyness,
We'll suck off the least handsome old men,
And sticking our nose deep into fleshy derrieres,
We'll breathe in a smell that doesn't offend.

One evening of fucking and making-up fun,
We'll go to an ancient lupanar retreat;
We'll rap a few times with cautious disquiet

And the rheumy-eyed madam who opens the door
Will be back with her broom, once we're done,
To sweep up dry semen and menstrual blood.

L. V.—P. V.

Le Sonnet du trou du cul

Obscur et froncé comme un œillet violet
Il respire, humblement tapi parmi la mousse,
Humide encor d'amour qui suit la pente douce
Des fesses blanches jusqu'au bord de son ourlet.

Des filaments pareils à des larmes de lait
Ont pleuré, sous l'autan cruel qui les repousse,
À travers de petits caillots de marne rousse,
Pour s'en aller où la pente les appelait.

Ma bouche s'accoupla souvent à sa ventouse,
Mon âme, du coït matériel jalouse,
En fit son larmier fauve et son lit de sanglots.

C'est l'olive pâmée et la flûte câline,
C'est le tube où descend la céleste praline,
Chanaan féminin dans les moiteurs éclos!

P. V.—A. R.

Sonnet on the Asshole

Dark and puckered like a purple carnation,
It breathes, humbly nestled in a setting of moss,
Still damp with a love that gently descends
The cheeks of white that slope right to its rim.

Threads that look like strings of milky tears
Wept, under a blast of cruel opposing wind,
Past what tiny clots of earthy rust were there
To drip then toward the slope's ensuing stop.

Often my mouth sought yours for our delight;
My soul, though, eager for the coupled thing,
Tore through the teary duct and the bed of sobs.

It's the olive in a swoon, the flute in tight caress,
It's the tube that's lined with almond cream—
A woman's promised land with a passage all our own.

P. V.—A. R.

From *Romances sans paroles*
[Songs Without Words]

Ariettes oubliées I

> Le vent dans la plaine
> Suspend son haleine.
>
> (FAVART.)

C'est l'extase langoureuse,
C'est la fatigue amoureuse,
C'est tous les frissons des bois
Parmi l'étreinte des brises,
C'est, vers les ramures grises,
Le chœur des petites voix.

Ô le frêle et frais murmure!
Cela gazouille et susurre,
Cela ressemble au cri doux
Que l'herbe agitée expire . . .
Tu dirais, sous l'eau qui vire,
Le roulis sourd des cailloux.

Cette âme qui se lamente
En cette plainte dormante,
C'est la nôtre, n'est-ce pas?
La mienne, dis, et la tienne,
Dont s'exhale l'humble antienne
Par ce tiède soir, tout bas?

From *Romances sans paroles*
[Songs Without Words]

Forgotten Ariettas I

> The wind on the plain
> Finds its breath soon restrained.
> (FAVART.)

This is the languid ecstasy,
The weary aftermath of love,
The woods all aquiver
Within the winds' embrace;
There is, high in hidden branches,
A chorus of the faintest voices.

Oh, that fresh and feeble murmur!
It babbles and whispers;
You think of the soundless cry
That rippling grass exhales.
You might say, under eddying water,
The muted play of pebbles.

The soul that mourns
In this dormant lament
Is our own, is it not?
Mine, isn't it—yours no less well,
Exhaling a humble anthem
Through the soft evening warmth?

Ariettes oubliées III

> Il pleut doucement sur la ville.
>
> (ARTHUR RIMBAUD.)

Il pleure dans mon cœur
Comme il pleut sur la ville,
Quelle est cette langueur
Qui pénètre mon cœur?

Ô bruit doux de la pluie
Par terre et sur les toits!
Pour un cœur qui s'ennuie
Ô le chant de la pluie!

Il pleure sans raison
Dans ce cœur qui s'écœure.
Quoi! nulle trahison?
Ce deuil est sans raison.

C'est bien la pire peine
De ne savoir pourquoi,
Sans amour et sans haine,
Mon cœur a tant de peine!

Forgotten Ariettas III

> It rains gently on the city.
>
> (ARTHUR RIMBAUD.)

The pain in my heart
Is like rain in the city.
What languor is this
That envelops my heart?

O soft sound of the rain
On the ground and on rooftops!
For a heart that's dismayed
O the song of the rain!

This pain has no reason
In a heart that's heart-sick.
What's this? No betrayal?
My grief's without reason.

It's by far the worst pain
Not to understand why,
With no love or complaint,
My heart's filled with such pain!

Ariettes oubliées IV

De la douceur, de la douceur, de la douceur.

(INCONNU.)

Il faut, voyez-vous, nous pardonner les choses:
De cette façon nous serons bien heureuses
Et si notre vie a des instants moroses,
Du moins nous serons, n'est-ce pas? deux pleureuses.

Ô que nous mêlions, âmes sœurs que nous sommes,
À nos yeux confus la douceur puérile
De cheminer loin des femmes et des hommes,
Dans le frais oubli de ce qui nous exile!

Soyons deux enfants, soyons deux jeunes filles
Éprises de rien et de tout étonnées
Qui s'en vont pâlir sous les chastes charmilles
Sans même savoir qu'elles sont pardonnées.

Ariettes oubliées VII

Ô triste, triste était mon âme
À cause, à cause d'une femme.

Je ne me suis pas consolé
Bien que mon cœur s'en soit allé,

Bien que mon cœur, bien que mon âme
Eussent fui loin de cette femme.

Je ne me suis pas consolé,
Bien que mon cœur s'en soit allé.

Forgotten Ariettas IV

> Softness, softness, softness.
> (UNKNOWN.)

You see, there are things you need to forgive us:
In that way, we can be really quite happy,
And if life comes along with moments of sadness,
At least, you'll agree, we'll be weeping together.

Oh, I'd like us, sister-souls that we are, to blend
With our ill-defined ends the childish delight
Of wandering far from women and men
To forget for a while what keeps us exiled!

Let's be two children, let's be two girls
Enraptured by nothing and awed by all things
Who walk off to swoon under maidenly bowers
Without even knowing they're already forgiven.

Forgotten Ariettas VII

Oh, sad, oh, sad, my wounded soul—
The cause, the cause, a woman's hold.

No consolation do I find,
Although my heart left her behind.

Although my heart, although my soul
Had flown to freedom from her hold.

No consolation do I find,
Although my heart left her behind.

Et mon cœur, mon cœur trop sensible
Dit à mon âme: Est-il possible,

Est-il possible—le fût-il,—
Ce fier exil, ce triste exil?

Mon âme dit à mon cœur: Sais-je
Moi-même, que nous veut ce piège

D'être présents bien qu'exilés,
Encore que loin en allés?

Ariettes oubliées VIII

Dans l'interminable
Ennui de la plaine,
La neige incertaine
Luit comme du sable.

Le ciel est de cuivre
Sans lueur aucune,
On croirait voir vivre
Et mourir la lune.

Comme des nuées
Flottent gris les chênes
Des forêts prochaines
Parmi les buées.

Le ciel est de cuivre
Sans lueur aucune,
On croirait voir vivre
Et mourir la lune.

My heart, my heart so sensitive
Addressed my soul: "Would you permit,

Would you permit that I abide
Such harsh exile, such sad exile?"

My soul replied: "Oh, heart, can I
Myself say why I can't deny

The trap of being kept behind
Though exiled far in thought and mind?"

Forgotten Ariettas VIII

In the featureless
Wearisome plain,
The tremulous snow
Glistens like sand.

A sky as of copper,
Not glistening at all—
Is this the life,
Or the death, of the moon?

As if they were clouds,
Grey oaks float by
Through the mist
Of the neighboring woods.

A sky as of copper,
Not glistening at all—
Is this the life,
Or the death, of the moon?

Corneille poussive
Et vous, les loups maigres,
Par ces bises aigres
Quoi donc vous arrive?

Dans l'interminable
Ennui de la plaine,
La neige incertaine
Luit comme du sable.

Ariettes oubliées IX

> Le rossignol qui du haut d'une branche se regarde
> dedans, croit être tombé dans la rivière. Il est au
> sommet d'un chêne et toutefois il a peur de se noyer.
>
> (CYRANO DE BERGERAC.)

L'ombre des arbres dans la rivière embrumée
    Meurt comme de la fumée,
Tandis qu'en l'air, parmi les ramures réelles,
    Se plaignent les tourterelles.

Combien, ô voyageur, ce paysage blême
    Te mira blême toi-même,
Et que tristes pleuraient dans les hautes feuillées
    Tes espérances noyées!

MAI, JUIN 72.

Short-winded crow
And you, hungry wolf,
In this bitter north wind,
What happens to you?

In the featureless
Wearisome plain,
The tremulous snow
Glistens like sand.

Forgotten Ariettas IX

> Looking down at himself from high up on his branch,
> the nightingale thinks he has fallen into the stream. He
> is at the top of an oak, yet fears he will drown.
> (CYRANO DE BERGERAC.)

The shadow of trees in a misty river
     Disappears just like steam,
While above, among all the real branches,
     Turtle-doves mourn what they've lost.

O traveler, this scene of a colorless landscape
     Reflected your colorless self,
While sadly there wept in the uppermost reaches
     Drowning hopes and all else.

MAY, JUNE 72.

Bruxelles—Chevaux de bois

> Par saint Gille,
> Viens-nous-en,
> Mon agile
> Alezan.
> (V. HUGO.)

Tournez, tournez, bons chevaux de bois,
Tournez cent tours, tournez mille tours,
Tournez souvent et tournez toujours,
Tournez, tournez au son des hautbois.

Le gros soldat, la plus grosse bonne
Sont sur vos dos comme dans leur chambre;
Car, en ce jour, au bois de la Cambre
Les maîtres sont tous deux en personne.

Tournez, tournez, chevaux de leur cœur,
Tandis qu'autour de tous vos tournois
Clignote l'œil du filou sournois,
Tournez au son du piston vainqueur.

C'est ravissant comme ça vous soûle
D'aller ainsi dans ce cirque bête!
Bien dans le ventre et mal dans la tête,
Du mal en masse et du bien en foule.

Tournez, tournez sans qu'il soit besoin
D'user jamais de nuls éperons
Pour commander à vos galops ronds,
Tournez, tournez, sans espoir de foin.

Brussels—Merry-Go-Round

By Saint-Gille,
Let's dash away
With vigor and zeal,
My handsome bay.
(V. HUGO.)

Turn, keep on turning, you horses of wood,
Turn five hundred turns, turn over a thousand,
Turn again and again, keep turning forever,
Turn, go on turning to the sound of the woods.

The broad-chested soldier, the full-breasted maid
Are riding your backs as if home and in charge;
On this day, in the park called the Cambre,
They've turned into masters, with roles deftly played.

Turn, keep on turning, you horses hard-pressed,
While round all about your whirls and your turns
There incessantly blinks a sly roguish eye.
Turn around at the sound of a blaring cornet!

So exciting it makes you giddy and loud,
Spinning like this through silly good times!
Great for the belly and an ache for the head,
Massive measure of ache, great joys in a crowd!

Turn, keep on turning, though without any need
Ever to use the spurs it might take
To command all your gallops and rounds.
Turn, go on turning, with no hope of real feed!

Et dépêchez, chevaux de leur âme:
Déjà, voici que la nuit qui tombe
Va réunir pigeon et colombe,
Loin de la foire et loin de madame.

Tournez, tournez! le ciel en velours
D'astres en or se vêt lentement.
Voici partir l'amante et l'amant.
Tournez au son joyeux des tambours.

CHAMP DE FOIRE DE SAINT-GILLES, AOÛT 1872.

Birds in the night

Vous n'avez pas eu toute patience,
Cela se comprend par malheur, de reste;
Vous êtes si jeune! et l'insouciance,
C'est le lot amer de l'âge céleste!

Vous n'avez pas eu toute la douceur,
Cela par malheur d'ailleurs se comprend;
Vous êtes si jeune, ô ma froide sœur,
Que votre cœur doit être indifférent!

Aussi, me voici plein de pardons chastes,
Non, certes! joyeux, mais très calme, en somme,
Bien que je déplore, en ces mois néfastes,
D'être, grâce à vous, le moins heureux homme.

*

Et vous voyez bien que j'avais raison
Quand je vous disais, dans mes moments noirs,
Que vos yeux, foyers de mes vieux espoirs,
Ne couvraient plus rien que la trahison.

Quick now, you horses, your souls' true delight!
Here now already the night's coming on,
Erasing the difference between pigeon and dove,
Far from the fair and from mistress's sight.

Turn, keep on turning! while the velvety sky
Slowly dresses itself in stars made of gold.
This is the time when the lovers depart.
Turn now to thump those drumbeats on high!

SAINT-GILLES FAIRGROUND, AUGUST 1872.

Birds in the Night

You did not have unlimited patience,
Which is understandable but too bad even so;
You are so young! and carefree behavior
Is the bitter trait of that heavenly age!

You did not have unlimited sweetness,
Which is too bad even if fast understood;
You are so young, my cold little sister,
That your heart must be callous and dull.

Here am I though, chastely ready to pardon,
No, of course, not happy, but calm, after all,
Yet deploring, in these ill-omened months,
How, thanks to you, I'm the least lucky of men.

*

And you see that I was right
When I told you, in my dark moments,
That your eyes, once the heart of my hopes,
Now covered no more than betrayal.

Vous juriez alors que c'était mensonge
Et votre regard qui mentait lui-même
Flambait comme un feu mourant qu'on prolonge,
Et de votre voix vous disiez: "Je t'aime!"

Hélas! on se prend toujours au désir
Qu'on a d'être heureux malgré la saison . . .
Mais ce fut un jour plein d'amer plaisir,
Quand je m'aperçus que j'avais raison!

*

Aussi bien pourquoi me mettrais-je à geindre?
Vous ne m'aimez pas, l'affaire est conclue,
Et, ne voulant pas qu'on ose me plaindre,
Je souffrirai d'une âme résolue.

Oui, je souffrirai, car je vous aimais!
Mais je souffrirai comme un bon soldat
Blessé, qui s'en va dormir à jamais,
Plein d'amour pour quelque pays ingrat.

Vous qui fûtes ma Belle, ma Chérie,
Encor que de vous vienne ma souffrance,
N'êtes-vous donc pas toujours ma Patrie,
Aussi jeune, aussi folle que la France?

*

Or, je ne veux pas,—le puis-je d'abord?—
Plonger dans ceci mes regards mouillés.
Pourtant mon amour que vous croyez mort
A peut-être enfin les yeux dessillés.

Mon amour qui n'est que ressouvenance,
Quoique sous vos coups il saigne et qu'il pleure
Encore et qu'il doive, à ce que je pense,
Souffrir longtemps jusqu'à ce qu'il en meure,

You swore then it was surely a lie,
And your glance, lying itself,
Flamed like a fire of slow-dying embers,
And you let your voice say: "I love you!"

Alas! it's easy to be fooled by the wish
To be happy, whatever the facts . . .
But the day's pleasure turned bitter
When I realized I was right!

*

Why, then, should I set about groaning?
You love me not, and the case is now closed,
And, lest anyone risk a show of some pity,
I'll continue to suffer with soul-deep resolve.

Yes, continue to suffer, as a man once in love!
But I shall suffer just like a good soldier
Wounded and ready for rest, drifting toward death
Full of love for some ungrateful land.

You were my Darling, my Sweetheart,
Even as my suffering stemmed all from you;
Aren't you still my very own homeland,
Just as young, just as mad, as is France?

*

No, I do not want (is it even possible?)
To dive into this matter with my tear-clouded eyes.
However, my love, which you think of as dead,
Is perhaps, at long last, no longer blind.

My love, which is no more than remembrance,
Although under your blows it bleeds and it weeps
Even yet and is bound, from what I can see,
To suffer for long until suffering kills it,

Peut-être a raison de croire entrevoir
En vous un remords (qui n'est pas banal)
Et d'entendre dire, en son désespoir,
À votre mémoire: "Ah! fi! que c'est mal!"

*

Je vous vois encor. J'entrouvris la porte.
Vous étiez au lit comme fatiguée.
Mais, ô corps léger que l'amour emporte,
Vous bondîtes, nue, éplorée et gaie.

Ô quels baisers, quels enlacements fous!
J'en riais moi-même à travers mes pleurs.
Certes, ces instants seront, entre tous,
Mes plus tristes, mais aussi mes meilleurs.

Je ne veux revoir de votre sourire
Et de vos bons yeux en cette occurrence
Et de vous enfin, qu'il faudrait maudire,
Et du piège exquis, rien que l'apparence.

*

Je vous vois encore! En robe d'été
Blanche et jaune avec des fleurs de rideaux.
Mais vous n'aviez plus l'humide gaîté
Du plus délirant de tous nos tantôts.

La petite épouse et la fille aînée
Était reparue avec la toilette
Et c'était déjà notre destinée
Qui me regardait sous votre voilette.

Is perhaps not mistaken to sense there's a hint
In you of more than some passing remorse
And in its despair, to hear your memory say:
"Oh, damn! what I did was all wrong!"

*

I see you once more. I opened the door.
You were lying in bed as though tired.
But what a lithe body when summoned by love!
You bounded up bare, eyes gleaming, aglow!

Oh, what kisses, what crazy embraces!
I was laughing myself right through my tears.
Those moments, no doubt, will be most of all
My most sad, but also my best.

All I want now to see of your smile
And your bright eyes when that happened
And, lastly, of you (worth my curse)
And your exquisite snare is just their appearance.

*

I see you again! In a flowered dress
For the summer, white and yellow.
But you no longer convey the sultry excitement
Of our feverish earlier times.

The little wife and elder daughter
Came back to me then in that outfit,
And it was already our fate
That, under your veil, had me in sight.

Soyez pardonnée! Et c'est pour cela
Que je garde, hélas! avec quelque orgueil,
En mon souvenir qui vous cajola,
L'éclair de côté que coulait votre œil.

*

Par instants je suis le Pauvre Navire
Qui court démâté parmi la tempête,
Et ne voyant pas Notre-Dame luire
Pour l'engouffrement en priant s'apprête.

Par instants je meurs la mort du Pécheur
Qui se sait damné s'il n'est confessé,
Et, perdant l'espoir de nul confesseur,
Se tord dans l'Enfer qu'il a devancé.

Ô mais! par instants, j'ai l'extase rouge
Du premier chrétien, sous la dent rapace,
Qui rit à Jésus témoin, sans que bouge
Un poil de sa chair, un nerf de sa face!

BRUXELLES–LONDRES, SEPTEMBRE–OCTOBRE 1872

Green

Voici des fruits, des fleurs, des feuilles et des branches
Et puis voici mon cœur qui ne bat que pour vous.
Ne le déchirez pas avec vos deux mains blanches,
Et qu'à vos yeux si beaux l'humble présent soit doux.

J'arrive tout couvert encore de rosée
Que le vent du matin vient glacer à mon front.
Souffrez que ma fatigue, à vos pieds reposée,
Rêve des chers instants qui la délasseront.

Be forgiven! For that surely explains
Why I recall, alas, with some pride,
Who it was that cajoled from you
The sidelong glance that flashed from your eye.

*

There are times when I am the Poor Ship
That unmasted sails ahead through the storm,
But not seeing Our Lady light its way,
Makes ready for sinking with prayer.

There are times when I die the death of the Sinner
Who knows he is damned not having confessed,
And, losing all hope of any confession,
Writhes through the Hell he's already felt.

Yes, but! there are times I feel the ecstatic burn
Of the earliest Christian, prey to ravenous beasts,
Who smiles to all-seeing Jesus as nothing disturbs
Any hair on his chest, any nerve in his face!

BRUSSELS–LONDON, SEPTEMBER–OCTOBER 1872

Green

Consider these fruits, these flowers and branches and leaves
And now consider my heart, beating only for you.
Don't tear it apart with your beautiful hands,
But treat it with the kindness it modestly seeks.

I arrive still covered with a new morning's dew
Which an early wind has let freeze on my brow.
Allow my fatigue, now at rest at your feet,
To dream of dear moments refreshingly new.

Sur votre jeune sein laissez rouler ma tête
Toute sonore encore de vos derniers baisers;
Laissez-la s'apaiser de la bonne tempête,
Et que je dorme un peu puisque vous reposez.

Spleen

Les roses étaient toutes rouges,
Et les lierres étaient tout noirs.

Chère, pour peu que tu te bouges,
Renaissent tous mes désespoirs.

Le ciel était trop bleu, trop tendre,
La mer trop verte et l'air trop doux.

Je crains toujours,—ce qu'est d'attendre!—
Quelque fuite atroce de vous.

Du houx à la feuille vernie
Et du luisant buis je suis las,

Et de la campagne infinie,
Et de tout, fors de vous, hélas!

Let my head roll about on your little young breast
Still alive with the sound of your final embrace;
Leave it there to repose from the tempest of love,
And I'll fall asleep while you take your rest.

Spleen

The roses were all red,
And the ivy, darker than lead.

My dear, you have only to stir,
And all my despair has recurred.

The sky was too blue—tender, too—
The sea too green, the air softer than dew.

I'm always afraid—it's a terrible wait!—
You will fly and leave me to ache.

The glossy leaves of a holly tree,
Like shiny box shrubs, weary me,

As do endless fields of grass
And whatever else—save you, alas!

Streets I

> Dansons la gigue!

J'aimais surtout ses jolis yeux,
Plus clairs que l'étoile des cieux,
J'aimais ses yeux malicieux.

> Dansons la gigue!

Elle avait des façons vraiment
De désoler un pauvre amant,
Que c'en était vraiment charmant!

> Dansons la gigue!

Mais je trouve encore meilleur
Le baiser de sa bouche en fleur,
Depuis qu'elle est morte à mon cœur.

> Dansons la gigue!

Je me souviens, je me souviens
Des heures et des entretiens,
Et c'est le meilleur de mes biens.

> Dansons la gigue!

SOHO.

Streets I

    Let's dance a jig!

I always loved her pretty eyes,
Brighter than stars high in the skies;
I loved those mischievous blue eyes.

    Let's dance a jig!

She really had her winning ways
Of putting a lover back in his place;
It took no more than her charming gaze.

    Let's dance a jig!

But better yet do I recall the kiss
That she could bring to smiling lips
Even once past the height of bliss.

    Let's dance a jig!

Do I recall . . . ? Yes, I recall
All those hours and all that talk—
Never was I so completely enthralled.

    Let's dance a jig!

SOHO.

A poor young shepherd

J'ai peur d'un baiser
Comme d'une abeille.
Je souffre et je veille
Sans me reposer:
J'ai peur d'un baiser!

Pourtant j'aime Kate
Et ses yeux jolis.
Elle est délicate,
Aux longs traits pâlis.
Oh! que j'aime Kate!

C'est Saint-Valentin!
Je dois et je n'ose
Lui dire au matin . . .
La terrible chose
Que Saint-Valentin!

Elle m'est promise,
Fort heureusement!
Mais quelle entreprise
Que d'être un amant
Près d'une promise!

J'ai peur d'un baiser
Comme d'une abeille.
Je souffre et je veille
Sans me reposer:
J'ai peur d'un baiser!

A Poor Young Shepherd

I'm afraid of a kiss
As I am of a bee.
I suffer without sleep
And can find no repose.
I'm afraid of a kiss!

For all that, I love Kate
And her pretty blue eyes.
She is gracious and wise,
With a pale, charming nose.
Oh! I do love my Kate!

It is Valentine's day!
I must say, but don't dare,
If I can, how I care—
Oh, the frightening thing
That is Valentine's day!

She is promised to me:
That's a fortunate fact!
But there's no holding back
When I'm close to the ring
Near Kate, promised to me!

I'm afraid of a kiss
As I am of a bee.
I suffer without sleep
And can find no repose.
I'm afraid of a kiss!

Beams

Elle voulut aller sur les flots de la mer,
Et comme un vent bénin soufflait une embellie,
Nous nous prêtâmes tous à sa belle folie,
Et nous voilà marchant par le chemin amer.

Le soleil luisait haut dans le ciel calme et lisse,
Et dans ses cheveux blonds c'étaient des rayons d'or,
Si bien que nous suivions son pas plus calme encor
Que le déroulement des vagues, ô délice!

Des oiseaux blancs volaient alentour mollement,
Et des voiles au loin s'inclinaient toutes blanches.
Parfois de grands varechs filaient en longues branches,
Nos pieds glissaient d'un pur et large mouvement.

Elle se retourna, doucement inquiète
De ne nous croire pas pleinement rassurés;
Mais nous voyant joyeux d'être ses préférés,
Elle reprit sa route et portait haut la tête.

DOUVRES–OSTENDE, À BORD DE LA "COMTESSE-DE-FLANDRE",

4 AVRIL 1873.

Beams

It was her choice to sail out on the sea,
So, braced by a breeze and bright clearing,
We all accepted her antic idea
And soon took the briny path east.

The sun shone bright in a calm and smooth sky
And her blond hair was dappled with gold,
So we could follow a course even calmer
Than the gradual pace of the waves—my, the delight!

White birds flew about in leisurely flight
And sails dipped their white hulls in the distance.
Sometimes stretches of kelp slid by in long branches;
Our feet slipped past in wide movements or tight.

She turned around, gently disturbed
That we were perhaps less than fully at ease;
But seeing us happy among her favorite beings,
She raised her head high and to her route she returned.

DOVER–OSTEND, ON BOARD THE *Countess of Flanders*,

APRIL 4, 1873.

Poems Contemporaneous with
Romances sans paroles

"Le son du cor . . ."

Le son du cor s'afflige vers les bois
D'une douleur on veut croire orpheline
Qui vient mourir au bas de la colline
Parmi la brise errant en courts abois.

L'âme du loup pleure dans cette voix
Qui monte avec le soleil qui décline
D'une agonie on veut croire câline
Et qui ravit et qui navre à la fois.

Pour faire mieux cette plainte assoupie,
La neige tombe à longs traits de charpie
À travers le couchant sanguinolent,

Et l'air a l'air d'être un soupir d'automne,
Tant il fait doux par ce soir monotone
Où se dorlote un paysage lent.

"La bise se rue . . ."

La bise se rue à travers
Les buissons tout noirs et tout verts,
Glaçant la neige éparpillée
Dans la campagne ensoleillée.
L'odeur est aigre près des bois,
L'horizon chante avec des voix,

Poems Contemporaneous with
Romances sans paroles

"The sound of the horn . . ."

The sound of the horn cries pain toward the woods
For a grief that bespeaks a bereavement,
Then dies away at the foot of the hill
'Mid scattering winds and baying distress.

The soul of the wolf laments in this voice
That grows loud as the sun goes down
In throes of death that are seemingly sweet,
Delighting and hurting at the very same time.

The better to hush this plaintive event,
The snow falls in long strings of white lint
Across the blood-tinctured sky of a setting sun;

And the air has the air of an autumn sigh,
So quiet and soft is this mild end of day,
When there nestles in stillness a landscape of rest.

"The wintry wind blasts . . ."

The wintry wind blasts across
The brush of dark-hued green,
Freezing smatterings of snow
In the sunlit countryside.
The woods exhale their pungency;
The horizon resounds with song;

Les coqs des clochers des villages
Luisent crûment sur les nuages.
C'est délicieux de marcher
À travers ce brouillard léger
Qu'un vent taquin parfois retrousse.
Ah! fi de mon vieux feu qui tousse!
J'ai des fourmis plein les talons.
Debout, mon âme, vite, allons!
C'est le printemps sévère encore,
Mais qui par instant s'édulcore
D'un souffle tiède juste assez
Pour mieux sentir les froids passés
Et penser au Dieu de clémence . . .
Va, mon âme, à l'espoir immense!

The cuckoo atop the village tower
Glares boldly through the clouds.
It's sheer delight to make my way
Through thin mist that here and there
A teasing wind lifts off the ground.
Ah, I've had enough of sputtering fires!
My wingèd heels are eager to be going.
Stand up, my soul! Fast now, ahead!
The season's still too far from spring,
But it sweetens now and then
With a breeze just soft enough
To call to mind what cold you've felt
And make you bow to God's new mercy . . .
Think, my soul, what hope we have!

After the Shooting

Vendanges

Les choses qui chantent dans la tête
Alors que la mémoire est absente,
Écoutez, c'est notre sang qui chante . . .
Ô musique lointaine et discrète!

Écoutez! c'est notre sang qui pleure
Alors que notre âme s'est enfuie,
D'une voix jusqu'alors inouïe
Et qui va se taire tout à l'heure.

Frère du sang de la vigne rose,
Frère du vin de la veine noire,
Ô vin, ô sang, c'est l'apothéose!

Chantez, pleurez! Chassez la mémoire
Et chassez l'âme, et jusqu'aux ténèbres
Magnétisez nos pauvres vertèbres.

Sonnet boiteux

Ah! vraiment c'est triste, ah! vraiment ça finit trop mal.
Il n'est pas permis d'être à ce point infortuné.
Ah! vraiment c'est trop la mort du naïf animal
Qui voit tout son sang couler sous son regard fané.

Londres fume et crie. Ô quelle ville de la Bible!
Le gaz flambe et nage et les enseignes sont vermeilles.

After the Shooting

Harvesting Grapes

The things that sing in our mind
Though memory itself is not present—
Listen! It's our blood that is singing . . .
O music far away and discreet!

Listen! It's our blood that is weeping,
Though our soul itself has departed,
In a voice never heard until now,
A voice sure to grow still in a moment.

Brother of the blood of the rose vine,
Brother of the wine of the black vein,
O wine! O blood! Apotheosis itself!

Sing now and weep! Drive away memory,
Drive away soul! And right to the dark
Make our poor bones a magnetic field.

Limping Sonnet

Oh, it's really too sad! and it ends very badly.
It just isn't right to have run so far out of luck.
Oh, it's really too much to have an animal die
With all its blood flowing as it wearily watches.

London smokes and it cries, a town right from the Bible!
Gas flames up and drifts, and the signs are discolored,

Et les maisons dans leur ratatinement terrible
Épouvantent comme un sénat de petites vieilles.

Tout l'affreux passé saute, piaule, miaule et glapit
Dans le brouillard rose et jaune et sale des Sohos
Avec des *indeeds* et des *all rights* et des *hâos*.

Non vraiment c'est trop un martyre sans espérance,
Non vraiment cela finit trop mal, vraiment c'est triste:
Ô le feu du ciel sur cette ville de la Bible!

Sur une statue de Ganymède

Eh quoi! Dans cette ville d'eaux,
Trêve, repos, paix, intermède,
Encor toi de face et de dos,
Beau petit ami Ganymède?

L'aigle t'emporte, on dirait comme
Amoureux, de parmi les fleurs,
Son aile, d'élans économe,
Semble te vouloir par ailleurs

Que chez ce Jupin tyrannique,
Comme qui dirait au Revard
Et son œil qui nous fait la nique
Te coule un drôle de regard.

Bah! reste avec nous, bon garçon,
Notre ennui, viens donc le distraire
Un peu de la bonne façon.
N'es-tu pas notre petit frère?

While the houses, all crumpled and shrunken,
Are as frightful as a club of little old women.

A whole dreadful past whines, whimpers, and yelps
In the fog—pink, yellow, and dirty—of Soho,
With endless "indeeds" and "all rights" and "how dos."

No, really, it's torture without any hope;
No, really, it ends very badly—a really sad close:
Oh, what fire from heaven on this town from the Bible!

On a Statue of Ganymede

What's this! Here at this spa,
Place of truce and calm rest,
You again, front and back,
Ganymede, my fine friend?

Carried off by the eagle as if by a lover,
Swept from your bower of flowers,
By powerful wings, however restrained,
That want you, it seems, elsewhere

Than in the talons of tyrannical Zeus
Flying aloft to the top of Revard,
While his eye, regardless of us,
Casts you a glance decidedly odd.

Well! Stay with us, my good fellow;
Come and dispel, as well you know how,
The weary state that's now ours.
Are you not our dear little brother?

À Arthur Rimbaud

Mortel, ange ET démon, autant dire Rimbaud,
Tu mérites la prime place en ce mien livre,
Bien que tel sot grimaud t'ait traité de ribaud
Imberbe et de monstre en herbe et de potache ivre.

Les spirales d'encens et les accords de luth
Signalent ton entrée au temple de mémoire
Et ton nom radieux chantera dans la gloire,
Parce que tu m'aimas ainsi qu'il le fallut.

Les femmes te verront grand jeune homme très fort,
Très beau d'une beauté paysanne et rusée,
Très désirable d'une indolence qu'osée!

L'histoire t'a sculpté triomphant de la mort
Et jusqu'aux purs excès jouissant de la vie,
Tes pieds blancs posés sur la tête de l'Envie!

À Arthur Rimbaud—Sur un croquis de lui par sa sœur

Toi mort, mort, mort! Mais mort du moins tel que tu veux,
En nègre blanc, en sauvage splendidement
Civilisé, civilisant négligemment . . .
Ah, mort! Vivant plutôt en moi de mille feux

D'admiration sainte et de souvenirs feux
Mieux que tous les aspects vivants même comment
Grandioses! De mille feux brûlant vraiment
De bonne foi dans l'amour chaste aux fiers aveux.

To Arthur Rimbaud

Mortal, angel AND demon—in other words, Rimbaud—
This book of mine is for you first of all,
Though by some fools you've been called
An ignorant kid, a bawdy brat of a drunk.

Incense rising in curls and the chords of a lute
Betoken your entry into memory's temple,
And your radiant name will be an anthem of glory,
Because you once loved me as you needed to do.

Women will find you, tall strong young man,
Handsome with the looks of a shrewd peasant fellow,
As desirable as indolence ever troubles to be.

History has portrayed you outwitting your death
And even to purest excess delighting in life,
Your white feet standing on the head of Envy.

To Arthur Rimbaud—On a Sketch of Him by His Sister

You—dead, dead, dead! But dead at least as you wished,
A black man who was white, a splendidly civilized
Savage, a casual bearer of civilization himself . . .
Ah! dead! But still living in me with countless sparks

Of sacred admiration and fated recollection
Greater than summoned by all other lives, however
Grand!—boldly bright with countless flames
Of faith in burning love and fierce avowals.

Poète qui mourus comme tu le voulais,
En dehors de ces Paris-Londres moins que laids,
Je t'admire en ces traits naïfs de ce croquis,

Don précieux à l'ultime postérité
Par une main dont l'art naïf nous est acquis,
Rimbaud! *pax tecum sit, Dominus sit cum te!*

À un passant

Mon cher enfant que j'ai vu dans ma vie errante,
Mon cher enfant, que, mon Dieu, tu me recueillis,
Moi-même pauvre ainsi que toi, purs comme lys,
Mon cher enfant que j'ai vu dans ma vie errante!

Et beau comme notre âme pure et transparente,
Mon cher enfant, grande vertu de moi, la rente
De mon effort de charité, nous, fleurs de lys!
On te dit mort . . . Mort ou vivant, sois ma mémoire!

Et qu'on ne hurle donc plus que c'est de la gloire
Que je m'occupe, fou qu'il fallut et qu'il faut . . .
Petit! mort ou vivant, qui fis vibrer mes fibres,

Quoi qu'en aient dit et dit tels imbéciles noirs,
Compagnon qui ressuscitas les saints espoirs,
Va donc, vivant ou mort, dans les espaces libres.

Poet who died just as you wished,
Far from all that Paris-London traveling,
I gaze at you in the simple lines of this small sketch,

A precious gift to all those coming later
From a hand whose untutored art is ours now.
Rimbaud! *pax tecum sit, Dominus sit cum te!*

To a Passerby

My dear child, whom I found in my wandering life,
My dear child, how, good God, you reached out to me,
Myself poor just like you, both pure as white lilies,
My dear child, whom I found in my wandering life!

And fine as our souls, just as pure and transparent,
My dear child, my great strength, the reward
For my effort at caring, two of us, white lilies both!
You are said to have died . . . Dead or alive, be memory's child!

So let them stop shouting that reputation is all
That's of interest to me, a madman then and now to be . . .
My boy! living or dead, you who quickened my being,

Whatever's been said or is said, by those idiots avid of doom,
O companion who revived my holiest hopes,
Go now, living or dead, into the wide realms of freedom.

Cellulairement

I.

Au Lecteur.

« Sué contiva donde apprendió á tener
paciencia en las adversidades
(Cervantes)

Ce n'est pas de ces dieux foudroyés,
Ce n'est pas encor une infortune
Poétique autant qu'inopportune :
O lecteur de bon sens, ne fuyez !

On sait trop tout le prix du malheur
Pour le perdre en disert gaspillage.
Vous n'aurez ni mes traits ni mon âge,
Ni le vrai mal secret de mon cœur.

Et de ce que ces vers maladifs
Furent faits en prison pour tout dire
On ne va pas crier au martyre :
Que Dieu vous garde des expansifs !

On vous donne un livre fait ainsi ;
Prenez-le pour ce qu'il vaut en somme.

From Prison
to Conversion

A day after wounding Rimbaud with two revolver shots in Brussels on July 10, 1873, Verlaine was arrested and incarcerated in the prison of the Petits-Carmes. He was subsequently sentenced to two years' imprisonment, not only for shooting his lover but also for "active and passive pederasty," according to forensic examination. In prison, first in Brussels and then in Mons, from October 1873 until January 1875, Verlaine wrote some of his most famous poems, including "Le ciel est, par-dessus le toit . . ." [The sky is, above the rooftop . . .] and "Art poétique" [Art of Poetry]. Most of these poems are included in the manuscript of *Cellulairement* [Cellularly], the prison book that Verlaine was planning to publish after being released in 1875, but which he later dismembered, scattering its poems throughout other collections, including *Sagesse* [Wisdom] (1880), *Jadis et Naguère* [Long Ago and Yesterday] (1884), and *Parallèlement* [In Parallel] (1889). The manuscript was rediscovered only in 2004.

It was in prison that Verlaine was informed of the judgment of separation from his wife and son in May 1873. The news left him devastated and led to his conversion to Catholicism, the religion of his childhood, in the course of the following months. The conversion is related in the ten sonnets, starting with "Jésus m'a dit . . ." [Jesus just told me . . .], which conclude *Cellulairement* and were subsequently included in *Sagesse*, the first of Verlaine's four Catholic collections, followed by *Amour* [Love] in 1888, *Bonheur* [Happiness] in 1891, and *Liturgies intimes* [Intimate Liturgies] in 1892.

In Prison (Poems from *Cellulairement* [Cellularly] and Other Poems)

Au lecteur

Ce n'est pas de ces dieux foudroyés,
Ce n'est pas encore une infortune
Poétique autant qu'inopportune,
Ô lecteur de bon sens, ne fuyez!

On sait trop tout le prix du malheur
Pour le perdre en disert gaspillage.
Vous n'aurez ni mes traits ni mon âge,
Ni le vrai mal secret de mon cœur.

Et de ce que ces vers maladifs
Furent faits en prison, pour tout dire,
On ne va pas crier au martyre.
Que Dieu vous garde des expansifs!

On vous donne un livre fait ainsi.
Prenez-le pour ce qu'il vaut en somme.
C'est l'*ægri somnium* d'un brave homme
Étonné de se trouver ici.

On y met, avec la "bonne foy,"
L'orthographe à peu près qu'on possède,
Regrettant de n'avoir à son aide
Que ce prestige d'être bien soi.

In Prison (Poems from *Cellulairement* [Cellularly] and Other Poems)

To the Reader

It isn't about those thunderstruck gods;
It isn't either about some woefully
Ill-timed poetic misfortune—
O sensible reader, don't go away!

Too well do I know the cost of bad luck
To waste it on meaningless chatter.
You won't have a picture of me or my age
Or the true secret pain in my heart.

And simply because these hapless lines
Were written in prison (yes, that's right),
I'm not about to start playing the martyr.
God keep you from unwarranted talk!

This is the book that I'll give you.
Take it for just what it's worth.
It's the nightmarish work of a decent man
Astonished to find himself here.

I've put into it, along with good faith,
The approximate spelling I know,
Regretting I've had no more help
Than the prestige of being myself.

Vous lirez ce libelle tel quel,
Tout ainsi que vous feriez d'un autre.
Ce vœu bien modeste est le seul nôtre,
N'étant guère après tout criminel.

Un mot encore, car je vous dois
Quelque lueur en définitive
Concernant la chose qui m'arrive:
Je compte parmi les maladroits.

J'ai perdu ma vie et je sais bien
Que tout blâme sur moi s'en va fondre:
À cela je ne puis que répondre
Que je suis vraiment né Saturnien.

BRUXELLES, DE LA PRISON DES PETITS-CARMES, JUILLET 1873.

Impression fausse

Dame souris trotte,
Noire dans le gris du soir,
Dame souris trotte,
Grise dans le noir.

On sonne la cloche,
Dormez, les bons prisonniers!
On sonne la cloche:
Faut que vous dormiez.

Pas de mauvais rêve,
Ne pensez qu'à vos amours.
Pas de mauvais rêve:
Les belles toujours!

You'll read this little book such as it is,
In the same way you'd read any other.
This modest wish is all that I have,
Since a criminal's not, after all, what I am.

One more word, for I do really
Owe you some clear information
On what's happened to me:
I'm a man of serial blunders.

I've wasted my life and well know
That all blame's coming down on my head;
The only thing I can say in reply
Is that I was truly born under Saturn.

BRUSSELS, FROM THE PRISON OF PETITS-CARMES, JULY 1873.

False Impression

Lady mouse trots about,
Dark in the evening grey;
Lady mouse trots about,
She's grey in the dark.

The bell sounds an order:
Lights out—end of day!
The bell sounds an order:
Time to sleep for the night!

No time for bad dreams;
Think only of lovers and love!
No time for bad dreams—
Only sweethearts will do!

Le grand clair de lune!
On ronfle ferme à côté.
    Le grand clair de lune
    En réalité!

    Un nuage passe,
Il fait noir comme en un four.
    Un nuage passe.
    Tiens, le petit jour!

    Dame souris trotte,
Rose dans les rayons bleus,
    Dame souris trotte:
    Debout, paresseux!

BR[UXELLES], 11 JUILLET 73. ENTRÉE EN PRISON.

Sur les eaux

    Je ne sais pourquoi
    Mon esprit amer
D'une aile inquiète et folle vole sur la mer.
    Tout ce qui m'est cher,
    D'une aile d'effroi
Mon amour le couve au ras des flots. Pourquoi, pourquoi?

    Mouette à l'essor mélancolique,
    Elle suit la vague, ma pensée,
    À tous les vents du ciel balancée,
    Et biaisant quand la marée oblique,
    Mouette à l'essor mélancolique.

    Ivre de soleil
    Et de liberté,

Bright light of the moon!
Heavy snoring in the bunk next to mine.
    Bright light of the moon
    In the free world outside!

    A cloud passes by;
It's as dark as inside an oven;
    A cloud passes by.
    Look, a glimmer of day!

    Lady mouse trots about,
Pink ringed in a setting of blue,
    Lady mouse trots about:
    Out of bed, lazy laggers!

BR[USSELS], JULY 11, 73. ENTERING THE PRISON.

Upon the Waters

    I don't know why
    My bitter spirit
With wild and worried wing takes flight across the sea.
    Everything that's dear to me
    My love protects
With fearful wing flying close to the waves. Why?

    Gull in melancholy flight
    Drifts with the waves like my thoughts,
    Propelled by the winds in the sky,
    And changes her route with the tide—
    Gull in melancholy flight.

    Drunken on sunlight
    And freedom,

Un instinct la guide à travers cette immensité.
        La brise d'été
        Sur le flot vermeil
Doucement la porte en un tiède demi-sommeil.

    Parfois si tristement elle crie
    Qu'elle alarme au lointain le pilote,
    Puis au gré du vent se livre et flotte
    Et plonge, et l'aile toute meurtrie
    Revole, et puis si tristement crie!

        Je ne sais pourquoi
        Mon esprit amer
D'une aile inquiète et folle vole sur la mer.
        Tout ce qui m'est cher,
        D'une aile d'effroi
Mon amour le cherche au ras des flots. Pourquoi, pourquoi?

BRUX[ELLES], JUILLET 1873.

Berceuse

> "Però non mi destar: Deh! Parla basso."
>
> (MICHEL-ANGE.)

Un grand sommeil noir
Tombe sur ma vie:
Dormez, tout espoir,
Dormez, toute envie!

Je ne vois plus rien,
Je perds la mémoire
Du mal et du bien . . .
Ô la triste histoire!

Instinct guides her through the vastness of the waters.
>Summer breeze
>On sunlit golden bronze
Softly lets her float in somnolescent warmth.

>Sometimes she cries so sadly
>That she alarms the distant pilot;
>Then, with the wind, she soars,
>She dives . . . with wounded wing
>She flies again, but oh, so sadly cries!

>I don't know why
>My bitter spirit
With wild and worried wing takes flight across the sea.
>Everything that's dear to me
>My love pursues
With fearful wing flying close to the waves. Why?

BRUSSELS, JULY 1873.

Lullaby

>Thus wake me not—ah! Speak softly.
>>(MICHELANGELO.)

A great dark sleep
Falls over my life.
Sleep, every hope,
Sleep, every wish!

I see nought anymore;
All memory's lost
Of right and of wrong . . .
Oh, sad, such a story!

Je suis un berceau
Qu'une main balance
Au creux d'un caveau:
Silence, silence!

BR[UXELLES], LE 8 AOÛT 1873.

"Le ciel est, par-dessus le toit"

Le ciel est, par-dessus le toit,
    Si bleu, si calme!
Un arbre, par-dessus le toit,
    Berce sa palme.

La cloche, dans le ciel qu'on voit,
    Doucement tinte.
Un oiseau, sur l'arbre qu'on voit,
    Chante sa plainte.

Mon Dieu, mon Dieu, la vie est là,
    Simple et tranquille.
Cette paisible rumeur-là
    Vient de la ville.

—Qu'as-tu fait, ô toi que voilà
    Pleurant sans cesse,
Dis, qu'as-tu fait, toi que voilà,
    De ta jeunesse?

148   PAUL VERLAINE

I am a cradle
Rocked by a hand
In the pit of a tomb.
Quiet now, quiet!

BRUSSELS, AUGUST 8, 1873.

"The sky is, above the rooftop"

The sky is, above the rooftop,
    So blue, so calm!
A tree, above the rooftop,
    Sways like a palm.

The bell I can see up there
    Softly chimes.
A bird perched on a limb up there
    Intones his lament.

My God, what life is out there,
    Quiet and simple!
Those tranquil sounds in the air
    Mount from the town.

—What have you done, you, standing there,
    Weeping no end?
What have you done, you, with a youth
    Too late to amend?

Dizain mil huit cent trente

Je suis né romantique et j'eusse été fatal
En un frac très étroit aux boutons de métal,
Avec ma barbe en pointe et mes cheveux en brosse.
Hablant español, très loyal et très féroce,
L'œil idoine à l'œillade et chargé de défis.
Beautés mises à mal et bourgeois déconfits
Eussent bondé ma vie et soûlé mon cœur d'homme.
Pâle et jaune, d'ailleurs, et taciturne comme
Un infant scrofuleux dans un Escurial . . .
Et puis j'eusse été si féroce et si loyal!

Invraisemblable mais vrai

Las! je suis à l'Index et dans les dédicaces
Me voici Paul V . . . pur et simple. Les audaces
De mes amis, tant les éditeurs sont des saints,
Doivent éliminer mon nom de leurs desseins.
Extraordinaire et saponaire tonnerre
D'une excommunication que je vénère
Au point d'en faire des fautes de quantité!
Vrai, si je n'étais pas (forcément) désisté
Des choses, j'aimerais, surtout m'étant contraire,
Cette pudeur du moins si rare de libraire.

Le dernier dizain

Ô Belgique qui m'as valu ce dur loisir,
Merci! J'ai pu du moins réfléchir et saisir
Dans le silence doux et blanc de tes cellules
Les raisons qui fuyaient comme des libellules
À travers les roseaux bavards d'un monde vain,
Les raisons de mon être éternel et divin,

Ten Lines on 1830

I was born a romantic and would have been deadly
In tails narrow and tapered, with buttons of metal,
With beard trimmed to a point and my hair in brush cut,
Babbling español, very loyal and ferocious,
With an eye more than made for provocative glances.
Beauties undone and upstanding grubbers unsettled
Would have crowded and sated my life as a man.
Pallid and yellow as well, no less sullen a child
Than a scrofulous prince in an Escorial . . .
And how I'd have been ferocious and loyal!

Hard to Believe, but True

Well, now! I've been placed on the Index! Dedications
Henceforth will call me nought but Paul V.! My brave friends
(And you know how pious all these publishers are)
Are now bound not to name me for the sales they intend.
Remarkable, this marvelous cleanser, this communication
Ex- or not, that I embrace and gladly take so to heart—
Even if it mean occasional mistakes in timing and measure!
True, had I not closed my eyes to things that might jar,
I would adore, all the more because it's meant to reprove,
That modest restraint so far from a bookman's regard.

The Last Ten Lines

O Belgium! What harsh leisure you've dealt me!
Many thanks for the chance to ponder and grasp
In the soft and white silence of your cells
The reasons as fleeting as dragonflies
Through the chattering reeds of a vacuous world,
Reasons for this being of mine, divine and eternal,

Et les étiqueter comme en un beau musée
Dans les cases en fin cristal de ma pensée.
Mais, ô Belgique, assez de ce huis clos têtu!
Ouvre enfin, car c'est bon pour une fois, sais-tu!

Art poétique

De la musique avant toute chose,
Et pour cela préfère l'Impair
Plus vague et plus soluble dans l'air,
Sans rien en lui qui pèse ou qui pose.

Il faut aussi que tu n'ailles point
Choisir tes mots sans quelque méprise:
Rien de plus cher que la chanson grise
Où l'Indécis au Précis se joint.

C'est des beaux yeux derrière des voiles,
C'est le grand jour tremblant de midi,
C'est, par un ciel d'automne attiédi,
Le bleu fouillis des claires étoiles!

Car nous voulons la Nuance encor,
Pas la Couleur, rien que la nuance!
Oh! la nuance seule fiance
Le rêve au rêve et la flûte au cor!

Fuis du plus loin la Pointe assassine,
L'Esprit cruel et le Rire impur,
Qui font pleurer les yeux de l'Azur,
Et tout cet ail de basse cuisine!

And to provide them with labels, as in a museum,
In my mind's crystal cases of thought.
But enough, O Belgium, of this stubborn reclusion!
Open up! It's a good thing for once, don't you know!

Art of Poetry

Music before everything else.
And to that end think odd and not even,
Uncertain of beat, dissolving more quickly,
With no weight to speak of, no feigning at all.

Here is a point you mustn't forget:
Choose all your words with some disregard;
No better choice than a somewhat blurred song
That treats clear and not-clear as but one.

It's bright eyes that you hide behind veils;
It's shimmering daylight of summer at noon,
Or, under the sky of a warm autumn evening,
The blue tumble of shining white stars!

And then it's nuance that we want;
Color's not wanted—only nuance!
That's what is needed to marry together
One dream and another, one flute and a horn!

Run far away from a word meant to kill,
From wit meant to hurt, from a laughing stiletto!
Tears do they bring to the blue eyes of heaven,
Like the rest of that garlic of low-class cuisine.

Prends l'éloquence et tords-lui son cou!
Tu feras bien, en train d'énergie,
De rendre un peu la Rime assagie.
Si l'on n'y veille, elle ira jusqu'où?

Ô qui dira les torts de la Rime?
Quel enfant sourd ou quel nègre fou
Nous a forgé ce bijou d'un sou
Qui sonne creux et faux sous la lime?

De la musique encore et toujours!
Que ton vers soit la chose envolée
Qu'on sent qui fuit d'une âme en allée
Vers d'autres cieux à d'autres amours.

Que ton vers soit la bonne aventure
Éparse au vent crispé du matin
Qui va fleurant la menthe et le thym . . .
Et tout le reste est littérature.

Take facile speech, that eloquent glibness,
Strangle it silent, and then, while you're at it,
Do what you can to discipline rhyme:
If you pay it no heed, it will hurt half your lines.

Oh, who can recite the abuses of rhyme?
What deaf little boy or woolly-brained fool
Ever forged us that cheap costume jewel
That rings hollow and fake if struck by a file?

Music once more and ever again!
Let your verse be that thing that takes off
And flies from a sensitive soul that's departed
Toward higher heavens and newer amours.

Let your verse be all the good fortune
Spread by crisp winds through the morning,
Fragrant of mint, fragrant with thyme . . .
And everything else is just an old story.

After the Conversion (Poems from *Sagesse* [Wisdom] and Other Poems)

"Jésus m'a dit . . ."

Jésus m'a dit: "Mon fils, il faut m'aimer. Tu vois
Mon flanc percé, mon cœur qui rayonne et qui saigne,
Et mes pieds offensés que Madeleine baigne
De larmes, et mes bras douloureux sous le poids

De tes péchés, et mes mains! Et tu vois la croix,
Tu vois les clous, le fiel, l'éponge, et tout t'enseigne
À n'aimer, en ce monde amer où la chair règne,
Que ma Chair et mon Sang, ma parole et ma voix.

Ne t'ai-je pas aimé jusqu'à la mort moi-même,
Ô mon frère en mon Père, ô mon fils en l'Esprit,
Et n'ai-je pas souffert, comme c'était écrit?

N'ai-je pas sangloté ton angoisse suprême
Et n'ai-je pas sué la sueur de tes nuits,
Lamentable ami qui me cherches où je suis?"

After the Conversion (Poems from *Sagesse* [Wisdom] and Other Poems)

"Jesus just told me . . ."

Jesus just told me: "My son, you must love me. You see
My side pierced, My heart shining forth and yet bleeding,
My feet crossed and wounded, bathed by the Magdalene's
Tears, and my arms painfully bearing all the weight

Of your sins; then consider my hands! Look at the cross,
See the nails, the gall and the sponge—and all of it teaches
To devote your love, in this bitter world where flesh reigns,
To my Flesh alone, to my Blood, to my word and my voice.

Have I not loved you, going even so far as to die,
O my brother in Father, O my son in the Spirit,
Have I not suffered as had been ever foretold?

Have I not shared the tears of your anguishing pain
And have I not been wet with the sweat of your nights,
O pitiful friend, you who seek me where I am?"

"Ô mon Dieu . . ."

Ô mon Dieu, vous m'avez blessé d'amour
Et la blessure est encore vibrante,
Ô mon Dieu, vous m'avez blessé d'amour.

Ô mon Dieu, votre crainte m'a frappé
Et la brûlure est encor là qui tonne,
Ô mon Dieu, votre crainte m'a frappé.

Ô mon Dieu, j'ai connu que tout est vil
Et votre gloire en moi s'est installée,
Ô mon Dieu, j'ai connu que tout est vil.

Noyez mon âme aux flots de votre Vin,
Fondez ma vie au Pain de votre table,
Noyez mon âme aux flots de votre Vin.

Voici mon sang que je n'ai pas versé,
Voici ma chair indigne de souffrance,
Voici mon sang que je n'ai pas versé.

Voici mon front qui n'a pu que rougir,
Pour l'escabeau de vos pieds adorables,
Voici mon front qui n'a pu que rougir.

Voici mes mains qui n'ont pas travaillé,
Pour les charbons ardents et l'encens rare,
Voici mes mains qui n'ont pas travaillé.

Voici mon cœur qui n'a battu qu'en vain,
Pour palpiter aux ronces du Calvaire,
Voici mon cœur qui n'a battu qu'en vain.

"O my God . . ."

O my God, you have wounded me with love,
And the wound is still searing,
O my God, you have wounded me with love.

O my God, fear of you has assailed me,
And the burn is still throbbing,
O my God, fear of you has assailed me.

O my God, I have seen how base everything is,
And yet how your glory has entered my heart,
O my God, I have seen how base everything is.

Drown my soul in the swell of your Wine,
Blend my life with the Bread on your table,
Drown my soul in the swell of your Wine.

Here is my blood that has never been spilled,
Here is my flesh unworthy of suffering,
Here is my blood that has never been spilled.

Here is my brow never reddened with shame,
To use as a stool for your venerable feet,
Here is my brow never reddened with shame.

Here are my hands which have never done labor,
To handle hot coals and rare kinds of incense,
Here are my hands which have never done labor.

Here is my heart always beating in vain,
To quiver in Calvary's nettles and brambles,
Here is my heart always beating in vain.

Voici mes pieds, frivoles voyageurs,
Pour accourir aux cris de votre grâce,
Voici mes pieds, frivoles voyageurs.

Voici ma voix, bruit maussade et menteur,
Pour les reproches de la Pénitence,
Voici ma voix, bruit maussade et menteur.

Voici mes yeux, luminaires d'erreur,
Pour être éteints aux pleurs de la prière,
Voici mes yeux, luminaires d'erreur.

Hélas, Vous, Dieu d'offrande et de pardon,
Quel est le puits de mon ingratitude,
Hélas, Vous, Dieu d'offrande et de pardon,

Dieu de terreur et Dieu de sainteté,
Hélas! ce noir abîme de mon crime,
Dieu de terreur et Dieu de sainteté,

Vous, Dieu de paix, de joie et de bonheur,
Toutes mes peurs, toutes mes ignorances,
Vous, Dieu de paix, de joie et de bonheur,

Vous connaissez tout cela, tout cela,
Et que je suis plus pauvre que personne,
Vous connaissez tout cela, tout cela,

Mais ce que j'ai, mon Dieu, je vous le donne.

Here are my feet, frivolous travelers,
To come running at the cries of your grace,
Here are my feet, frivolous travelers.

Here is my voice, deceitful and sullen,
To set forth the sins I'd repent for,
Here is my voice, deceitful and sullen.

Here are my eyes, lamplights of error,
To be quenched by the tears of my prayer,
Here are my eyes, lamplights of error.

You, alas, God of sacrifice and of pardon,
What is the depth of my failure of thanks,
You, alas, God of sacrifice and of pardon.

God of terror, God of all that is holy,
Alas! the black abyss of my crime,
God of terror, God of all that is holy,

You, God of happiness, of peace and of joy,
All my fears, all the things I know not,
You, God of happiness, of peace and of joy,

You are aware of all that, of all that,
And know that I am poorer than anyone else,
You are aware of all that, of all that,

But whatever I have, my God, I give to you.

"Beauté des femmes . . ."

Beauté des femmes, leur faiblesse, et ces mains pâles
Qui font souvent le bien et peuvent tout le mal,
Et ces yeux, où plus rien ne reste d'animal
Que juste assez pour dire: "assez" aux fureurs mâles!

Et toujours, maternelle endormeuse des râles,
Même quand elle ment, cette voix! Matinal
Appel, ou chant bien doux à vêpre, ou frais signal,
Ou beau sanglot qui va mourir au pli des châles! . . .

Hommes durs! Vie atroce et laide d'ici-bas!
Ah! que du moins, loin des baisers et des combats,
Quelque chose demeure un peu sur la montagne,

Quelque chose du cœur enfantin et subtil,
Bonté, respect! Car, qu'est-ce qui nous accompagne,
Et vraiment, quand la mort viendra, que reste-t-il?

"La vie humble . . ."

La vie humble aux travaux ennuyeux et faciles
Est une œuvre de choix qui veut beaucoup d'amour.
Rester gai quand le jour, triste, succède au jour,
Être fort, et s'user en circonstances viles,

N'entendre, n'écouter aux bruits des grandes villes
Que l'appel, ô mon Dieu, des cloches dans la tour,
Et faire un de ces bruits soi-même, cela pour
L'accomplissement vil de tâches puériles,

Dormir chez les pêcheurs étant un pénitent,
N'aimer que le silence et converser pourtant;

"Beauty of women . . ."

Beauty of women, their weakness, those delicate hands
That often do what is right but can also work harm,
And those eyes, with no animal glance anymore
But to say "no, that's enough" to men who press hard!

And ever the motherly soother of sensitive throats,
And that voice, even when led into lies! Her call
In the morning, lullaby late at night, a clear nod,
A deeply felt sob trailing off in the pleats of a shawl . . .

Men rough and harsh! Life ugly, so hard here below!
Ah, at least let there be, far from combat and kiss,
Something still to be sensed in that far-off place,

Something subtle, as if from the heart of a child—
Goodness, respect! What, after all, do we carry away,
And in truth, at the last, what have we that stays?

"A humble life . . ."

A humble life of tasks tiresome but simple
Is an employment of choice that calls for much love.
Keeping good cheer when grey day follows grey,
Starting strong, then declining in base occupations,

Attending to nothing in the sounds of the city
But the call—O my God!—of the bells in the tower,
And hearing in one of those rings your own summons
To accomplish such low and puerile duties,

Sleeping with sinners, though no longer a sinner,
Loving but silence, yet open to much conversation—

Le temps si long dans la patience si grande,

Le scrupule naïf aux repentirs têtus,
Et tous ces soins autour de ces pauvres vertus!
—Fi, dit l'Ange gardien, de l'orgueil qui marchande!

"L'échelonnement des haies . . ."

L'échelonnement des haies
Moutonne à l'infini, mer
Claire dans le brouillard clair
Qui sent bon les jeunes baies.

Des arbres et des moulins
Sont légers sur le vert tendre
Où vient s'ébattre et s'étendre
L'agilité des poulains.

Dans ce vague d'un Dimanche
Voici se jouer aussi
De grandes brebis aussi
Douces que leur laine blanche.

Tout à l'heure déferlait
L'onde, roulée en volutes,
De cloches comme des flûtes
Dans le ciel comme du lait.

STICKNEY, 75.

So long a time in the fullness of patience,

Innocent scruples, insistent repentance,
And all that attention to penniless virtue!
—Away, says the guardian Angel, with such mercantile pride!

"Hedges ranged . . ."

Hedges ranged in staggered rows
Billow toward infinity, a brilliant
Sea in the brightening mist
Fragrant now of bayleaf blooms.

Windmills and flowering trees
Sit light on the newly green field
Where colts cavort and prance
And sport with the vigor of youth.

Here too you'll see at play,
In this open field of a Sunday,
Full-grown sheep soft and sweet
As their snowy white fleece.

Just now the breaking waves
Sent twists and curls to blend
Like flutes with all the bells
On high in a milk-colored sky.

STICKNEY, 75.

Londres

. . . un grave Anglais correct, bien mis, beau linge.

(VICTOR HUGO.)

Un dimanche d'été, quand le soleil s'en mêle,
Londres forme un régal offert aux délicats:
Les arbres forts et ronds sur la verdure frêle,
Vert tendre, ont l'air bien loin des brumes et des gaz,

Tant ils semblent plantés en terre paysanne.
Un soleil clair, léger dans le ciel fin, bleuté
À peine. On est comme en un bain où se pavane
Le parfum d'une lente infusion de thé.

Dix heures et demie, heure des longs services
Divins. Les cloches par milliers chantent dans l'air
Sonore et volatil sur d'étranges caprices,
Les psaumes de David s'ébrouent en brouillard clair.

Argentines comme on n'en entend pas en France,
Pays de sonnerie intense, bronze amer,
Font un concert très doux de joie et d'espérance,
Trop doux peut-être, il faut la crainte de l'Enfer.

L'après-midi, cloches encor. Des files d'hommes,
De femmes et d'enfants bien mis glissent plutôt
Qu'ils ne marchent, muets, on dirait économes
De leur voix réservée aux amen de tantôt.

Tout ce monde est plaisant dans sa raide attitude
Gardant, bien qu'erroné, le geste de la foi
Et son protestantisme à la fois veule et rude
Met quelqu'un tout de même au-dessus de la loi.

London

. . . a grave Englishman, proper, well-dressed.

(VICTOR HUGO.)

On a Sunday in summer, when the sun lets it happen,
London is a treat for its delicate souls:
Trees sturdy and tall rising from grass that's
Tender and green, far from mists and gaseous ills

They seem, looking so rooted in newly turned earth.
Bright sunshine there, airy light in a fine warm sky,
Barely blue . . . May we call it a bath whence there
Rises and spreads the scent of a tea gently brewed?

Ten thirty: it's time for that long Sunday service—
Divine, need we add? Too many bells sing out loud
Strange caprices that take wing in the resonant air;
The psalms of King David splash about in bright fog.

Silver bells, of a sort we don't hear in France,
A tolling land of sharp and bitter bronze,
Produce a soft and gentle sound of joyful hope,
Perhaps too soft, as it neglects all dread of Hell.

Afternoon and bells again. Long rows of men
And women and their tidied young not stroll,
But glide along, their silence meant to save
Their vocal strength for the amens that wait.

This whole world is a bit of a laugh, with its
Stiff-collared creed of mistaken belief
And a Protestant faith both crude and too weak
That sets one being above the reach of the law.

Espoir du vrai chrétien, riche vivier de Pierre,
Poisson prêt au pêcheur qui peut compter dessus,
Saint-Esprit, Dieu puissant, versez-leur la lumière
Pour qu'ils apprennent à comprendre enfin Jésus.

Six heures. Les buveurs regagnent leur buvette,
La famille son home et la rue est à Dieu:
Et dans le ciel sali quelque étoile seulette
Pronostique la pluie aux gueux sans feu ni lieu.

"L'immensité . . ."
L'immensité de l'humanité,
Le Temps passé, vivace et bon père,
Une entreprise à jamais prospère:
Quelle puissante et calme cité!

Il semble ici qu'on vit dans l'histoire.
Tout est plus fort que l'homme d'un jour.
De lourds rideaux d'atmosphère noire
Font richement la nuit alentour.

Ô civilisés que civilise
L'Ordre obéi, le Respect sacré!
Ô dans ce champ si bien préparé,
Cette moisson de la seule Église!

LONDRES, 75–77.

Hope of the Christian, the true, Peter's rich pond,
Fish all set for the fisher who's left with no doubt,
Holy Spirit, O powerful God, send them your light
So they'll finally learn to understand Jesus!

Six o'clock in the evening. The drinkers are back;
The family's home, and the street's in God's hands.
And in a sky full of soot some solitary star
Foretells more rain for the lightless and homeless.

"The immensity . . ."

The immensity of humankind,
Time past, a living good and kind father,
An enterprise forever thriving—
What calm power in this city!

Here it appears they all live in history.
Everything is stronger than the man of one day.
Curtains of air in heavy black
Surround the day with densest night.

Oh, so civilized! civilized by
Obedience to Order and sacred Respect!
Oh, in this field so deeply furrowed,
What a harvest for the only Church!

LONDON, 75–77.

"La 'grande ville' . . ."

La "grande ville"! Un tas criard de pierres blanches
Où rage le soleil comme en pays conquis.
Tous les vices ont leurs tanières, les exquis
Et les hideux, dans ce désert de pierres blanches.

Des odeurs. Des bruits vains. Où que vague le cœur,
Toujours ce poudroiement vertigineux de sable,
Toujours ce remuement de la chose coupable
Dans cette solitude où s'écœure le cœur!

De près, de loin, le Sage aura sa Thébaïde
Parmi le fade ennui qui monte de ceci,
D'autant plus âpre et plus sanctifiante aussi
Que deux parts de son âme y pleurent, dans ce vide!

PARIS, 77.

"Et j'ai revu l'enfant unique . . ."

Et j'ai revu l'enfant unique: il m'a semblé
Que s'ouvrait dans mon cœur la dernière blessure,
Celle dont la douleur plus exquise m'assure
D'une mort désirable en un jour consolé.

La bonne flèche aiguë et sa fraîcheur qui dure!
En ces instants choisis elles ont éveillé
Les rêves un peu lourds du scrupule ennuyé,
Et tout mon sang chrétien chanta la Chanson pure.

"'Big city' . . ."

"Big city"—a flashy pile of blinding stone
Where a harsh sun rules over conquered land!
Vices, however alluring, however repugnant,
Are denned in this desert of blinding stone.

Smells. Pointless noise. Where roams the heart,
It is ever the same sand-covered dizzying void,
Ever the same stirring of the guilt-laden thing,
In this lonely expanse that disheartens the heart!

Nearby or not, the desert Sage can hardly avoid
The tasteless boredom rising from this place,
All the more bitter and more purifying, too,
As two parts of his soul shed tears in this void!

PARIS, 77.

"Once more I have seen my sole child . . ."

Once more I have seen my sole child: I felt
The last wound in my heart spread open again,
The one so piercingly painful that I am sure
Only longed-for death will bring consolation.

It's a very sharp arrow and a fresh hurt that endures.
In those few special moments they wakened
Dreams somewhat heavy with tiresome scruples,
And my Christian blood sang forth the pure Song.

J'entends encor, je vois encor! Loi du devoir
Si douce! Enfin, je sais ce qu'est entendre et voir,
J'entends, je vois toujours! Voix des bonnes pensées!

Innocence, avenir! Sage et silencieux,
Que je vais vous aimer, vous un instant pressées,
Belles petites mains qui fermerez nos yeux!

Un veuf parle

Je vois un groupe sur la mer.
Quelle mer? Celle de mes larmes.
Mes yeux mouillés du vent amer
Dans cette nuit d'ombres et d'alarmes
Sont deux étoiles sur la mer.

C'est une toute jeune femme
Et son enfant déjà tout grand
Dans une barque où nul ne rame,
Sans mât ni voile, en plein courant . . .
Un jeune garçon, une femme!

En plein courant dans l'ouragan!
L'enfant se cramponne à sa mère
Qui ne sait plus où, non plus qu'en . . .
Ni plus rien, et qui, folle, espère
En le courant, en l'ouragan.

Espérez en Dieu, pauvre folle,
Crois en notre Père, petit.
La tempête qui vous désole,
Mon cœur de là-haut vous prédit
Qu'elle va cesser, petit, folle!

Again I hear, again I see! That so gentle Law
Of duty! Now I know what it means to hear and to see!
Yes, I see—yes, I hear, the voices of all that is right!

Innocence and future! Courteous and quiet,
How I do love you—you, those tightly pressed
Little hands that one day will open to close our eyes.

A Widower Speaks

I see a couple on the sea.
What sea? The sea of the tears in my eyes.
My eyes, made wet by the bitter wind
Of this night of dark shadows and frights,
Are two bright stars upon the sea.

I see a young woman, oh, very young,
And with her a child already grown,
Alone in a boat, alone with no oar,
With no mast and no sail, adrift on the tide . . .
Just a boy, just a woman too young!

Adrift on the tide in hurricane season!
The child clings to his mother in fear.
No knowledge has she of where or if . . .
Or whatever else, as distraught, but with hope,
She floats adrift in hurricane season.

Have hope in the Lord; be not distraught!
Have faith in our Father, young lad!
The storm that is sure to inflict such distress—
My heart has heard from above and predicts
It will end, lad and mother; be not distraught!

Et paix au groupe sur la mer,
Sur cette mer de bonnes larmes!
Mes yeux joyeux dans le ciel clair,
Par cette nuit sans plus d'alarmes,
Sont deux bons anges sur la mer.

"Né l'enfant . . ."

Né l'enfant des grandes villes
Et des révoltes serviles,
J'ai là tout cherché, trouvé,
De tout appétit rêvé . . .
Mais, puisque rien n'en demeure,

J'ai dit un adieu léger
À tout ce qui peut changer,
Au plaisir, au bonheur même,
Et même à tout ce que j'aime
Hors de vous, mon doux Seigneur!

La Croix m'a pris sur ses ailes
Qui m'emporte aux meilleurs zèles,
Silence, expiation,
Et l'âpre vocation
Pour la vertu qui s'ignore.

Douce, chère Humilité,
Arrose ma charité,
Trempe-la de tes eaux vives,
Ô mon cœur, que tu ne vives
Qu'aux fins d'une bonne mort!

I ask peace for the couple upon the sea,
On that sea of tears, of good tears!
My joyful eyes in the open sky,
In this night of no more shadows and frights,
Are two bright angels upon the sea!

"Born the child . . ."

Born the child of big cities
And servers' revolts,
I there sought and there found,
There dreamt of, every desire . . .
But since it all came to nought,

I bade an easy goodbye
To everything apt ever to change:
To pleasure, good fortune itself,
Even all that I love—
Save You, my gentle dear Lord!

The wings of the Cross have
Carried me off to worthier ends:
Silence, amending my ways,
And the harsh drive to strive
For a virtue yet to be known.

Dear, sweet Humility,
Water the love in my heart;
Steep it in your own living waters!
O my heart, may you live your whole
Life for the right sort of death!

"Prince mort . . ."

Prince mort en soldat à cause de la France,
    Âme certes élue,
Fier jeune homme si pur tombé plein d'espérance,
    Je t'aime et te salue!

Ce monde est si mauvais, notre pauvre patrie
    Va sous tant de ténèbres,
Vaisseau désemparé dont l'équipage crie
    Avec des voix funèbres,

Ce siècle est un tel ciel tragique où les naufrages
    Semblent écrits d'avance . . .
Ma jeunesse, élevée aux doctrines sauvages,
    Détesta ton enfance,

Et plus tard, cœur pirate épris des seules côtes
    Où la révolte naisse,
Mon âge d'homme, noir d'orages et de fautes,
    Abhorrait ta jeunesse.

Maintenant j'aime Dieu dont l'amour et la foudre
    M'ont fait une âme neuve,
Et maintenant que mon orgueil réduit en poudre,
    Humble, accepte l'épreuve,

J'admire ton destin, j'adore, tout en larmes
    Pour les pleurs de ta mère,
Dieu qui te fit mourir, beau prince, sous les armes,
    Comme un héros d'Homère.

"Prince brought down . . ."

Prince brought down as a soldier for France,
    Blessèd soul,
Proud pure young man fallen while still full of hope,
    Accept my love, accept my salute!

This world is so evil, our poor nation
    So covered in darkness,
A vessel adrift whose crew cries out
    In funereal tones,

Beneath so tragic a sky, where wrecks seem
    Inscribed in advance . . .
When a youth, imbued with undisciplined dogmas,
    I abhorred your high birth,

And later, with piratical heart drawn only to shores
    Where revolt might break out,
As a man blackened by storms and by sins,
    I detested your youth.

Now, with God's love and his thunderous power,
    My soul is renewed,
And now that my pride, reduced to mere powder,
    Humbly accepts the event,

I admire your fate; I worship, as I weep for
    The tears of your mother,
The God who slew you, good Prince, under arms,
    Like a hero of Homer.

Et je dis, réservant d'ailleurs mon vœu suprême
　　Au lys de Louis Seize:
Napoléon, qui fus digne du diadème,
　　Gloire à ta mort française!

Et priez bien pour nous, pour cette France ancienne,
　　Aujourd'hui vraiment "Sire,"
Dieu qui vous couronna, sur la terre païenne,
　　Bon chrétien, du martyre!

Prologue de "Jadis"

En route, mauvaise troupe!
Partez, mes enfants perdus!
Ces loisirs vous étaient dus:
La Chimère tend sa croupe.

Partez, grimpés sur son dos,
Comme essaime un vol de rêves
D'un malade dans les brèves
Fleurs vagues de ses rideaux.

Ma main tiède qui s'agite
Faible encore, mais enfin
Sans fièvre, et qui ne palpite
Plus que d'un effort divin,

Ma main vous bénit, petites
Mouches de mes soleils noirs
Et de mes nuits blanches. Vites,
Partez, petits désespoirs,

And I say, as I pronounce my ultimate tribute
    Before Louis Sixteenth:
Glory, Napoleon, who merited the crown,
    Glory to your death as a Frenchman!

Pray now for us, for this France ages-old,
    Now truly Sire,
Crowned by our God in the land of the pagans,
    Christian forever, and martyr!

Prologue of "Long Ago"

Move along, wicked band!
On your way, my rudderless children!
This time off was due you:
The Chimera is showing his rump.

On your way! hanging onto his back
Like a swarm of bad dreams
Among the ill-defined flowers
Of a patient's bed curtains!

My tepid hand, still weak,
But moving finally free
Of its fever, is yet only nimble
With heaven-helped effort.

With that hand I bless you,
My little spots of black suns
And white nights. Quick now,
On your way, little bits of despair!

Petits espoirs, douleurs, joies,
Que dès hier renia
Mon cœur quêtant d'autres proies . . .
Allez, *ægri somnia.*

Prologue de "Naguère"

Ce sont choses crépusculaires,
Des visions de fin de nuit.
Ô Vérité, tu les éclaires
Seulement d'une aube qui luit

Si pâle dans l'ombre abhorrée
Qu'on doute encore par instants
Si c'est la lune qui les crée
Sous l'horreur des rameaux flottants,

Ou si ces fantômes moroses
Vont tout à l'heure prendre corps
Et se mêler au chœur des choses
Dans les harmonieux décors

Du soleil et de la nature;
Doux à l'homme et proclamant Dieu
Pour l'extase de l'hymne pure
Jusqu'à la douceur du ciel bleu.

À la louange de Laure et de Pétrarque

Chose italienne où Shakespeare a passé
Mais que Ronsard fit superbement française,
Fine basilique au large diocèse,
Saint-Pierre-des-Vers, immense et condensé,

Little hopes, pains, and joys
Renounced but now by my heart
As it seeks other prey . . .
Be on your way, bitter dreams!

Prologue of "Yesterday"

They are crepuscular things,
Things we see when night ends.
In truth, they come to light
Only when dawn first appears,

Appears so pale in the detested dark
That still we sometimes wonder
If they're created by the moon
To frighten us with spectral boughs,

Or if these doleful ghosts
Are going soon to take on flesh
And join all things in hearty song
In harmony with the waiting stage,

This stage of sun and all of nature—
Welcome to man, proclaiming the Lord
In a pure, ecstatic anthem,
Reaching up to a heaven of blue.

In Praise of Laura and Petrarch

An Italian invention that Shakespeare used, too,
But was made proudly French by Ronsard,
Spiraling church drawing devout from afar,
Saint Peter of Verse, immense text to construe,

Elle, ta marraine, et Lui qui t'a pensé,
Dogme entier toujours debout sous l'exégèse
Même edmondschéresque ou francisquearceyse,
Sonnet, force acquise et trésor amassé,

Ceux-là sont très bons et toujours vénérables,
Ayant procuré leur luxe aux misérables
Et l'or fou qui sied aux pauvres glorieux,

Aux poètes fiers comme les gueux d'Espagne,
Aux vierges qu'exalte un rhythme exact, aux yeux
Épris d'ordre, aux cœurs qu'un vœu chaste accompagne.

Your godmother She, and He it was made you,
A full dogma still standing after the scars
Scratched by one or another critical star,
Sonnet! with strength and treasure imbued,

Those two are good and due veneration,
Having given new wealth to poetic creation,
And fool's gold to the pitifully supreme,

Pitiful poets as proud as the vagrants of Spain,
And virgins excited only by rhythm, eyes keen
On order, and hearts with a single chaste aim.

From *Amour* [Love] and Other Poems

À propos d'un "centenaire" de Calderon (1600–1681)

Ce poète terrible et divinement doux,
Plus large que Corneille et plus haut que Shakespeare,
Grand comme Eschyle avec ce souffle qui l'inspire,
Ce Calderon mystique et mythique est à nous.

Oui, cette gloire est nôtre, et nous voici jaloux
De le dire bien haut à ce siècle en délire:
Calderon, catholique avant tout, noble lyre
Et saints accents, et bon catholique avant tous,

Salut! Et qu'est ce bruit fâcheux d'académies,
De concours, de discours, autour de ce grand mort
En éveil parmi tant de choses endormies?

Laissez rêver, laissez penser son Œuvre fort
Qui plane, loin d'un siècle impie et ridicule,
Au-dessus, au-delà des colonnes d'Hercule!

MAI 1881.

À Victor Hugo, en lui envoyant "Sagesse" (1881)

Nul parmi vos flatteurs d'aujourd'hui n'a connu
Mieux que moi la fierté d'admirer votre gloire:
Votre nom m'enivrait comme un nom de victoire,
Votre œuvre, je l'aimais d'un amour ingénu.

From *Amour* [Love] and Other Poems

About a Calderón Centenary (1600–1681)

This powerful poet, divinely benign,
More inclusive than Corneille, more lofty than Shakespeare,
Great as was Aeschylus, with his inspiring breath,
This Calderón, mystic and mythic, is ours.

Yes, this glory is ours, and here we are, eager
To say so out loud in this delirious world:
Calderón, Catholic above all, noble lyre,
Sacred rhythms, and good Catholic most of all,

Hail to you! But what is this harsh academical stir,
Contests and speeches, while the great long-deceased
Stands awake and alert amid so much that's asleep?

Let his strong Work dream on, let it still think
As it glides, far from an impious, ridiculous world,
High above, high beyond the Pillars of Hercules!

MAY 1881.

To Victor Hugo, upon Sending Him "Sagesse" (1881)

None of those now flattering you has known
Better than I the pride of admiring your glory:
Your name was as thrilling as a victory's name;
Your works: with what innocent love did I love them!

Depuis, la Vérité m'a mis le monde à nu.
J'aime Dieu, son église, et ma vie est de croire
Tout ce que vous tenez, hélas! pour dérisoire,
Et j'abhorre en vos vers le Serpent reconnu.

J'ai changé. Comme vous. Mais d'une autre manière.
Tout petit que je suis j'avais aussi le droit
D'une évolution, la bonne, la dernière.

Or, je sais la louange, ô maître, que vous doit
L'enthousiasme ancien; la voici franche, pleine,
Car vous me fûtes doux en des heures de peine.

À Ernest Delahaye

Dieu, nous voulant amis parfaits, nous fit tous deux
Gais de cette gaîté qui rit pour elle-même,
De ce rire absolu, colossal et suprême,
Qui s'esclaffe de tous et ne blesse aucun d'eux.

Tous deux nous ignorons l'égoïsme hideux
Qui nargue ce prochain même qu'il faut qu'on aime
Comme soi-même: tels les termes du problème,
Telle la loi totale au texte non douteux.

Et notre rire étant celui de l'innocence,
Il éclate et rugit dans la toute-puissance
D'un bon orage plein de lumière et d'air frais.

Pour le soin du Salut, qui me pique et m'inspire,
J'estime que, parmi nos façons d'être prêts,
Il nous faut mettre au rang des meilleures ce rire.

Truth, since that time, has re-cast my world.
I love God, love his Church, and fully believe
All that you hold, alas, open to scorn,
And I abhor, in your verse, the Serpent I see there.

I have changed. As have you. But not the same way.
Small as I am, I too had the right to evolve.
This change is correct—and is the last.

I do know all the praise, Master, that my fervor of old
Owes to you. Here it is now, offered freely and fully,
For you were gentle to me in my hours of pain.

To Ernest Delahaye

God, with His will that we be perfect friends, made us both
Mirthful with that mirth that laughs for no sake but its own,
With that absolute laugh, supreme and colossal,
That finds everyone fun and is hurtful to none.

We both pay no heed to that egotistical grossness
That derides the same neighbor it's our duty to love
As we love ourself: such are the terms of the problem;
Such is the law that's beyond doubt or question.

And since our laughter is innocent laughter,
It bursts out and roars with the almighty power
Of a beneficent storm full of light and fresh air.

As for Salvation, my goad and ever true inspiration,
I believe, among all the ways we may have to prepare,
There's probably none more effective than our laughter.

Langueur

Je suis l'Empire à la fin de la décadence,
Qui regarde passer les grands Barbares blancs
En composant des acrostiches indolents
D'un style d'or où la langueur du soleil danse.

L'âme seulette a mal au cœur d'un ennui dense.
Là-bas on dit qu'il est de longs combats sanglants.
Ô n'y pouvoir, étant si faible aux vœux si lents,
Ô n'y vouloir fleurir un peu cette existence!

Ô n'y vouloir, ô n'y pouvoir mourir un peu!
Ah! tout est bu! Bathylle, as-tu fini de rire?
Ah! tout est bu, tout est mangé! Plus rien à dire!

Seul, un poème un peu niais qu'on jette au feu,
Seul, un esclave un peu coureur qui vous néglige,
Seul, un ennui d'on ne sait quoi qui vous afflige!

Parsifal

Parsifal a vaincu les Filles, leur gentil
Babil et la luxure amusante—et sa pente
Vers la Chair de garçon vierge que cela tente
D'aimer les seins légers et ce gentil babil;

Il a vaincu la Femme belle, au cœur subtil,
Étalant ses bras frais et sa gorge excitante;
Il a vaincu l'Enfer et rentre sous sa tente
Avec un lourd trophée à son bras puéril,

Languor

I am the Empire as Decadence ends,
Watching the tall blond invaders pass through
While I sit composing indifferent acrostics
With a stylus of gold in a slow sunlit dance.

The solitary soul is disheartened and aching.
They say over there that bloody fights are to come.
Oh, we can't, with our weakness and hesitant wishes—
Oh, we won't turn this life into flowered denial!

Oh, we won't—oh, we can't—lie down and die!
Ah! it's all drunk! is your laughing, Bathyllus, now done?
Ah! it's all drunk! it's all eaten! No more can we say!

There's only a dumb poem that belongs in the fire;
There's only a slave with an eye not for you;
There's only an ache with no name—but it hurts!

Parsifal

Parsifal has defeated the Maidens, their agreeable
Babble, their lustful amusement—and his own
Virginal weakness for Flesh, which tempts him
To love youthful breasts and agreeable babble;

He has defeated the beautiful woman of wiles,
Displaying warm arms and provocative bosom;
He has defeated Hell and returned to his tent,
A still-childlike arm bearing a trophy too heavy

Avec la lance qui perça le Flanc suprême!
Il a guéri le roi, le voici roi lui-même,
Et prêtre du très saint Trésor essentiel.

En robe d'or il adore, gloire et symbole,
Le vase pur où resplendit le Sang réel.
—Et, ô ces voix d'enfants chantant dans la coupole!

Ballade—À propos de deux ormeaux qu'il avait

Mon jardin fut doux et léger,
Tant qu'il fut mon humble richesse:
Mi-potager et mi-verger,
Avec quelque fleur qui se dresse
Couleur d'amour et d'allégresse,
Et des oiseaux sur des rameaux,
Et du gazon pour la paresse.
Mais rien ne valut mes ormeaux.

De ma claire salle à manger
Où du vin fit quelque prouesse,
Je les voyais tous deux bouger
Doucement au vent qui les presse
L'un vers l'autre en une caresse,
Et leurs feuilles flûtaient des mots.
Le clos était plein de tendresse.
Mais rien ne valut mes ormeaux.

Hélas! Quand il fallut changer
De cieux et quitter ma liesse,
Le verger et le potager
Se partagèrent ma tristesse,
Et la fleur couleur charmeresse,
Et l'herbe, oreiller de mes maux,

With the Spear that pierced the heavenly Side!
The king is now healed; he himself is now king
And now priest of the holiest Treasure.

In golden robe, he bows low before glory and symbol:
The pure vessel containing the real gleaming blood.
But, oh, those boys' voices singing under the dome!

Ballade—About Two Elms That He Had

My garden was a restful delight,
My well-loved and humble possession:
It gave what the kitchen required,
And grew too a remarkable bloom
Colored in love and in joy,
And there were birds on the boughs,
And grass for cushioned repose.
But it was my elms I loved most.

In my bright dining room,
Where the pleasure of wine had a place,
I'd watch them both gently sway
As the wind urged them on, one
Toward the other, in a binding caress,
As their leaves trilled their sighs.
Such was the love the garden enclosed,
But it was my elms I loved most.

Alas! When the time came to leave
This abode and the bliss that it brought,
The orchard and the vegetable garden
Shared my sadness between them,
And the flower colored enchantment
And the grass that pillowed my pain

Et l'oiseau, surent ma détresse.
Mais rien ne valut mes ormeaux.

Envoi

Prince, j'ai goûté la simplesse
De vivre heureux dans vos hameaux:
Gaîté, santé que rien ne blesse.
Mais rien ne valut mes ormeaux.

Ballade Sappho

Ma douce main de maîtresse et d'amant
Passe et rit sur ta chère chair en fête,
Rit et jouit de ton jouissement.
Pour la servir tu sais bien qu'elle est faite,
Et ton beau corps faut que je le dévête
Pour l'enivrer sans fin d'un art nouveau
Toujours dans la caresse toujours prête.
Je suis pareil à la grande Sappho.

Laisse ma tête errant et s'abîmant
À l'aventure, un peu farouche, en quête
D'ombre et d'odeur et d'un travail charmant
Vers les saveurs de ta gloire secrète.
Laisse rôder l'âme de ton poète
Partout par là, champ ou bois, mont ou vau,
Comme tu veux et si je le souhaite.
Je suis pareil à la grande Sappho.

Je presse alors tout ton corps goulûment,
Toute ta chair contre mon corps d'athlète
Qui se bande et s'amollit par moment,
Heureux du triomphe et de la défaite

And the birds understood all my woes.
But it was my elms I loved most.

Envoy

Prince, I have known how simple it was
To live in your hamlets and happy,
With good health and cheer unopposed.
But it was my elms I loved most.

Sappho Ballade

Mistress or lover, I pass my hand gently
Over the feast of your flesh, and I smile;
I smile and enjoy the enjoyment you feel.
My hand, need I say? was intended for that.
And I need to unclothe your beautiful form
For unending arousal with a skill always
New, with an art of caresses ever renewed.
I follow the way of great Sappho.

Let my head wander and burrow
Wherever it will, even wildly, will, in quest
Of shadow and scent and the charm of exertion
Toward the taste of your glorious secret.
Let the soul of your poet now roam
Everywhere, field or wood, hill or vale,
Just as you like and if it's my wish as well.
I follow the way of great Sappho.

Then I'll hungrily press your whole body,
Your whole flesh, against the athlete I am,
Stiffening now, softening after,
Happy in triumph as in concluding

En ce conflit du cœur et de la tête.
Pour la stérile étreinte où le cerveau
Vient faire enfin la nature complète
Je suis pareil à la grande Sappho.

Envoi

Prince ou princesse, honnête ou malhonnête,
Qui qu'en grogne et quelque soit son niveau,
Trop su poète ou divin proxénète,
Je suis pareil à la grande Sappho.

Guitare

Le pauvre du chemin creux chante et parle.
Il dit: "Mon nom est Pierre et non pas Charle,
Et je m'appelle aussi Duchatelet.
Une fois je vis, moi qu'on croit très laid,
Passer vraiment une femme très belle.
(Si je la voyais telle, elle était telle.)
Nous nous mariâmes au vieux curé.
On eut tout ce qu'on avait espéré,
Jusqu'à l'enfant qu'on m'a dit vivre encore.
Mais elle devint la pire pécore
Indigne même de cette chanson,
Et certain beau soir quitta la maison
En emportant tout l'argent du ménage
Dont les trois quarts étaient mon apanage.
C'était une voleuse, une sans-cœur,
Et puis, par des fois, je lui faisais peur.
Elle n'avait pas l'ombre d'une excuse,
Pas un amant ou par rage ou par ruse.
Il paraît qu'elle couche depuis peu
Avec un individu qui tient lieu

In this contest of head and of heart.
For the sterile embrace in which mind
Comes at last to complement nature.
I follow the way of great Sappho.

Envoy

Prince or princéss, truthful or not,
Whoever may grumble and of whatever condition,
Too well-known a poet or divine go-between,
I follow the way of great Sappho.

Guitar

Down in the hollow there's a poor fellow who sings
As he says: "My name is not Roger but Peter,
And as for the rest, I call myself Castle.
One time I saw, I who was thought very homely,
A woman pass by who was remarkably lovely.
(If that's how I saw her, that's how she was.)
We were soon married by the old local priest
And had whatever we'd hoped for,
Even the child who I hear's still alive.
But she became the most stupid of sows,
Unworthy even of this poor song of mine;
Then came the day she picked up and left,
Carrying off the household's last funds.
Most of that money was mine by all rights.
What a thief, this woman without any heart!
True enough, I may sometimes have scared her.
Still, she didn't have the slightest excuse,
No lover to run to, no rage or unoriginal ruse.
It appears she's been recently living
With some creature who stands in

D'époux à cette femme de querelle.
Faut-il la tuer ou prier pour elle?"

Et le pauvre sait très bien qu'il priera,
Mais le diable parierait qu'il tuera.

Gais et contents

Une chanson folle et légère
Comme le drapeau tricolore
Court furieusement dans l'air,
Fifrant une France âpre encor.

Sa gaîté qui rit d'elle-même
Et du reste en passant se moque
Pourtant veut bien dire: Tandem!
Et vaticine le grand choc.

Écoutez! le flonflon se pare
Des purs accents de la Patrie,
Espèce de chant du départ
Du gosse effrayant de Paris.

Il est le rhythme, il est la joie,
Il est la Revanche essayée,
Il est l'entrain, il est tout, quoi!
Jusqu'au juron luron qui sied,

Jusqu'au cri de reconnaissance
Qu'on pousse quand il faut qu'on meure
De sang-froid, dans tout son bon sens,
Avec de l'honneur plein son cœur!

As a mate for this troublesome woman.
Should I put her to death or pray for her soul?"

And the poor fellow's quite sure that he'll pray,
But the devil is betting on death.

Cheerful and Glad

A song that's as foolish and frilly
As our flag of three colors
Is making the rounds in the city,
Fifing a France still bitter and fierce.

Her good cheer is a laugh at herself,
While she couldn't care less for the rest—
Which makes quite a pair of concerns,
With pompous pronouncements aplenty.

Just listen! the band wants to blare
The bold sounds of the Nation,
A goodbye kind of outgoing shout
From the capital's creepiest kid.

It's got rhythm, it's got joy;
It's got the would-be Avenger himself;
It's got gusto, it's got go—
Right down to a fitting wild oath!

Right down to the shout "Now I see!"
When your time's come to bow out—
A brave, forthright cry that says clearly
What honor resides in your heart.

À Emmanuel Chabrier

Chabrier, nous faisions, un ami cher et moi,
Des paroles pour vous qui leur donniez des ailes,
Et tous trois frémissions quand, pour bénir nos zèles,
Passait l'Ecce Deus et le Je ne sais quoi.

Chez ma mère charmante et divinement bonne,
Votre génie improvisait au piano,
Et c'était tout autour comme un brûlant anneau
De sympathie et d'aise aimable qui rayonne.

Hélas! ma mère est morte et l'ami cher est mort.
Et me voici semblable au chrétien près du port,
Qui surveille les tout derniers écueils du monde,

Non toutefois sans saluer à l'horizon,
Comme une voile sur le large au blanc frisson,
Le souvenir des frais instants de paix profonde.

À Fernand Langlois

Vous vous êtes penché sur ma mélancolie,
Non comme un indiscret, non comme un curieux,
Et vous avez surpris la clef de ma folie,
Tel un consolateur attentif et piteux;

Et vous avez ouvert doucement ma serrure,
Y mettant tout le temps, non ainsi qu'un voleur,
Mais ainsi que quelqu'un qui préserve et rassure
Un triste possesseur peut-être recéleur.

To Emmanuel Chabrier

Chabrier, I wrote, with a dear friend of mine,
Words to which you would give wings,
And all three we were stirred when, to bless our efforts,
We heard your "Ecce Deus" and "Je ne sais quoi."

In the home of my charming, divinely good mother,
Your genius would improvise at the piano,
And all around us would burn bright a circle
Of radiant warmth and comfort and ease.

Alas! my mother is gone, and gone is my friend.
And here am I, like the Christian alert at the port,
Looking out at the very last reefs in the world,

Not, though, without saluting, on the horizon,
The fluttering white sail out at sea, bringing back
The remembrance of deep moments of peace.

To Fernand Langlois

You took a close look at my sadness,
Not wanting to be indiscreet or to meddle,
And you uncovered the key to my madness;
You consoled me with attention and pity;

You gently unlocked what was hidden,
Slowly prying and searching, not as a thief
But as someone intent on being of help
To an unhappy hoarder of miserable secrets.

Soyez aimé d'un cœur plus veuf que toutes veuves,
Qui n'avait plus personne en qui pleurer vraiment,
Soyez béni d'une âme errant au bord des fleuves
Consolateurs si mal avec leur air dormant;

Que soient suivis des pas d'un but à la dérive
Hier encor, vos pas eux-mêmes tristes, ô
Si tristes, mais que si bien tristes, et que vive
Encore, alors! mais par vous pour Dieu, ce roseau,

Cet oiseau, ce roseau sous cet oiseau, ce blême
Oiseau sur ce pâle roseau fleuri jadis,
Et pâle et sombre, spectre et sceptre noir: Moi-même!
Surrexit hodie, non plus: *de profundis*.

Fiat! La défaillance a fini. Le courage
Revient. Sur votre bras permettez qu'appuyé
Je marche en la fraîcheur de l'expirant orage,
Moi-même comme qui dirait défoudroyé.

Là, je vais mieux. Tantôt le calme s'en va naître.
Il naît. Si vous voulez, allons à petits pas,
Devisant de la vie et d'un bonheur peut-être
Non, sans doute, impossible, en somme, n'est-ce pas?

Oui, causons de bonheur. Mais vous? pourquoi si triste,
Vous aussi? Vous si jeune et si triste, ô pourquoi,
Dites? Mais cela vous regarde; et si j'insiste,
C'est uniquement pour vous plaire et non pour moi.

Discrétion sans borne, immense sympathie!
C'est l'heure précieuse, elle est unique, elle est
Angélique. Tantôt l'avez-vous pressentie?
Avez-vous comme su—moi je l'ai—qu'il fallait

Accept the love of a heart more bereft than a widow's,
Who could no longer find a breast for his weeping;
Be blessed by a soul adrift on rivers meant to console
But doing so poorly with their air of uncaring;

May your steps, in their sadness, soon be followed
By steps that only yesterday, and still sadder, were
Wandering, oh, so lost!—and may this reed, with
Thanks to you, live on and celebrate God's will!

That bird, that reed under the bird, colorless bird
Atop the pale reed that was once in full bloom,
Now pale and somber, specter and dark scepter: Myself!
Surrexit hodie, no more: *de profundis.*

Fiat! The crisis has passed. Assurance
Is back. Allow me, with the help of your arm,
To encounter the freshness that follows the storm,
My self, so to speak, renewed and unthundered.

There, I feel better. Give it a moment; calm will return.
It's returning. If you wish, let's proceed step by step,
Discoursing on life and perhaps happiness, too—
Well, no! is it not, in the end, an impossible thing?

Yes, that's our topic. You, though, why are you sad,
Sad as I am? You, so young and so sad, why, oh why?
Tell me. But that's your concern; and if I persist,
It's for you to be pleased, and not for my sake.

Boundless discretion, broad and deep fellow-feeling!
The moment is precious, strangely one of a kind,
Gift of an angel. Could you have known in advance?
Could you have known—as I knew—that this was a need?

Peut-être bien, sans doute, et quoique, et puisque, en somme
Éprouvant tant d'estime et combien de pitié,
Laisser monter en nous, fleur suprême de l'homme,
Franchement, largement, simplement, l'Amitié.

Lucien Létinois

XV

Puisque encore déjà la sottise tempête,
Explique alors la chose, ô malheureux poète.

Je connus cet enfant, mon amère douceur,
Dans un pieux collège où j'étais professeur.
Ses dix-sept ans mutins et maigres, sa réelle
Intelligence, et la pureté vraiment belle
Que disaient et ses yeux et son geste et sa voix,
Captivèrent mon cœur et dictèrent mon choix
De lui pour fils, puisque, mon vrai fils, mes entrailles,
On me le cache en manière de représailles
Pour je ne sais quels torts charnels et surtout pour
Un fier départ à la recherche de l'amour
Loin d'une vie aux platitudes résignée!
Oui, surtout et plutôt pour ma fuite indignée
En compagnie illustre et fraternelle vers
Tous les points du physique et moral univers,
—Il paraît que des gens dirent jusqu'à Sodome,—
Où mourussent les cris de Madame Prudhomme!

Je lui fis part de mon dessein. Il accepta.

Il avait des parents qu'il aimait, qu'il quitta
D'esprit pour être mien, tout en restant son maître
Et maître de son cœur, de son âme peut-être,

A need, very likely, although and because (and what else?)
We felt such esteem and were so deeply moved,
To let blossom in us that finest, that greatest flower of man,
Fully and frankly, broadly and simply: Friendship.

Lucien Létinois

XV

Since once again stupidity's raging,
Tell us, O poet, what the storm is about!

I met this young boy, my bitter-sweet love,
In a confessional school where I worked as a teacher.
Cheeky and twiggy at seventeen years, really
Bright, though, and beautifully, honestly pure,
As said his eyes and his gestures and voice, which
Then captured my heart and dictated my choice
Of him as my son, since the actual fruit of my loins
Was hidden from me as a kind of revenge
For some sort of sins of the flesh and even more
For a proud goodbye in the interest of love,
Far from a life that's resigned to clichés—
Yes, but especially, for my indignant flight
In company well-known and fraternal, toward
All points of the moral and physical world where
It seems some people said we'd go even to Sodom—
Enough to send Ms. Oh-So-Proper into a spin!

I spoke to the lad of my plan. He agreed.

He had parents whom he loved, whom in spirit
He left to be mine; he remained his own master—
Master he was, of his heart and his soul, master,

Mais de son esprit, plus.

                    Ce fut bien, ce fut beau,
Et c'eût été trop bon, n'eût été le tombeau.
Jugez.

     En même temps que toutes mes idées
(Les bonnes!) entraient dans son esprit, précédées
De l'Amitié jonchant leur passage de fleurs,
De lui, simple et blanc comme un lys calme aux couleurs
D'innocence candide et d'espérance verte,
L'Exemple descendait sur mon âme entr'ouverte
Et sur mon cœur qu'il pénétrait, plein de pitié,
Par un chemin semé des fleurs de l'Amitié;
Exemple des vertus joyeuses, la franchise,
La chasteté, la foi naïve dans l'Église,
Exemple des vertus austères, vivre en Dieu,
Le chérir en tout temps et le craindre en tout lieu,
Sourire, que l'instant soit léger ou sévère,
Pardonner, qui n'est pas une petite affaire!

Cela dura six ans, puis l'ange s'envola,
Dès lors je vais hagard et comme ivre. Voilà.

XVI
Cette adoption de toi pour mon enfant
Puisque l'on m'avait volé mon fils réel,
Elle n'était pas dans les conseils du ciel,
Je me le suis dit, en pleurant, bien souvent;

Je me le suis dit toujours devant ta tombe
Noire de fusains, blanche de marguerites;
Elle fut sans doute un de ces démérites
Cause de ces maux où voici que je tombe.

What's more, of his spirit.
                          All was well, all was fine,
And it would have been ideal, if not for the grave.
Just think.
                  At the same time my ideas (the right ones!)
Were finding their way through his mind, guided
By Friendship, with flowers strewn on the way;
His simple example, calm, lily-white,
With purity's candor and the green hue of hope,
Swept down upon my now welcoming soul
And pierced my heart with compassionate feeling.
On a road sown with the flowers of Friendship,
His example of the virtues of joy and of frankness,
Chastity, unquestioning faith in the Church—
Example of virtues austere and anchored in God,
Loving him always and fearing him wherever,
Smiling through light moments or heavy,
Granting pardon—not a painless affair!

It lasted six years and then the angel took flight.
Haggard I stay, as if I were drunk. Come now what may.

XVI
My adoption of you as my child
Since my real son had been stolen away,
Was never intended by heaven;
The thought often brings me to tears.

That is my thought as I look at your tomb,
Charcoal-black and white with daisy bouquets;
The adoption was surely one of those errors
Causing the ills that have now brought me low.

Ce fut, je le crains, un faux raisonnement.
À bien réfléchir je n'avais pas le droit,
Pour me consoler dans mon chemin étroit,
De te choisir même, ô si naïvement,

Même ô pour ce plan d'humble vertu cachée:
Quelques champs autour d'une maison sans faste
Que connaît le pauvre, et sur un bonheur chaste
La grâce de Dieu complaisamment penchée!

Fallait te laisser, pauvre et gai, dans ton nid,
Ne pas te mêler à mes jeux orageux,
Et souffrir l'exil en proscrit courageux,
L'exil loin du fils né d'un amour bénit.

Il me reviendrait, le fils des justes noces,
À l'époque d'être au moment d'être un homme,
Quand il comprendrait, quand il sentirait comme
Son père endura des sottises féroces!

Cette adoption fut le fruit défendu;
J'aurais dû passer dans l'odeur et le frais
De l'arbre et du fruit sans m'arrêter auprès.
Le ciel m'a puni . . . J'aurais dû, j'aurais dû!

I'm afraid that my thinking was wrong.
The fact is, I see, it wasn't my right
To seek consolation for my too-narrow path
By turning even to you, oh, so naively,

Even, oh, for our veiled humble virtue,
A few fields around a small modest house,
A poor man's house, and observing our chaste
Joy, God's grace looks on with approval!

Should 've left you, poor and content, in your nest,
Not draw you in to my tempestuous games
To suffer my exile as a courageous outsider,
An exile far from the son of legitimate love.

Will he return, that son of proper conception,
When the time comes to grow into a man,
When he can grasp, when he can finally feel
What ferocious stupidities his father endured?

This adoption was truly the forbidden fruit;
I should have gone past the fresh fragrance
Of the tree and its fruit with no halt for a taste.
I've been punished by God for an awful mistake!

À Georges Verlaine

Ce livre ira vers toi comme celui d'Ovide
        S'en alla vers la Ville.
Il fut chassé de Rome; un coup bien plus perfide
        Loin de mon fils m'exile.

Te reverrai-je? Et quel? Mais quoi? moi mort ou non,
        Voici mon testament:
Crains Dieu, ne hais personne, et porte bien ton nom
        Qui fut porté dûment.

To Georges Verlaine

This book will go to you as Ovid's book
> Went out to the City.
He was run out of Rome; a scheme more treacherous still
> Banishes me far from my son.

Will I see you again? Whatever occurs, dead or alive,
> I give you this final word:
Fear God; hate no one; and bear your name with honor,
> For so was it borne.

From *Bonheur* [Happiness]

Noël—à Rodolphe Salis

La neige à travers la brume
Tombe et tapisse sans bruit
Le chemin creux qui conduit
À l'église où l'on allume
Pour la messe de minuit.

Londres sombre flambe et fume:
Ô la chère qui s'y cuit
Et la boisson qui s'ensuit!
C'est Christmas et sa coutume
De minuit jusqu'à minuit.

Sur la plume et le bitume,
Paris bruit et jouit.
Ripaille et Plaisant Déduit
Sur le bitume et la plume
S'exaspèrent dès minuit.

Le malade en l'amertume
De l'hospice où le poursuit
Un espoir toujours détruit
S'épouvante et se consume
Dans le noir d'un long minuit . . .

From *Bonheur* [Happiness]

Christmas—To Rodolphe Salis

Snow falls through the mist
And silently carpets
The sunken lane that leads
To the church they're lighting now
For mass at midnight.

Darkening London flames and frizzles:
Oh, the feast that's before us
And the drink that will follow!
It's Christmas and its customs
From midnight to midnight.

Whether in bed or the street,
Paris is buzzing and busy with fun.
They make merry and frolic
Whether in street or in bed,
Going too far as soon as it's midnight.

Bitterly a patient in the bed
Of the hospice where he's pursued
By a hope that's destroyed once again
Takes fright and wastes now away
In the long darkness of midnight.

La cloche au son clair d'enclume
Dans la tour fine qui luit,
Loin du péché qui nous nuit,
Nous appelle en grand costume
À la messe de minuit.

DÉCEMBRE, HÔPITAL BROUSSAIS.

XX

I

Je voudrais, si ma vie était encore à faire,
Qu'une femme très calme habitât avec moi,
Plus jeune de dix ans, qui portât sans émoi
La moitié d'une vie au fond plutôt sévère.

Notre cœur à tous deux dans ce château de verre,
Notre regard commun, franchise et bonne foi,
Un et double, dirait comme en soi-même: Voi!
Et répondrait comme à soi-même: Persévère!

Elle se tiendrait à sa place, mienne aussi,
Nous serions en ceci le couple réussi
Que l'inégalité, parbleu! des caractères

Ne saurait empêcher l'équilibre qu'il faut,
Ce point étant compris d'esprits en somme austères
Qu'au fond et qu'en tout cas l'indulgence prévaut.

The bell with its anvil-bright bang
In the tower glowing on high,
Far removed from the sin that besets us,
Is a summons to come in full dress
To mass at midnight.

DECEMBER, BROUSSAIS HOSPITAL.

XX

I

I would like, if my life were still lying ahead,
To find a wife quite calm to abide with me,
Ten years my junior and ready to spend
Half a lifetime resigned and somewhat severe.

Two hearts together in that castle of glass,
Two views converging in honest good faith,
Each and the other in wordless accord—yes!,
Responding as one to the same "Persevere!"

She'd know her place, as I would know mine;
Thus we would be a success as a couple;
For dissimilar traits might very well show,

But that couldn't prevent the balance we'd need,
As that point would be made by sensible spirits,
And in any case tempered by unfailing indulgence.

II

L'indulgence qui n'est pas de l'indifférence
Et qui n'est pas non plus de la faiblesse, ni
De la paresse pour un devoir défini,
Monitoire au plaisir, bénin à la souffrance.

Non plus le scepticisme et ni préjugé rance
Mais grand'délicatesse et bel accord béni,
Et ni la chair honnie et ni l'ennui banni,
Toute mansuétude et comme vieille France.

Nous serions une mer en deux fleuves puissants
Où le Bonheur et le Malheur, têtes de flotte,
Nous passeraient sans heurts, montés par le Bon Sens,

Ubiquiste équipage, ubiquiste pilote,
Ubiquiste amiral sous ton sûr pavillon,
Amitié, non plus sous le vôtre, Amour brouillon.

III

L'amitié, mais entre homme et femme elle est divine!
Elle n'empêche rien, aussi bien, des rapports
Nécessaires, et sous les mieux séants dehors
Abrite les secrets aimables qu'on devine.

Nous mettrions chacun du nôtre, elle très fine,
Moi plus naïf, et bien réglés en chers efforts
Lesdits rapports dès lors si joyeux sans remords
Dans la simplesse ovine et la raison bovine.

Si le bonheur était d'ici, ce le serait!
Puis nous nous en irions sans l'ombre d'un regret,
La conscience en paix et de l'espoir plein l'âme,

II

Indulgence that isn't indifference
And that's neither weakness nor sloth,
Whatever the task or duty in question,
Caution for pleasure, kind help in distress . . .

Neither skeptical look nor jaundiced prejudgment,
But a delicate welcome and blessèd accord,
Neither shame of the flesh nor denial of dullness,
All kindness and goodness as tradition requires . . .

We're like a sea joining two powerful streams,
Where Good Fortune and Bad, sailing ahead,
Could steam past without ramming Good Sense.

Ubiquitous crew, ubiquitous pilot,
Ubiquitous admiral under a reliable flag:
Friendship! no longer that muddle-head, Love!

III

Friendship between woman and man is truly divine!
It stops nothing, prevents no relations of the usual
Sort, and under the most proper of poses
Keeps all the secrets you'll find it easy to guess.

Each of us does what we can: she with finesse,
I rather grossly; and with dearly planned efforts,
The relations just said offer joy without question,
As do artless young sheep and clever new oxen.

Were happiness at home here—and yes, it could be!
We'd go out for a time with no hint of regret,
With conscience at peace and soul full of hope,

Comme les bons époux d'il n'y a pas longtemps,
Quand l'un et l'autre d'être heureux étaient contents
Qui vivaient, sans le trop chanter, l'épithalame.

XXXIII

Voix de Gabriel
Chez l'humble Marie,
Cloches de Noël,
Dans la nuit fleurie,
Siècles, célébrez
Mes sens délivrés!

Martyrs, troupe blanche,
Et les confesseurs,
Fruits d'or de la branche,
Vous, frères et sœurs,
Vierges dans la gloire,
Chantez ma victoire!

Les Saints ignorés,
Vertus qu'on méprise,
Qui nous sauverez
Par votre entremise,
Priez, que la foi
Demeure humble en moi.

Pécheurs, par le monde,
Qui vous repentez,
Dans l'ardeur profonde
D'être rachetés,
Or, je vous contemple,
Donnez-moi l'exemple.

Like good husbands and wives of not long ago,
When both were content to hymn their good fortune
And live the quiet notes of their marital anthem . . .

XXXIII

Voice of Gabriel
Alongside Mary the humble,
Bells of Noël
In flower-covered night,
Time and the age, celebrate
My senses' new freedom!

White troop of martyrs,
Confessors as well,
Golden fruits on the branch,
You, brothers and sisters,
Virgins in glory,
Sing of my triumph!

Saints disregarded,
Virtues disdained,
You who shall save us
Through your intervention,
Pray that my faith
Keep me humble.

Sinners everywhere
Who repent
In the deep ardent hope
Of redemption,
I consider you now;
Offer me your example.

Nature, animaux,
Eaux, plantes et pierres,
Vos simples travaux
Sont d'humbles prières.
Vous obéissez:

Pour Dieu, c'est assez.

Nature and animals,
Plants, water, and stones,
The simple works you perform
Are humble prayers.
You comply:

For God, that suffices.

From *Liturgies intimes* [Intimate Liturgies]

À Charles Baudelaire

Je ne t'ai pas connu, je ne t'ai pas aimé,
Je ne te connais point et je t'aime encore moins:
Je me chargerais mal de ton nom diffamé,
Et, si j'ai quelque droit d'être entre tes témoins,

C'est que, d'abord, et c'est qu'ailleurs, vers les Pieds joints
D'abord par les clous froids, puis par l'élan pâmé
Des femmes de péché—desquelles ô tant oints,
Tant baisés, chrême fol et baiser affamé!—

Tu tombas, tu prias, comme moi, comme toutes
Les âmes que la faim et la soif sur les routes
Poussaient belles d'espoir au Calvaire touché!

—Calvaire juste et vrai, Calvaire où, donc, ces doutes,
Ci, çà, grimaces, art, pleurent de leurs déroutes.
Hein? mourir simplement, nous, hommes de péché.

Rois

La myrrhe, l'or et l'encens
Sont des présents moins aimables
Que de plus humbles présents
Offerts aux Yeux adorables
Qui souriront plutôt mieux
À de simples vœux pieux.

From *Liturgies intimes* [Intimate Liturgies]

To Charles Baudelaire

I never met you; I didn't like you;
I don't know you now, and I like you even less:
I wouldn't readily take on a name so defamed
And if I have any right to be one of your witnesses,

Above all, it's because once, observing those Feet
Nailed so coldly together, and urged by the swoon
Of those women of sin (who anointed them so
With oil become holy, and so hungrily kissed!),

You fell to your knees and prayed, as I did,
Like all souls whom hunger and thirst on their way
Push, radiant with hope, toward Calvary's cross:

Calvary just, Calvary true, Calvary where doubts
On all sides, frowns and art too lament their lost way . . .
Death, is it? It's simple for us, men of sin that we are.

Kings

Myrrh, gold, and incense
Are less worthy gifts
Than gifts much more humble
Unveiled before precious Eyes
That will more gladly smile
Upon vows of simple piety.

Le voyage des Rois Mages
Certes agrée au Seigneur.
Il accepte ces hommages
Et les tient en haut honneur;
Mais d'un pécheur qui s'amende
Pour lui la gloire est plus grande.

Dans ce sublime concours
D'adorations premières,
Jésus goûtera toujours
Davantage les prières
Des misérables et leur
Garde un royaume meilleur.

Les anges et les archanges
Qui réveillent les bergers,
Voix d'espoir et de louanges
Aux hommes encouragés,
Priment dans l'azur sans voile
La miraculeuse étoile . . .

Riches, pauvres, faisons-nous
Néant, devant Toi, le Maître,
De Ton Saint Nom seuls jaloux;
Tu sauras bien reconnaître
Et magnifier les tiens,
Riches, pauvres, tous chrétiens.

The journey of the Magi
Is of course pleasing to the Lord.
He accepts such homage
And holds it in high honor;
But the glory of a sinner who repents
Is to Him a yet greater good.

In the sublime encounter
Of competing adorations,
Jesus will always show
A preference for the prayers
Of the feeble and beset
And offer them a richer kingdom.

The angels and archangels
Who waken the shepherds
With voices of hope and of praise
Give to those thus enheartened
First place in an unclouded heaven
Facing the miraculous star.

Both rich and poor, we become
Naught in Your sight, our Master,
Claiming alone Your Holy Name;
You can always recognize and
Give strength to Your faithful,
Rich or poor, all Christians together.

Gloria in excelsis

Gloire à Dieu dans les hauteurs,
Paix aux hommes sur la terre!

Aux hommes qui l'attendaient
Dans leur bonne volonté,

Le salut vient sur la terre . . .
Gloire à Dieu dans les hauteurs!

Nous te louons, bénissons,
Adorons, glorifions,

Te rendons grâce et merci
De cette gloire infinie!

Ô Seigneur, Dieu, roi du ciel,
Père, Puissance éternelle,

Ô Fils unique de Dieu,
Agneau de Dieu, Fils du Père,

Vous effacez les péchés:
Vous écouterez nos vœux.

Vous, à la droite du Père,
Vous aurez pitié de nous.

Car vous êtes le seul Saint,
Seul Seigneur et seul Très Haut,

Gloria in excelsis

Glory to God on high,
Peace to all men on earth!

To men lying in wait,
To men of good will

Salvation has come down to earth . . .
Glory to God on high!

We praise you and bless you,
Worship and glorify you,

Offer you thanks and are grateful
For your infinite glory!

O Lord, our God, ruler of heaven,
Power and Father eternal,

O God's only Son,
Lamb of God, Son of the Father,

You wipe out our sins;
You will grant our wishes.

You, to the right of the Father,
You will take pity on us.

For you are the sole Saint,
Sole Lord and sole Being on high,

Ô Jésus, qui fûtes oint
De très loin et de très haut,

Dieu des cieux, avec l'Esprit,
Dans le Père,
Ainsi soit-il.

Credo

Je crois ce que l'Église catholique
M'enseigna dès l'âge d'entendement :
Que Dieu le Père est le fauteur unique
Et le régulateur absolument
De toute chose invisible et visible,
Et que, par un mystère indéfectible,

Il engendra, ne fit pas Jésus-Christ
Son Fils unique avant que la lumière
Ne fût créée, et qu'il était écrit
Que celui-ci mourrait de mort amère,
Pour nous sauver du malheur immortel,
Sur le Calvaire et, depuis, sur l'Autel ;

Enfin je crois en l'Esprit, qui procède
Et du Père et du Fils et qui parlait
Par les prophètes, et ma foi qui s'aide
De charité croit le dogme complet
De l'Église de Rome, au saint baptême,
En la vie éternelle.
                              Vœu suprême.

O Jesus, you who were anointed
From afar and on high,

God of creation, along with the Spirit.
And within the Father,
Amen.

Credo

I believe what the Catholic Church
Taught me at the earliest age:
God the Father is the sole maker,
The one-and-only controller,
Of everything seen and unseen;
Then, through inscrutable mystery,

He begot, but made not, Jesus Christ,
His sole Son, before light was created;
At a following time was it put into writing
That the Son would die the bitterest death,
Us to deliver from deathless despair,
On Calvary hill and since then on our altars;

I believe too in the Ghost, who proceeds
From Father and Son and who spoke through
The prophets, and my faith, with charity
Girded, accepts the whole dogma of Rome
And its Church; I believe in holy baptism
And in life everlasting.
                    Supreme, this belief.

Agnus Dei

L'agneau cherche l'amère bruyère,
C'est le sel et non le sucre qu'il préfère,
Son pas fait le bruit d'une averse sur la poussière.

Quand il veut un but, rien ne l'arrête,
Brusque, il fonce avec des grands coups de sa tête,
Puis il bêle vers sa mère accourue inquiète . . .

Agneau de Dieu, qui sauves les hommes,
Agneau de Dieu, qui nous comptes et nous nommes,
Agneau de Dieu, vois, prends pitié de ce que nous sommes,

Donne-nous la paix et non la guerre,
Ô l'Agneau terrible en ta juste colère,
Ô toi, seul Agneau, Dieu le seul fils de Dieu le père.

Agnus Dei

The lamb seeks bitter briar,
Drawn to the saline and not to the sweet;
The sound of his step is the sound of a downpour on dust.

In pursuit of a goal, nothing can stop him;
He lowers his head, rushes and strikes straight ahead,
Then bleats toward his mother, who runs to protect him.

Lamb of God, you who save all mankind,
Lamb of God, you who number and name us,
Lamb of God, look upon us with pity for all that we are.

Grant us peace rather than war,
O Lamb, terrifying in your wrath of the righteous,
O you, only Lamb, God the sole son of God our Father.

PART 4

The Last Years

OPENING IMAGE: Frédéric-Auguste Cazals, *Verlaine au café Voltaire*, 1891. In *Les Derniers Jours de Paul Verlaine* (Paris: Mercure de France, 1923).

Since the mid-1880s, following the publication of the anthology *Les Poètes maudits* [The Accursed Poets] in 1883–84, Verlaine had finally achieved some critical recognition, becoming the acknowledged master of the Decadent movement (see the sonnet "À Stéphane Mallarmé" [To Stéphane Mallarmé]). Nevertheless, the poet spent the last ten years of his life, until his death in January 1896, in poverty, burdened with debt, moving from one hovel to another and often recovering from illness at the hospital (see, in particular, the volume *Dans les limbes* [In Limbo] for the winter 1892–93). The many anecdotal collections of verse by Verlaine published in the 1890s (*Dédicaces* [Dedications] in 1890, *Chansons pour Elle* [Songs for Her] in 1891, *Odes en son honneur* [Odes in Her Honor] and *Élégies* in 1893, *Dans les limbes* and *Épigrammes* [Epigrams] in 1894, as well as the posthumous *Chair* [Flesh] and *Invectives* [Invective] in 1896) were thus first of all expedients of survival rather than long-meditated books, each bringing a few hundred francs to the author, which he would immediately spend on drinking and prostitutes.

But the poet had not disappeared for all that. After the chaste and spiritual inspiration of the Catholic triptych *Sagesse, Amour,* and *Bonheur,* Verlaine partially recovered his sensual, even erotic vein in his last collections, notably in the pieces inspired by his last lovers: Eugénie Krantz (*Chansons pour Elle*) and Philomène Boudin (*Odes en son honneur* and *Élégies*). Moreover, the occasional and autobiographical poems composed by Verlaine in his last years, mostly included in *Dédicaces, Épigrammes,* and *Invectives,* offer a moving account of the everyday life of an aging and ill poet who, in all his years, was never able to overcome his condition of "accursed poet."

From *Dédicaces* [Dedications]

À Jules Tellier

Quand je vous vois de face et penché sur un livre
Vous m'avez l'air d'un loup qui serait un chrétien;
Pardon, rectifiez: qui serait un païen,
En tout cas d'un loup peu garou qui saurait vivre.

Je vous vois de profil: un faune m'apparaît,
Mais un faune select, au complet sans reproche
Avec, pour plus de chic, une main dans la poche
Et promenant à pas discrets son vœu secret.

Vu de dos, vous semblez un sage qui médite,
À jamais affranchi des fureurs d'Aphrodite
Et du soin de penser uniquement jaloux.

Vu de loin, on vous veut de près à justes titres,
Et, car la vie, hélas! a de sombres chapitres,
Quand je ne vous vois pas je me souviens de vous.

Ier JANVIER 1889.

À Villiers de L'Isle-Adam

Tu nous fuis comme fuit le soleil sous la mer
Derrière un rideau lourd de pourpres léthargiques,
Las d'avoir splendi seul sur les ombres tragiques
De la terre sans verbe et de l'aveugle éther.

From *Dédicaces* [Dedications]

To Jules Tellier

When I see you full-face hunched over a book,
I have the impression of a wolf as a Christian—
No, sorry: I mean made up as a pagan;
In any case, not much on the prowl but very alive.

I see you in profile, and now you're a faun,
But a faun of the best, in impeccable dress
And, to back up that chic, one hand in a pocket
And the casual glance of some hidden desire.

Seen from the back, you're a sage in meditation,
Forever cut free from Aphroditian passions
And eager for nothing but study and thought.

Seen from afar, I want you close for good reason:
Since life, alas, is a book with frightening chapters,
When I don't see you, you are still on my mind.

JANUARY 1, 1889.

To Villiers de L'Isle-Adam

You disappeared from our view as the sun disappears
Past lethargical crimson curtains at sea,
Tired of shining alone over tragical shadows
Of an Earth with no voice and an Ether that's blind.

Tu pars, âme chrétienne on m'a dit résignée
Parce que tu savais que ton Dieu préparait
Une fête enfin claire à ton cœur sans secret,
Une amour toute flamme à ton amour ignée.

Nous restons pour encore un peu de temps ici,
Conservant ta mémoire en notre esprit transi,
Tels les mourants savourent l'huile du Saint-Chrême.

Villiers, sois envié comme il aurait fallu
Par tes frères impatients du jour suprême
Où saluer en toi la gloire d'un élu.

À Germain Nouveau

Ce fut à Londres, ville où l'Anglaise domine,
Que nous nous sommes vus pour la première fois,
Et, dans King's Cross mêlant ferrailles, pas et voix,
Reconnus dès l'abord sur notre bonne mine.

Puis, la soif nous creusant à fond comme une mine,
De nous précipiter, dès libres des convois,
Vers des bars attractifs comme les vieilles fois
Où de longues misses plus blanches que l'hermine

Font couler l'ale et le bitter dans l'étain clair
Et le cristal chanteur et léger comme l'air,
—Et de boire sans soif à l'amitié future!

Notre toast a tenu sa promesse. Voici
Que, vieillis quelque peu depuis cette aventure,
Nous n'avons ni le cœur ni le coude transi.

You left, Christian soul resigned, I've been told,
Because you knew that your God was preparing
A now radiant feast for your secretless heart,
A love full of fire for the flame of your love.

We remain here for yet some more time,
Your memory kept in our mind now benumbed,
Just as the dying enjoy the oil that says life.

Villiers, accept the well-grounded envy
Of your brothers impatient to face the last day
And greet in your glory a man chosen by God.

To Germain Nouveau

It was in London, a city subject to women,
That we spotted each other for the very first time,
And, at King's Cross, 'mid the din of rails, steps, and voices,
Hale and hearty regards quickly brought us together.

Then, with thirst drilling us dry as a mine,
We dashed, once away from the trains,
Toward the bars, as appealing as ever,
Where willowy misses whiter than ermine

Were serving pale ale and bitters in silver-grey pewter
And singing crystal there was, lighter than air—
Thirsty or not, we drank to a long future as friends!

Our toast has indeed kept its promise. Now today,
Some years having passed since that moment,
We're neither chilled at the heart nor stiff at the elbow.

À François Coppée

Les passages Choiseul aux odeurs de jadis,
Oranges, parchemins rares,—et les gantières!
Et nos "débuts," et nos verves primesautières,
De ce Soixante-sept à ce Soixante-dix,

Où sont-ils? Mais où sont aussi les tout petits
Événements et les catastrophes altières,
Et le temps où Sarcey signait S. de Suttières,
N'étant encore pas mort de la mort d'Athys!

Or vous, mon cher Coppée, au sein du bon Lemerre
Comme au sein d'Abraham les justes d'autrefois,
Vous goûtez l'immortalité sur des pavois.

Moi, ma gloire n'est qu'une humble absinthe éphémère
Prise en catimini, crainte des trahisons,
Et, si je n'en bois pas plus, c'est pour des raisons.

À Stéphane Mallarmé

Des jeunes—c'est imprudent!—
Ont, dit-on, fait une liste
Où vous passez symboliste.
Symboliste? Ce pendant

Que d'autres, dans leur ardent
Dégoût naïf ou fumiste
Pour cette pauvre rime iste,
M'ont bombardé décadent.

Soit! Chacun de nous, en somme,
Se voit-il si bien nommé?
Point ne suis tant enflammé

To François Coppée

Yesterday's aromas in the Passage Choiseul,
Citrus and old parchment and oh! those glove ladies!
And our "first times," our impulsive excitement
As we went to explore one address and another—

Where are they now? But also where are the little
Events and the world-shaking disasters,
And the time when Sarcey chose to sign as Souttières
Even before the death of Atys was a fact!

You, now, Coppée my friend, dear to good man Lemerre
As were to Abraham's heart the just of times past,
You enjoy all the trappings of deathless renown.

In my case, fame's found in a fleeting green drink
That I took on the sly, to avoid a betrayer's detection,
And, if I no longer indulge, I've got a good reason.

To Stéphane Mallarmé

Some young fellows (how imprudent!)
Have, I am told, made a list
Where you are labeled a symbolist.
Symbolist? Yes that, whereas

Others, in their ardent
Disgust (naïve or pretended)
For that poor rhyme in *ist*,
Tagged me just as decadent.

Well! Is any of us, after all,
As well named as he'd like?
I'm not now nearly so worked up

Que ça vers les n...ymphes, comme
Vous n'êtes pas mal armé
Plus que Sully n'est Prud'homme.

Fernand L'Anglois

Haut comme le soleil, pâle comme la lune,
Comme dit vaguement le proverbe espagnol,
Il a presque la voix tendre du rossignol,
Tant son cœur fut clément à ma triste fortune.

Je l'écoute toujours, cette voix opportune
Qui me parlait naguère, est-ce en ut, est-ce en sol?
Et qui sut relever, furieux sur le sol,
Mon cœur, ce cœur sauvage et fou de roi de Thune!

Mais rions! car mon livre est un livre amusant,
Et dès lors que ce souvenir doux et cuisant
D'un suicide prévenu de mains pieuses

Me remonte ce soir, peut-être pire encor
Dans un absurde et vraiment sinistre décor,
Paix là, pour ces mains-là, mes mains calamiteuses!

Sur un buste de moi—pour mon ami Niederhausern

Ce buste qui me représente
Auprès de la postérité
Lui montre une face imposante
Pleine de quelle gravité!

Devant cette tête pesante
Du poids tous les jours augmenté

As when I look at the nymphs
And see you're no more poorly armed
Than Sully, an upstanding fellow.

Fernand L'Anglois

High as the sun, pale as the moon,
As the vague saying in Spanish would have it,
His tender voice almost sounds like a bird's,
So kind was his heart to this sad fate of mine.

I listen still now for that timely nightingale voice
That addressed me but lately (was it in C or in G?)
And was able to raise, enraged and prostrate,
My wild and mad heart, cheap plaything of vice!

But let's laugh! My book is meant to amuse,
And now that this memory, smarting but sweet,
Of a suicide stopped in time by still pious hands

Resurfaces tonight, perhaps this time even worse
In such an absurd and truly sinister setting—
But that's it now for my hands, calamitous hands!

On a Bust of Me—For My Friend Niederhausern

This bust, here for posterity
To have a look at me,
Shows an imposing face
And much impressive gravity.

Standing before this heavy head
That constant thought

D'une pensée, ô pas puissante,
D'un souci plutôt entêté,

Qu'est-ce que vont dire les femmes
Et les hommes des temps futurs?
"Au fait, on sent, sous ces traits durs

Et derrière ces yeux aux flammes
Noires, un monsieur malveillant,
Mais le sculpteur eut du talent."

À G...

Tu m'as plu par ta joliesse
Et ta folle frivolité.
J'aime tes yeux pour leur liesse
Et ton corps pour sa vénusté.

Mais j'ai détesté tout de suite
La gourmandise de ta chair.
J'abhorre ton besoin de cuite
(Non pas celui qui m'est cher,

Le besoin d'être avec cet homme
Encore vert qui serait moi),
J'abomine, pour parler comme
Il faut, ton goût pour trop d'émoi

Joyeux, gamin, charmant sans doute . . .
Au fait, j'y pense, je suis vieux
Tant (cinquante ans!) et t'es en route
Pour tes dix-huit ans . . . pauvre vieux!

Weighs down—though, more potently,
My stubborn care instead—

Men in future times
And women, too, will say:
"In fact, those surly traits betray,

As do those darkly flaming eyes,
Ill-will and arrant malice . . .
But the sculptor was a man of talent."

To G . . .

I liked you right off for your looks
And acting so flighty and care-free.
I'm drawn to your eyes for their sparkle
And the rest for your Venus-like grace.

But I was put off right away
By your ever-unsatisfied flesh.
I abhor your need to be soused
(Not the one that I crave—

The need just to be with the man
Still spry and alive that I am.)
I detest, to use polite words,
Your taste for excessive excitement,

Lively, childish, and charming no doubt . . .
But the fact, I admit, is I'm old
(Fifty years), and you're on your way
To the age of eighteen . . . Poor fellow!

Anniversaire—à William Rothenstein

> "Et j'avais cinquante ans quand cela m'arriva."

Je ne crois plus au langage des fleurs
Et l'Oiseau bleu pour moi ne chante plus.
Mes yeux se sont fatigués des couleurs
Et me voici las d'appels superflus.

C'est, en un mot, la triste cinquantaine.
Mon âge mûr, pour tous fruits tu ne portes
Que vue hésitante et marche incertaine
Et ta frondaison n'a que feuilles mortes!

Mais des amis venus de l'étranger,
—Nul n'est, dit-on, prophète en son pays—
Du moins ont voulu, non encourager,
Consoler un peu ces lustres haïs.

Ils ont grimpé jusques à mon étage
Et des fleurs plein les mains, d'un ton sans leurre,
Souhaité gentiment à mon sot âge
Beaucoup d'autres ans et santé meilleure,

Et comme on buvait à ces vœux du cœur
Le vin d'or qui rit dans le cristal fin,
Il m'a semblé que des bouquets, en chœur,
S'élevaient des voix sur un air divin;

Et comme le pinson de ma fenêtre
Et le canari, son voisin de cage,
Pépiaient gaiement, je crus reconnaître
L'Oiseau bleu qui chantait dans le bocage.

PARIS, 30 MARS 1894.

Birthday—To William Rothenstein

> "And I was fifty years old when this happened to me."

I no longer believe in the language of flowers,
And the Blue Bird, for me, is no longer singing.
My eyes have grown tired of colors,
And I've long had enough of meaningless urges.

In a word, it's a sad thing to turn fifty.
O ripe age of mine, the only fruit that you bring
Is weakening eyesight and an unsteady step
And a capital wreath of dead leaves.

But friends who have come from abroad
(No one, they say, is a prophet at home)
Have at least tried not to encourage,
But to console us a bit for these hated old years.

They have climbed all the way up to my floor
And with flowers in hand and no ulterior motive,
Pleasantly wished me, at my silly old age,
Many more years and improving good health.

As we were drinking with heartfelt good wishing
The golden wine bubbling in crystalline goblets,
I had the impression that from choral bouquets
Voices were rising in heavenly song;

And just as the finch at my window
And its cage-mate canary
Were cheerily chirping, I thought I could hear
The Blue Bird filling the grove with its song.

PARIS, MARCH 30, 1894

À Edmond Lepelletier

Mon plus vieil ami survivant
D'un groupe déjà de fantômes
Qui dansent comme des atomes
Dans un rais de lune devant

Nos yeux assombris et rêvant
Sous les ramures polychromes
Que l'automne arrondit en dômes
Funèbres où gémit le vent,

Bah! la vie est si courte en somme
—Quel sot réveil après quel somme!—
Qu'il ne faut plus penser aux morts

Que pour les plaindre et pour les oindre
De regrets exempts de remords,
Car n'allons-nous pas les rejoindre?

To Edmond Lepelletier

My oldest friend surviving
In a group now made of ghosts
Who dance like specks of dust
In a moonbeam visible to

Darkened eyes a-dreaming
Below the many-colored boughs
That autumn fashions into rounded
Domes of groaning funerary wind . . .

Stop there! Life is just too brief
—Pointless waking after pointless sleep—
To go on thinking of the dead

Except to mourn them and anoint them
With regrets exempt from all remorse—
For are we not soon to join them?

From *Chansons pour Elle* [Songs for Her]

II

Compagne savoureuse et bonne
À qui j'ai confié le soin
Définitif de ma personne,
Toi mon dernier, mon seul témoin,
Viens çà, chère, que je te baise,
Que je t'embrasse long et fort,
Mon cœur près de ton cœur bat d'aise
Et d'amour pour jusqu'à la mort:
  Aime-moi,
  Car, sans toi,
  Rien ne puis,
  Rien ne suis.

Je vais gueux comme un rat d'église
Et toi tu n'as que tes dix doigts;
La table n'est pas souvent mise
Dans nos sous-sols et sous nos toits;
Mais jamais notre lit ne chôme,
Toujours joyeux, toujours fêté
Et j'y suis le roi du royaume
De ta gaîté, de ta santé!
  Aime-moi,
  Car, sans toi,
  Rien ne puis,
  Rien ne suis.

From *Chansons pour Elle* [Songs for Her]

II

Delectable, good companion,
To whom I've entrusted
The ultimate care of my person,
You, my last and my only support,
Come close, love, and I'll give you
A long and deep kiss;
My heart next to yours beats with comfort
And love right up to death.

> Love me!
> Without you,
> I'm helpless,
> I'm nameless.

I'm a tramp, as poor as a church mouse
And you, all you have is ten fingers;
There is not much food on the table
Or anything much in basement or attic;
But our bed is never at rest:
It's always a joy, always a feast
And there I am king of the realm
Of pleasure and health!

> Love me!
> Without you,
> I'm helpless,
> I'm nameless.

Après nos nuits d'amour robuste
Je sors de tes bras mieux trempé,
Ta riche caresse est la juste,
Sans rien de ma chair de trompé,
Ton amour répand la vaillance
Dans tout mon être, comme un vin,
Et, seule, tu sais la science
De me gonfler un cœur divin.
      Aime-moi,
      Car, sans toi,
      Rien ne puis,
      Rien ne suis.

Qu'importe ton passé, ma belle,
Et qu'importe, parbleu! le mien:
Je t'aime d'un amour fidèle
Et tu ne m'as fait que du bien.
Unissons dans nos deux misères
Le pardon qu'on nous refusait
Et je t'étreins et tu me serres
Et zut au monde qui jasait!
      Aime-moi,
      Car, sans toi,
      Rien ne puis,
      Rien ne suis.

VII

Je suis plus pauvre que jamais
    Et que personne;
Mais j'ai ton cou gras, tes bras frais,
    Ta façon bonne
De faire l'amour, et le tour
    Leste et frivole

After our nights of exuberant love,
I leave your arms much better disposed;
Your caresses are rich and are right,
Never leaving my flesh disappointed.
Your love spreads courage and strength
Through my whole being, much like wine,
And you alone have the knowledge
To make my heart swell divinely.

Love me!
Without you,
I'm helpless,
I'm nameless.

Your past doesn't matter, my darling,
Any more, good lord! than does mine:
I love you with a love that is true
And you have brought me nothing but good.
Let's find together in our two woeful lots
The forgiveness that others refuse us;
I'll embrace you and you will hold me,
And if there's any objection, too bad!

Love me!
Without you,
I'm helpless,
I'm nameless.

VII

I am poorer than ever before,
    Poorer than anyone else;
But I have the cool flesh of your arms and your neck
    And your wee wicked way
Of love-making, and the care-free,
    Casual play

Et la caresse, nuit et jour,
    De ta parole.

Je suis riche de tes beaux yeux,
    De ta poitrine,
Nid follement voluptueux,
    Couche ivoirine
Où mon désir, las d'autre part,
    Se ravigore
Et pour d'autres ébats repart
    Plus brave encore . . .

Sans doute tu ne m'aimes pas
    Comme je t'aime,
Je sais combien tu me trompas
    Jusqu'à l'extrême.
Que me fait, puisque je ne vis
    Qu'en ton essence,
Et que tu tiens mes sens ravis
    Sous ta puissance?

XIII

        Es-tu brune ou blonde?
        Sont-ils noirs ou bleus,
            Tes yeux?
Je n'en sais rien, mais j'aime leur clarté profonde,
Mais j'adore le désordre de tes cheveux.

        Es-tu douce ou dure?
        Est-il sensible ou moqueur,
            Ton cœur?

And daily caress, night and day,
Of your words.

I am rich with your beautiful eyes
And your breast,
That madly voluptuous nest,
That ivory couch
Where my desire, elsewhere grown tired,
Gathers fresh strength
And goes off to new frolic and sport
Now even bolder . . .

I have no doubt you don't love me
The way I love you;
I know how unfaithful you've been
And how far you have gone.
But what does it matter, for I live
Only through you
And you hold all my senses in thrall
Under your rule?

XIII

Are you blonde or brunette?
And your eyes,
Are they dark, are they blue?
That I can't say, but I love their deep brightness,
And I adore the hair that tangles 'round your neck.

Are you tender or tough?
And your heart,
Is it gentle, is it spiteful?

Je n'en sais rien, mais je rends grâce à la nature
D'avoir fait de ton cœur mon maître et mon vainqueur.

Fidèle, infidèle?
Qu'est-ce que ça fait,
Au fait,
Puisque, toujours disposée à couronner mon zèle,
Ta beauté sert de gage à mon plus cher souhait.

XVI

L'été ne fut pas adorable
Après cet hiver infernal
Et quel printemps défavorable!
Et l'automne commence mal.
Bah! nous nous réchauffâmes
En mêlant nos deux âmes.

La pauvreté, notre compagne
Dont nous nous serions bien passés,
Vainement menait la campagne
Durant tous ces longs mois glacés . . .
Nous incaguions l'intruse,
Son astuce et sa ruse.

Et, riches de baisers sans nombre,
—La seule opulence, crois-moi,—
Que nous fait que le temps soit sombre
S'il fait soleil en moi, chez toi,
Et que le plaisir rie
À notre gueuserie?

That I can't say, but I thank mother nature
Who has made your heart my lord and my master.

Are you faithful or not?
But in fact
It can't really matter,
Since, always prepared to comfort my desire,
Your beauty never fails to sense my dearest wish.

XVI

The summer was not very lovely
After that winter from hell,
Then a thoroughly disagreeable spring!
And autumn's now starting off poorly . . .
So what! we found warmth,
Weaving two souls into one.

Poverty, a constant companion
We would gladly have lived on without,
Tried his best, but in vain, to intrude
Through those shivering months . . .
We couldn't care less for that fool,
With his wiles and designs!

And rich in numberless kisses
—Our only wealth, need I say?—
It's no matter to us that the times are so dark,
If the sun goes on shining in you and in me
And pleasure just laughs
At our mendicity!

XVIII

Si tu le veux bien, divine Ignorante,
Je ferai celui qui ne sait plus rien
Que te caresser d'une main errante,
En le geste expert du pire vaurien,

Si tu le veux bien, divine Ignorante.

Soyons scandaleux sans plus nous gêner
Qu'un cerf et sa biche ès bois authentiques.
La honte, envoyons-la se promener.
Même exagérons et, sinon cyniques,

Soyons scandaleux sans plus nous gêner.

Surtout ne parlons pas littérature.
Au diable lecteurs, auteurs, éditeurs
Surtout! Livrons-nous à notre nature
Dans l'oubli charmant de toutes pudeurs,

Et, ô! ne parlons pas littérature.

Jouir et dormir ce sera, veux-tu?
Notre fonction première et dernière,
Notre seule et notre double vertu,
Conscience unique, unique lumière,

Jouir et dormir, m'amante, veux-tu?

XVIII

If it's all right with you, divine Simpleton,
I'll be an ignoramus like you, knowing just
The flesh to caress with the wandering hands
And deft touch of a ne'er-do-well bum.

If it's all right with you, divine Simpleton.

Let's misbehave—and with no greater care
Than a stag and his doe in antlered embrace.
We won't be put off by concerns about shame,
But go even further, though not cynical ever:

Let's misbehave—and with no further care!

Let's not talk—above all!—about literary matters.
Editors, authors, readers and more can all go to hell!
Let's give ourselves up—above all!—to our nature
And forget the constraints of everyday shame.

And—oh, no!—no talk about literary matters!

Coming and sleeping—how's that for a time?
The two ends of our first and last function,
Our only, our double virtue and strength,
A single awareness, our sole source of light,

Coming and sleeping—how's that, love of mine?

XX

Tu crois au marc de café,
   Aux présages, aux grands jeux:
Moi je ne crois qu'en tes grands yeux.

Tu crois aux contes de fées,
   Aux jours néfastes, aux songes:
Moi je ne crois qu'en tes mensonges.

Tu crois en un vague Dieu,
   En quelque saint spécial,
En tel *Ave* contre tel mal.

Je ne crois qu'aux heures bleues
   Et roses que tu m'épanches
Dans la volupté des nuits blanches!

Et si profonde est ma foi
   Envers tout ce que je croi
Que je ne vis plus que pour toi.

XX

You believe in coffee grounds,
In omens and in big-board games;
I believe only in your big bright eyes.

You believe in fairy tales,
In unlucky days and in dreams;
I believe only in your fibs and your lies.

You believe in God, I guess,
In some special saint or another,
In this or that prayer contra woes yet to arise.

I believe just in the blue and rose
Moments that you spread over me
In the sensual joy of our insomnolent nights.

And so profound is my faith
In all things I believe
That only through you am I now truly alive.

From *Odes en son honneur* [Odes in Her Honor] and *Élégies*

IX

Tu fus souvent cruelle,
Même injuste parfois,
Mais que fait, ô ma belle,
Puisqu'en toi seule crois

Et puisque suis ta chose.

Que tu me trompes avec Pierre,
Louis, *et cætera punctum*,
Le sais, mais, là! n'en ai que faire:
Ne suis que l'humble factotum

De ton humeur gaie ou morose.

S'il arrive que tu me battes,
Soufflettes, égratignes, tu
Es le maître dans nos pénates,
Et moi le cocu, le battu,

Suis content et vois tout en rose.

Et puis dame! j'opine
Qu'à me voir ainsi si
Tien, finiras, divine,
Par m'aimoter ainsi

Qu'on s'attache à sa chose.

From *Odes en son honneur* [Odes in Her Honor] and *Élégies*

IX

You've often been cruel,
Sometimes even unfair,
But what matter, my sweet?
I believe in you—

Actually now, I belong to you!

Deceive me with Peter,
With Lou or whomever—
Oh, I know, but so what?
I'm just a lowly do-all,

Whether your mood is cheerful or blue.

If you happen to hit me,
Slap me or scratch me, you,
After all, run the show,
And I'm just a cuckold and sucker.

I can't complain: it's perfectly true.

Oh what the heck! It's my guess
That, seeing me thus, so utterly
Yours, you'll wind up, my muse,
With the same touch of love

You might have for a broken-in shoe.

XI

Riche ventre qui n'a jamais porté,
Seins opulents qui n'ont pas allaité,
Bras frais et gras, purs de tout soin servile,

Beau cou qui n'a plié que sous le poids
De lents baisers à tous les chers endroits,
Menton où la paresse se profile,

Bouche éclatante et rouge d'où jamais
Rien n'est sorti que propos que j'aimais,
Oiseux et gais—et quel nid de délices!

Nez retroussé quêtant les seuls parfums
De la santé robuste, yeux plus que bruns
Et moins que noirs, indulgemment complices,

Front peu penseur mais pour cela bien mieux,
Longs cheveux noirs dont le grand flot soyeux
Jusques aux reins lourdement se hasarde,

Croupe superbe éprise de loisir
Sauf aux travaux du suprême plaisir,
Aux gais combats dont c'est l'arrière-garde,

Jambes enfin, vaillantes seulement
Dans le plaisant déduit au bon moment
Serrant mon buste et ballant vers la nue,

Puis, au repos,—cuisses, genoux, mollets,—
Fleurant comme ambre et blanches comme lait:
—Tel le pastel d'après ma femme nue.

XI

Bounteous belly that has never borne fruit—
Opulent bosom that has never breast-fed—
Fresh and plump arms free of workaday tasks—

Beautiful neck that has never been bent but
To bestow warmest kisses on places of choice—
Chin that shows signs of deliberate languor—

Lips brilliantly red whence never at all
Have sounds issued save words that I loved
For their indolent cheer and endless delights—

Turned-up little nose seeking sweet odors
Of solid good health—eyes darker than brown
And lighter than black, an indulgent abettor—

Brow not that of a thinker but better for that—
Hair long and black whose great silken stream
Ventures heavily down the length of her back—

Backside superb and given to leisure
Save when engaged in the greatest of pleasures,
Those happy wars where it serves as rear guard—

Legs, in the end, only sturdy and strong
For the enjoyable sport at just the right time,
Clasping my trunk and dancing toward heaven—

Then back at rest, thighs, knees, and calves
Perfumed like amber and white as pure milk—
A very pastel of my bare lissome wife.

XIII

Nos repas sont charmants encore que modestes,
Grâce à ton art profond d'accommoder les restes
Du rôti d'hier ou de ce récent pot-au-feu
En hachis et ragoûts comme on n'en trouve pas chez Dieu.

Le vin n'a pas de nom, car à quoi sert la gloire?
Et puisqu'il est tiré, ne faut-il pas le boire?
Pour le pain, comme on n'en a pas toujours mangé,
Qu'il nous semble excellent me semble un fait archijugé.

Le légume est pour presque rien, et le fromage:
Nous en usons en rois dont ce serait l'usage.
Quant aux fruits, leur primeur ça nous est bien égal,
Pourvu qu'il y en ait dans ce festin vraiment frugal.

Mais le triomphe, au moins pour moi, c'est la salade:
Comme elle en prend! sans jamais se sentir malade,
Plus forte en cela que défunt Tragaldabas,
Et j'en bâfre de cœur tant elle est belle en ces ébats.

Et le café, qui pour ma part fort m'indiffère,
Ce qu'elle l'aime, mes bons amis, quelle affaire!
Je m'en amuse et j'en jouis pour elle, vrai!
Et puis je sais si bien que la nuit j'en profiterai,

Je sais si bien que le sommeil fuira sa lèvre
Et ses yeux allumés encor d'un brin de fièvre
Par la goutte de rhum bue en trinquant gaîment
Avec moi, présage gentil d'un choc bien plus charmant.

XIII

Our meals are delightful (though really quite light),
Thanks to your artful way with whatever remains
Of yesterday's roast or a recent ragout
Turned into mincemeat or hash or a new sort of stew.

The wine is unlabeled, but what's the point of a name?
Once it's been poured, it's to be drunk all the same.
As for the bread, since we don't always have it,
Whether it's good or first-class, seems not much to matter.

Vegetables cost just a pittance, and so does the cheese;
We consume them like kings for whom they're the norm.
For fruits, it matters not much how early they are,
Provided they figure in a feast that's actually frugal.

But the triumph, at least as I see it, is the salad:
How she does wolf it—enough to grow ill, but she doesn't!
She clearly outdoes in that way the late Tragaldabas,
And gladly I follow her lead, so lovely is she in such revels.

But coffee, which leaves me wholly indifferent—
How she loves it, good friends, what a busy to-do!
It's entertaining, and I enjoy it for her—oh, how true!
Besides, I well know what a boon it will be come the night.

And well do I know how sleep will run from her lips
And her eyes still aglow with a suggestion of fever
Begun by the fun tippling of rum that together we did
As an enjoyable hint of the wonderful clash still to come.

XIX

Ils me disent que tu me trompes.
D'abord, qu'est-ce que ça leur fait,
Chère frivole, que tu rompes
Un serment que tu n'as pas fait?

Ils me disent que t'es méchante
Envers moi,—moi, qui suis si bon!
Toi, méchante! Qu'un autre chante
Ce refrain très loin d'être bon.

Méchante, toi qui toujours m'offres
Un sourire amusant toujours,
Toi, ma reine, qui de tes coffres
Me puises des trésors toujours.

Ils me disent et croient bien dire,
Ô toi, que tu ne m'aimes pas.
Que m'importe, j'ai ton sourire,
Et puis, tu ne m'aimerais pas?

Tu ne m'aimes pas? Et la grâce
Et la force de ta beauté,
Tu me les donnes, grande et grasse
Et voluptueuse beauté.

Tu ne m'aimes pas? Et quand même
Ce serait vrai, qu'est-ce que fait?
"Si tu ne m'aimes pas, je t'aime."
—Mais tu m'aimes, dis, par le fait.

XIX

They tell me you're unfaithful.
Well, what is it to them,
My silly little dear, if you break
A vow you never swore to keep?

They tell me that you're spiteful
To me, while I'm goodness itself!
You, full of spite! Let someone else
Sing that tune so far from the truth.

Spiteful, you who always smile me
A smile that's always delightful—
You, my fair queen, always finding
New treasures for me in your chest.

They tell me, and wanting to be right,
That you, my love, don't love me.
But it matters not—I have your smile,
It cannot be your love is not real!

You, not love me? But you grant me
The grace and appeal of your great
And well-rounded beauty, all that
Full and voluptuous beauty.

You, not love me? But let's say
It were true, how would it matter?
"Love me or not, I'm in love with you!"
—But you do love me, not true?

Élégies IV

Notre union plutôt véhémente et brutale
Recèle une douceur que nulle autre n'étale,
Nos caractères détestables à l'envi
Sont un champ de bataille où tout choc est suivi
D'une trêve d'autant meilleure que plus brève.
Le lourd songe oppressif s'y dissout en un rêve
Élastique et rafraîchissant à l'infini.
Je croirais pour ma part qu'un ange m'a béni
Que des Cieux indulgents chargeraient de ma joie,
En ces moments de calme où ses ailes de soie
Abritent la caresse enfin que je te dois.
Et toi, n'est-ce pas, tu sens de même; ta voix
Me le dit et ton œil me le montre, ou si j'erre
Plaisamment? Et la vie alors m'est si légère
Que j'en oublie, avec les choses de tantôt,
Tout l'ancien passé, son naufrage et son flot
Battant la grève encore et la couvrant d'épaves.
Et toi, n'est-ce pas, tu sens de même ces graves
Moments de nonchaloirs voluptueux, ou c'est
Qu'un mensonge plus vrai que du vrai me berçait?
Comme un air de pardon flotte comme un arôme
Sur le cœur affranchi du poids de tel fantôme,
Et, ô l'incube et le succube du présent,
C'est toi, c'est moi dans le bon spasme renaissant
Après les froids contacts de deux âmes froissées.
Vite, vite, accourez, nos plus tendres pensées,
Nos maux les plus naïfs, nos mieux luisants regards.
Plus de manières ni de tics, plus d'airs hagards.
Que d'armistice en armistice, une paix franche
Éternise ce nid d'oiseaux bleus sur la branche.

Elegies IV

Our union, however fervid and rough,
Harbors a softness that no other displays;
Our detestable natures, one worse than the other,
Are a field where combat is followed
By a truce at its best when most brief.
Oppressive reflection dissolves into a dream
That's elastic and endlessly bracing.
I could imagine myself blessed by an angel
That Heaven's indulgence had tasked with my joy
In moments of calm when his diaphanous wings
Enfold the caress that I hold to be yours.
And you—am I wrong?—feel what I feel:
Your voice and your eyes make it clear—or is this
A silly mistake? But life then is so easy to bear
That I forget, with these latest events,
The whole former story, the waves of its wreck
Still beating the shore and leaving débris.
And you—am I wrong?—feel, as I do, these
Serious moments of sensuous calm—or is it
A lie only too true, rocking me quiet?
A suggestion of pardon floats like a fragrance
On a heart freed of the weight of a phantom.
O the incubus and succubus of the latest event!
It is you, it is I, in a marvelous burst of rebirth
After the frozen relations of two wounded souls.
Fast now, come running, O tenderest thoughts,
Most artless of our ills, most receptive of looks!
No more airs, affectation nor haggard allure!
May a true peace, from one truce to the next,
Give lasting life to our bluebirds' nest on the branch.

From *Dans les limbes* [In Limbo]

II

Hélas! tu n'es pas vierge ni
Moi non plus. Surtout tu n'es pas
La Vierge Marie et mes pas
Marchent très peu vers l'infini

De Dieu; mais l'infini d'amour,
Et l'amour c'est toi, cher souci,
Ils y courent, surtout d'ici,
Lieu blême où sanglote le jour.

Ils y courent comme des fous,
Saignant de n'être pas ailés,
Puis s'en reviennent désolés
De la porte fermée à tous

Espoirs certains, et résistant
À tels efforts pour t'enfin voir
En plein grand jour par un beau soir
Mué tôt en nuit douce tant!

Ah! Limbes où non baptisés
Du platonisme patient
Vont, pitoyablement criant
Et pleurant, mes désirs brisés.

DÉCEMBRE 1892.

From *Dans les limbes* [In Limbo]

II

Alas! no virgin, you—but I'm
Not, either. What's more, you're not
The Virgin Mary, and my steps
Are headed not toward God's

Infinity, but that of love,
And love means you, my only care!
They run toward you, away from here,
This faceless place of sobbing days.

They run, my feet, as madmen run,
Bleeding for want of wings;
They then turn back disconsolate,
The door slammed shut to every

Certain hope, and they resist
Attempts at last to meet you
In full light of day transmuted soon
By twilight into softest night.

Ah! Limbo, where, unbaptized
By patient Platonism,
Go, piteously wailing and
Weeping, the shreds of my desires.

DECEMBER 1892.

IX

Des méchants, ou, s'ils aiment mieux, des indiscrets,
Sinon des envieux que je pardonnerais,
S'ils ne te faisaient pas, bon chéri, de la peine,
Tant leur manège est nul, tant leur malice est vaine,
Ont essayé, même s'efforcent d'essayer
À nouveau de nous désunir, d'entre-bâiller
La porte à la querelle, au soupçon qui gourmande,
À la colère à qui, lors, l'ouvrir toute grande,
Et qui rugit avec un couteau dans la main.

Honnêtes Iagos, passez votre chemin.
Comme si ce n'était assez de mes misères,
Des ennuis de partout me griffant de leurs serres
En attendant de m'emporter je ne sais où,
Voici sortir je ne sais quels serpents d'un trou
Pour taquiner mes pieds clapotant dans leurs vases.
Heureusement, amie, ô toi, tu les écrases,
Femme bonne que le mépris arme et défend,
Femme bonne qui me défends comme un enfant,
Femme douce qui me souris, femme sublime,
Ô ma femme, qui recevras mon souffle ultime!

X

Ils ont rampé jusques ici,
Dans ces limbes où je soupire
Après toi lointaine, ô martyre!
Ils ont rampé jusques ici,

Guettant ta venue et l'instant
Propice pour, devant ma face,
T'insulter, limiers sur ta trace,
Guettant ta venue et l'instant.

IX

Some spiteful people or, if they prefer, indiscreet,
Envious, perhaps—people I'd no doubt forgive
If they didn't cause you, my dear, such pain,
So pointless is their game, so worthless their hate—
Have attempted, indeed with considerable effort
Once more, to sever our bond, to push the door
Ajar to discord and suspicion, berating and ranting,
To anger, which will throw it open wide
To one of us roaring with knife well in hand.

Honest Iagos, go on your way.
As if my misfortunes were not countless enough
—Manifold troubles tearing me with their claws
Before bearing me off to a destination unknown—
Here now from their pit emerge serpents unnamed
To lap at my feet in their sludge.
Happily, love, you know how to crush them,
Good wife well armed and defended by scorn,
Good wife defending me just like a child,
Sweet wife smiling at me, my wife so sublime,
O my wife, you will reap the last breath of my life.

X

They crept all the way here,
Into my limbo of sighs
For faraway you—my despair!
They crept all the way here,

On watch for your coming
And just the right moment to
Hurt you, hounds on your track,
On watch for your coming.

T'insulter, or, c'est m'insulter
Au centuple, et certes pour ce
Ils auront lieu d'apprendre que
T'insulter, or, c'est m'insulter.

Viens, bien-aimée, et, va, vivons
En paix loin du monde imbécile:
"La vie est là, simple et tranquille."
Viens, bien-aimée, et, va, vivons!

XI

Oh! tu n'es pas une savante
Et je t'en félicite fort,
Et je t'en loue et je t'en vante,
Et qui me censure il a tort,

Car ta finesse toute nue
Sans vains mots et sans gestes faux,
Car ta ruse mieux qu'ingénue,
Car ta rouerie aux plans nouveaux,

Car jusqu'à ta "méchanceté,"
Comme ces bons pantes-là disent,
Nous défendent de leur bêtise . . .
Ta méchanceté? ta bonté!

Car ces vertus d'entre les tiennes,
Me vont mieux, te vont mieux aussi,
Bien qu'on n'en chante pas l'antienne,
Que d'autres fleurant le moisi.

An insult to you is an insult to me
But greater by far, and for that, for sure,
They'll have reason to learn that
An insult to you is an insult to me.

Come, my belovèd, let us go live
In peace far from this imbeciles' world:
"Life is out there, quiet and simple."
Come, my belovèd, let us go live!

XI

Oh, no intellectual, you!
Congratulations, I say,
With admiration and boasting!
And to critics I say, But it's true!

Since your forthright approach,
With no meaningless words or fake moves,
Your more than innocent cunning,
Your wily new ways without self-reproach,

Your "spiteful" turn of mind,
As the dear know-nothings say,
Defend us against all such drivel . . .
Spiteful, you? you, good and kind!

Your virtues—as long as they hold—
Suit me better, and better suit you,
Though the tune's not always the same,
Than others, smelling of mold.

Ils disent encore, les gens,
Que tu n'es pas intelligente;
Eux, ce qu'ils sont intelligents,
C'en est une chose touchante.

Il paraît que tu ne comprends
Pas les vers que je te soupire,
Soit! et cette fois je me rends!
Tu les inspires, c'est bien pire.

XIII

> Ô! l'absence! le moins clément de tous les maux!
>
> (LA BONNE CHANSON.)

J'ai dit jadis que l'absence
Est le plus cruel des maux,
On s'y berce avec des mots,
C'est l'horreur de l'impuissance

Sans la consolation
Du moins de quelque caresse,
On meurt sans qu'il y paraisse
On est mort, dis-je, et si on

Feint de respirer encore,
C'est bien machinalement.
Ô ce découragement
À voir se lever l'aurore!

Or, depuis que dans ces lieux
Je souffre,—dès toi venue,—
Par quelle force inconnue
Allé-je infiniment mieux?

Those people also say
That you lack an intelligent brain.
Oh, aren't they brilliant themselves!
What a terribly touching display!

It appears that you fail to understand verse—
All those poems I sigh just for you.
All right! What if this time they're right?
You inspire me—and that's even worse!

XIII

> Oh, absence—the least merciful of all ills!
> (THE GOOD SONG.)

I once said that absence
Is the cruelest of ills;
You try to find comfort in words;
But without power, there's only horror,

And there is no consolation
From even the slightest caress;
Death comes unnoticed, it's stealthy;
You're dead, as I said, and yet

You pretend some breath is still left.
It's a mechanical tic.
Oh, how heart-rending
To see the sun rise again!

Now, to this place of my pain,
You came, and with you new hope:
To what force I can't name do I owe
So profound a new start?

C'est l'histoire de l'éphèbe
Mourant de la vierge au loin!
Qu'elle arrive et soit témoin,
Comme il nargue et fuit l'Érèbe!

Et tant que j'y resterai,
Accours en ce limbe blême:
Moi qui déjà t'aime et t'aime,
Ô que je t'adorerai!

It is the story of the youth
Dying far from the virgin!
She has but to arrive and take note,
And he runs from the realm of the dead.

And now that I'm here at the pale
Edge of dawn, hurry to join me!
I am already in love—and with you.
Oh, you'll be mine to adore!

In England (1893)

Souvenir du 19 novembre 1893 (Dieppe–Newhaven)

Mon cœur est gros comme la mer,
Qui s'exile de l'être cher!
Gros comme elle et plus qu'elle amer.

Ma tête est comme la tempête,
Elle est folle et forte, ma tête,
Plus qu'elle, effrénée, inquiète ...

Furieuse et triste d'avoir
Ce doux et douloureux devoir
De m'exiler au pays noir ...

Mais puisqu'il le faut pour ma reine,
Embarquons d'une âme sereine,
Et fi de toute crainte vaine!

Ah! quoi que fasse le bateau
Ivre des colères de l'eau
Qui tantôt s'érige en tombeau,

Tantôt se creuse, affreuse fosse,
Embarquons sans nulle peur fausse,
Sans nul regret menteur! Se hausse

Au ciel ou s'abîme en l'enfer
Le bateau douloureux et fier
Moins que mon cœur, moins que la mer!

In England (1893)

Memory of November 19, 1893 (Dieppe–Newhaven)

My heart is heavy as the sea,
Soon exiled from the dearest one!
Heavy, yes—more bitter yet.

My head is like the very storm;
It's riotous, my head, and roiled,
More agitated yet, more wroth . . .

Furious and sad to have
This soft but oh, so painful task:
Exiling me to a land that's dark . . .

But if that's what's needed for my queen,
Let us set sail with soul serene
And pay no heed to pointless fear!

Ah! however the boat behaves,
Battered drunk by the water's wrath,
Now rising like an undug grave,

Now buried in a frightful pit,
Let us set sail with no false fear,
With no untrue regret! The boat

May rise on high or plunge toward hell;
It hurts, yet remains both proud and fierce
But less than my heart, less than the sea!

Or, je pars pour ma souveraine
Et reviendrai l'âme sereine,
Chargé pour cette douce reine

De diamants, de perles, d'ors!
Et bercé, mer, en tes bras forts,
Et rêvant de trésors, je dors.

Paul Verlaine's Lecture at Barnard's Inn

Dans ce hall trois fois séculaire,
Sur ce fauteuil dix fois trop grand,
À ce pupitre révérend
Qu'une lampe, vieux cuivre, éclaire,

J'étais comme en quel temps ancien!
Et l'âme, un peu, du Moyen Âge
M'investissait d'un parrainage
Grave, à mes airs mûrs séant bien.

Ma parole en l'antique enceinte
Ne jurait pas trop, célébrant
La Foi du passé, sûr garant,
L'éternel Beau, vérité sainte!

J'entretenais de mon pays,
De cette France athénienne,
Une élite londonienne
Dont les vœux furent obéis,

Puisque de l'estrade sévère
Il ne tombait, conformément
Au réel devoir du moment,
Que ces mots: "Bien dire et bien faire,"

Now I leave without pointless fear
And I'll come back with soul serene,
Laden, for my gentle queen,

With diamonds, pearls, and rings of gold!
And rocked, sea, in your motherly arms,
I'll dream of treasure as I sleep.

Paul Verlaine's Lecture at Barnard's Inn

In this hall three hundred years of age,
On this seat ten times too large,
At this reverend rostrum
Lighted by a copper lamp of old,

I was as if in some long-distant past
Whose medieval soul now granted me
The auspicial look of new-found gravity
That suited my years very well.

My address was not too far at odds
With this venerable site in its praise
Of the rock-solid Faith of the past,
Its Beauty eternal, its truth that is sacred.

I was speaking of my country,
That France of Athenian spirit,
To a London elite
Whose wishes were dutifully served,

Since from that serious platform
There fell nothing more, in line
With what the moment called for,
Than the words "Do as you say,"

Et tel bel autre et cætera
Dont s'esjouit la bonne salle,
—Coin de la ville colossale
Où, ce soir, l'Esprit se terra...

Je conserverai la mémoire
Bien profondément et longtemps
De ces miens sérieux instants
Où j'ai revécu de l'histoire.

LONDON, NOVEMBER 1893, ON THE 21TH. [*sic*]

Oxford

Oxford est une ville qui me consola,
Moi rêvant toujours de ce Moyen Âge-là.

En fait de Moyen Âge, on n'est pas difficile
Dans ce pays d'architecture un peu fossile

À dessein, c'est la mode et qui s'en moque fault,
Mais Oxford c'est sincère, et tout l'art y prévaut;

Mais Oxford a la foi, du moins en a la mine
Beaucoup, et sa science en joyau se termine,

En joyau précieux, délicieux: les cieux
Ici couronnent d'un prestige précieux

L'étude et le silence exigés comme on aime,
Et la sagesse récompense le problème,

La sagesse qu'il faut, cette douce raison
Que la Cathédrale termine en oraison.

And every further apothegm
That brought delight to that good room
One corner of colossal London
Where, that day, sharp wit went dull . . .

I shall retain the memory,
Deep within and for long a time,
Of those serious instants of mine
When I relived a hint of history.

LONDON, NOVEMBER 21, 1893.

Oxford

Oxford is a city where I found consolation,
I, with its Middle Ages still alive in my dreams.

No, that time is no problem, no stranger
To this town of old architectural age

By design; it's a style that is wrong to deride;
Oxford is earnest, and that art is meaningful there;

But Oxford has faith—at least, a great presence
Thereof—and its knowledge leads up to a jewel,

A precious and wondrous jewel, for here
Heaven crowns with precious prestige

Study and silence, exactly as desired,
And wise thought resolves a possible problem,

The wisdom that's called for, satisfaction
Through sweet reason by a Cathedral in prayer.

Sous les arceaux romans qui virent tant de choses
Et les rinceaux gothiques, fins d'apothéoses

De Saints mieux vénérés peut-être qu'on ne croit,
Et mon cœur s'humilie et mon désir s'accroît

De devenir et de redevenir, loin d'elle,
Cette cité glorieuse d'être infidèle,

Paris! l'enfant ingrat qui s'imaginerait
Briser les sceaux sacrés et tenir le secret—

De devenir et de redevenir la chose
Agréable au Seigneur, quelle qu'en soit la cause,

Et par cela même être encore doux et fort,
Ô toi, cité charmante et mémorable, Oxford!

NOVEMBRE 1893.

Souvenir de Manchester—à Theodore C. London

Je n'ai vu Manchester que d'un coin de Salford,
Donc très mal et très peu, quel que fût mon effort
À travers le brouillard et les courses pénibles
Au possible, en dépit d'hansoms inaccessibles
Presque, grâce à ma jambe male et mes pieds bots.
N'importe, j'ai gardé des souvenirs plus beaux
De cette ville que l'on dit industrielle,—
Encore que de telle ô qu'intellectuelle
Place où ma vanité devait se pavaner
Soi-disant mieux—et dussiez-vous vous étonner
Des semblantes naïvetés de cette épître,

Under the Roman arches witness to so much
And sculpted Gothic scrolls of apotheotic ends

Of Saints more widely worshiped than we think,
My heart is humbled and my desire grows

To become once and again, though far from her,
That city glorious in her faithlessness—

Paris! the ungrateful child who might imagine
Breaking sacred seals to seize the secret—

Of becoming once and again a thing apt
To find favor with the Lord, for whatever cause,

And thereby be once more gentle, strong once again,
O you, city of memory, city of charm—O Oxford!

NOVEMBER 1893.

Memory of Manchester—To Theodore C. London

A mere corner of Salford let me see all I could
Of this city—a poor and scant view, whatever my effort
Through fog and impossibly tiring drives across town,
With only rare thanks to those cabs I could barely access
With a comfortless leg and my terrible club of a foot.
No matter. I've kept pleasanter thoughts in my mind
Of this city they pass off as industrial
Than of that other oh! so intellectual place
Where my pride could better display a vainglorious strut
—And were you to wonder at the signs of naïveté
You might find in this missive . . . No, no, friend!

Ô vous! quand je parlais du haut de mon pupitre
Dans cette salle où l'"élite" de Manchester
Applaudissait en Verlaine l'auteur d'*Esther*,
Et que je proclamais, insoucieux du pire
Ou du meilleur, mon culte énorme pour Shakespeare.

30 JANVIER 1894.

When presenting my lecture from the prestigious chair
In that hall where the city's "elite" had come to applaud
Their French guest Verlaine as the author of *Esther*,
I was proclaiming, with no regard for compare,
How much I revere, indeed worship, Shakespeare.

JANUARY 30, 1894.

From *Épigrammes* [Epigrams]

III—À Edmond de Goncourt

Lourd comme un crapaud, léger comme un oiseau,
Exquis et hideux, l'art japonais effraie
Mes yeux de Français dès l'enfance acquis au
Beau jeu de la Ligne en l'air clair qui l'égaie.

Au cruel fracas des trop vives couleurs,
Dieux, héros, combats, et touffus gynécées,
Je préférerais, d'entre les œuvres leurs,
Telles scènes d'un bref pinceau retracées.

Un pont plie et fuit sur un lac lilial,
Un insecte vole, une fleur vient d'éclore,
Le tout fait d'un trait unique et génial.
Vivent ces aspects que l'esprit seul colore!

Si je blasonnais cet art qui m'est ingrat
Et cher par instants, comme le fit Racine
Formant son écu d'un cygne et non d'un rat,
Je prendrais l'oiseau léger, laissant le lourd crapaud dans sa piscine.

VII—À Francis Poictevin

Il ne me faut plus qu'un air de flûte,
Très lointain en des couchants éteints.
Je suis si fatigué de la lutte
Qu'il ne me faut plus qu'un air de flûte
Très éteint en des couchants lointains.

From *Épigrammes* [Epigrams]

III—To Edmond de Goncourt

Heavy as a toad, light as a bird,
Delicate and ugly, Japanese art is a fright
To French eyes accustomed since childhood to
The beautiful play of Line in clear and bright air.

To the cruel commotion of colors too vivid,
Gods, heroes, battles, and overstuffed harems,
I would prefer, among their various works,
Such scenes reconceived with a quieter brush.

A bridge folds and fades on a lily-white lake;
An insect flies and a flower's just blossomed;
The whole picture's done with a single ingenious line.
Wonderful features given color just by the mind!

If I gave noble value to this art I dislike
But also hold dear, I would do as Racine, who
For his arms chose a swan instead of a rat,
I would take the light bird and leave the heavy toad in its pool.

VII—To Francis Poictevin

All I need now is to hear a flute play
Far away, where the sun's gone to rest.
The struggle has left me so tired that
All I want now is to hear a flute play
And then rest like the sun in the west.

Ah, plus le clairon fou de l'aurore!
Le courage est las d'aller plus loin.
Il veut et ne peut marcher encore
Au son du clairon fou de l'aurore:
C'est d'un chant berceur qu'il a besoin.

La rouge action de la journée
N'est plus qu'un rêve courbaturé
Pour sa tête encor que couronnée,
Et la victoire de la journée
Flotte en son demi-sommeil lauré.

Femme, sois ce héros qui bute
D'avoir marché sans cesse en avant,
L'huile sur son corps après la lutte:
—Plus du clairon fou: la molle flûte!
La paix dans son cœur dorénavant.

XI—À François Coppée

La ville que Vauban orna d'un beau rempart,
De ceux qu'on démolit chez nous pour la plupart
En y campant dessus industrie et culture
Au lieu de la vivace et profonde verdure
Avec ses murs moins hauts que les hauts peupliers
Le long du ruisseau clair aux bouillons familiers,
La ville a l'air, depuis qu'elle est ainsi châtrée,
Toute autre. Ce n'est plus la tourelle échancrée;
Le grand beffroi dit l'heure, on croirait, pour ailleurs;
Tambours et clairons ont comme des sons railleurs
De ne plus avoir un écho pour leur répondre;
Et le soleil couchant, quand dans l'or il s'effondre,
Pleure du sang de n'ouïr plus, les soirs d'été,
Monter vers lui l'air sombre et gai répercuté.

Ah, there's the mad trumpet of dawn!
Weary spirit can push no farther than this.
It wants to, but can't, move ahead
To the sound of the mad trumpet of dawn;
What it needs is a soft cradle song.

The heated action of the day
Is now but a tired old dream
For his head, though crowned it may be,
And the happy triumph of the day
Floats on garlands in wide-awake sleep.

Woman, be this hero, who stumbles,
Having walked without ceasing ahead,
His body oiled once fighting is done:
Mad trumpet no, not now—the soft flute!
His heart is at peace for all time ahead.

XI—To François Coppée

The city adorned with Vauban's handsome rampart,
One of those structures they're destroying these days,
Stonework of old falling to smokestacks and farmland,
All the new overtaking deep green in profusion
With its walls far less high than the tall poplar trees
Along the clear stream with the eddies we know—
Oh, the city's been altered; once vigorously virile, it is
Now very different. The old creneled turret is gone;
The great belfry tolls the hour, but not in this town;
Bugles and drums blare out as if meaning to mock,
For they sound with no echo coming back in response;
And the sun, as it sets and sinks into gold,
Weeps blood no longer to hear, on long summer eves,
Its dark ancient air, like its light, rise high and rebound.

XIII

Quand nous irons, si je dois encor la voir,
    Dans l'obscurité du bois noir,

Quand nous serons ivres d'air et de lumière
    Au bord de la claire rivière,

Quand nous serons d'un moment dépaysés
    De ce Paris aux cœurs brisés,

Et si la bonté lente de la nature
    Nous berce d'un rêve qui dure,

Alors, allons dormir du dernier sommeil!
    Dieu se chargera du réveil.

XVI.vii—Nascita di Venere (Botticelli)

Vénus, debout sur le plus beau des coquillages,
Aborde, nue, au moins sauvage des rivages,
Ne cachant de son corps avec ses longs cheveux
Que juste ce qu'il faut pour qu'y dardent nos vœux.
Une nymphe, éployant un clair manteau, s'empresse
À vêtir en impératrice la déesse;
Et deux vents accourus, beaux éphèbes ailés,
Des cuisses et des bras l'un à l'autre mêlés,
De qui l'un est Zéphyre et dont l'autre est Borée,
Soufflent l'amour divin et la haine sacrée.
Le visage est suavement indifférent,
Comme attendant le culte à venir que lui rend
Toute herbe et toute chair depuis cette naissance,
Et se pare d'une inquiétante innocence.

XIII

When we go off, if I'm to see her again,
 Into the dark and shadowy wood;

When we are drunk on air and on light
 On the gleaming bright bank of the stream;

When we are for a moment removed from our Paris
 Of sad, broken hearts;

And if the slow goodness of nature
 Lulls us into permanent dreaming,

Then let us accept this sleep everlasting:
 God will see to our waking.

XVI.vii—Birth of Venus (Botticelli)

Venus, atop the most beautiful shell,
Stands nude on the calmest of shores,
Her long tresses concealing those parts alone
That most sharply attract our desiring eyes.
A nymph, holding out a bright cloak, is eager
To dress the goddess as empress;
Two winds have come, too, winged handsome ephebes,
With intertwined thighs and arms crossed together,
Zephyrus from the west, Boreas from the north
Breathe divine love and hatred that's sacred.
Her visage is smooth and impassive,
As expecting the forthcoming worship
Of plant and of flesh starting here with this birth,
And disquieting innocence is what it expresses.

XXII—À Sully Prudhomme

Schopenhauer m'embête un peu
Malgré son épicuréisme,
Je ne comprends pas l'anarchisme,
Je ne fais pas d'Ibsen un dieu.

Ce n'est pas du Nord aujourd'hui
Que m'arriverait la lumière;
Du Midi non plus, en dernière
Analyse. Du Centre, oui?

Non. Mais d'où? De nulle part,—là!
Rien n'égale ma lassitude:
Laissez-moi rentrer dans l'étude
Du bon vieux temps qu'on persifla.

J'aime les livres lus et sus,
Je suis fou de claires paroles,
J'adore la Croix sans symboles:
Un gibet et Jésus dessus.

XXVIII—Sur un exemplaire des *Fleurs du Mal* (première édition)

Je compare ces vers étranges
Aux étranges vers que ferait
Un marquis de Sade discret
Qui saurait la langue des anges.

XXII—To Sully Prudhomme

Schopenhauer is a bit of a bore
Despite his epicurism;
I don't understand anarchism,
And Ibsen's a god I refuse to adore.

No, it is not from the North
That enlightenment can reach me;
Nor from the South, in actual truth.
Is it a third place—or even a fourth?

No. Then from where? Nowhere—that's it!
My fatigue is unequaled;
Just let me return to the study
Of past time people now find unfit.

I love books that teach as I read;
I'm obsessed with words that are clear;
I worship the Cross without other symbols,
For a gallows and Jesus are all that I need.

XXVIII—On a Copy of *The Flowers of Evil* (First Edition)

I regard these strange verses
As if they were made
By a circumspect Marquis de Sade
Who knew the language of angels.

From *Invectives* [Invective]

Portrait académique

Fleur de cuistrerie et de méchanceté
Au parfum de lucre et de servilité,
Et poussée en plein terrain d'hypocrisie,

Cet individu fait de la poésie
(Qu'il émet d'ailleurs sous un faux nom "pompeux,"
Comme dit Molière à propos d'un fossé bourbeux).*

Sous l'Empire il émargea tout comme un autre,
Mais en catimini, car le bon apôtre
Se donnait des airs de farouche républicain:

Depuis il a retourné son casaquin
Et le voici plus et moins qu'opportuniste.
Mais de ses hauts faits j'arrête ici la liste
Dont Vadius et Trissotin seraient jaloux.

Pour conclure, un chien couchant aux airs de loups.

> *Je sais un paysan qu'on appelait Gros Pierre,
> Qui, n'ayant pour tout bien qu'un seul quartier de terre,
> Y fit tout à l'entour faire un fossé bourbeux
> Et de Monsieur de l'Isle en prit le nom pompeux.
> (ÉCOLE DES FEMMES.)

From *Invectives* [Invective]

Academic Portrait

Flower of pedantry and spite
With a fragrance of cash and compliance,
And grown in a hypocrite's hothouse,

This character's a composer of poetry
(Which he writes, by the way, under a 'pompous' false name,
To quote Molière on a certain fool's muddy ditch).*

Under the Empire he was as much on the take as another,
But on the sly, for the fair-haired apostle
Preferred to pretend he was fiercely republican;

Since that time, he's turned his coat
And here he is now, an opportunist as before.
But here I'll end the list of all his noble deeds,
Which would put Vadius and Trissotin to shame.

My final word: a sleeping dog who claims to be a wolf.

> *I know of a farmer they once called Gros Pierre,
> Who, owning nothing but a small plot of terre,
> Had it surrounded with a mucky excavation,
> Then took Lord of the Isle as his due appellation.
> (*THE SCHOOL FOR WIVES*, TRANS. M. ZRAFA)

Sonnet pour larmoyer

Juge de paix mieux qu'insolent
Et magistralement injuste,
Qui va massif, ventre ballant,
Jambes cagneuses—et ce buste!

Je veux dire ton maltalent,
Ta manière rustique et fruste
D'être pédant . . . et somnolent,
Et sot, que de façon robuste!

Je n'ai pas oublié, non, non!
(Ce compliment de sorte neuve
Que je te rime en est la preuve.)

Je n'ai pas oublié ton nom,
Tes rengaines ni ta bedaine,
Ni ta dégaine—ni ma haine!

Griefs

On me dit vieux, qui ça? Les jeunes d'aujourd'hui!
Homère est vieux aussi, je réclame de lui,
Non dans des termes équivoques ni baroques,
Mon esprit qui n'a pas besoin de leurs breloques
Pour tinter et briller au vrai soleil d'été.
Cinquante ans, non sonnés, non pas trop hébété,
Que je sache, l'esprit dont Dieu fit mon partage.

On me dit vieux, qui ça? Les amants de cet âge-
Ci, mannequins transis, de Gomorrhe venus.
Or je suis tout plein vert, j'en atteste Vénus
Et les dames. On me dit vieux, qui ça? Ce maître

Sonnet for Weeping

More than insolent, this justice of the peace,
And magisterially unjust,
With heavy tread and sagging paunch,
With knock-kneed legs—and oh, that chest!

I'll go on about the animus you show,
Your crude, unlettered way
With pedantry . . . and half-asleep at that!
A fool, I say—a true and thorough ass!

No way could I forget—no, no!
(And it's no compliment to you
That you figure in a rhyme of mine),

No way could I forget your name,
Your hackneyed talk, your ugly paunch,
Your gawky walk—or my unending hate!

Grievances

Old? Who calls me old? These youngsters today!
Homer's old, too, whom I'll take as my model,
Not in questionable terms or baroque,
But my spirit has no need of their trinkets
To tinkle and glisten in the real summer sun.
Not yet fifty in age, not too deadened or dazed,
Seems I still have the mind that God allotted to me.

Old? Who calls me old? Lovers these days!
Frozen dummies, right out of Gomorrah!
But I am full of green sap, as Venus well knows,
Like the ladies. Old? Who calls me old? That

Ès-Anarchie (un mot suranné), petit traître
À la patrie en deuil, au pauvre qu'il voudrait
Faire méchant au lieu des soins qu'il lui faudrait,
Conseils doux, Dieu montré, pain, vin, la main tendue
Et la bonne mort patiemment attendue
Comme la délivrance en une vie enfin
Heureuse!

On me dit vieux, qui ça? Cet aigrefin
Imberbe, mais pêcheur émérite en eau trouble,
Qui me plaint de mon indigence triple et double,
Unique! sans songer un instant, le pauvret,
Que je suis riche, étant honnête. Âpre secret,
Recette pas drôle, être riche puisque honnête!
On me dit vieux encore. Encore qui de bête?
Ah oui, parfois moi-même, alors surtout que j'ai
Mal agi, mal parlé, garrulé comme un geai,
Trottiné comme un âne à travers telle et telle
Préoccupation, sordeur ou bagatelle.
Mais j'ai tôt reverdi d'entre ce détritus
Et je me bande en presque enfantines vertus,
En efforts bien adolescents, et très viriles
Actions contre mes propres propos futiles!

Je demande pardon pour leur peu haute voix
Et le ton vif,—mais on n'est jeune qu'une fois.

À F.-A. Cazals

Ils avaient escompté ma mort
Qui n'arrivait pas assez vite.
Pour quel vil et quel sale effort
Avaient-ils escompté ma mort?
Ils voulaient te salir, toi, fort

Master of Anarchical Arts (if I may), petty traitor
To the nation in mourning, to the poor fellow
He'd denounce and not offer the care that he needs:
Mild advice, face of God, bread and wine, out-
Stretched hand, a good death awaited with patience
Like deliverance at the end of a life that is
Happy at last!

Old? Who calls me old? That beardless
Shark but veteran fisher in deep troubled water,
Who pities me for my penury—triple and double,
No: single!—without thinking an instant, poor fool,
That I'm rich, because honesty is. What an odd secret,
A curious pair: being rich and honest as well!
They still call me old. Still, who is so stupid?
Oh yes, sometimes I myself am, especially when
I've acted ill, spoken wrong, chattered like a jay,
Jogged along like an ass through this or that
Labor, a sordid affair or a trifle.
But I've quickly sprung back from such wreckage
And I bandage myself in virtues of childhood,
In adolescent endeavors and manly demands
Opposed to my own futile efforts!

Pardon, please, for their voice too restrained and
Their tone a bit sharp—but we're young only once!

To F.-A. Cazals

They'd been counting on my death,
But it wasn't coming fast enough.
With what low and nasty plan in mind
Had they been counting on my death?
They wanted you besmirched for all

De mon amitié, point en fuite.
Ils avaient escompté ma mort
Qui n'arrivait pas assez vite.

Même elle a fait faux-bond, ma mort,
À tel type et telle drôlesse
Près de mon lit, rués au bord.
Elle a fait quel faux-bond, ma mort!
J'allais de tribord à bâbord,
Mais je vis, c'est le point qui blesse.
Même elle a fait faux-bond, ma mort,
À tel type et telle drôlesse.

Mon Cazals, tu sais qu'en dépit
De tout je t'aime mieux qu'un frère.
Cette amitié-là, sans répit
Ni trêve, en crédit ou débit,
Elle est au cœur qui la fourbit,
S'il le faut, en arme de guerre.
Mon Cazals, tu sais qu'en dépit
De tout je t'aime mieux qu'un frère.

Chanson à manger

Nos repas furent sommaires
Cette semaine: enfoncés
Les Marguerys et les Maires
Aux menus par trop foncés.

Fi de la sole normande,
Fi de l'entrecôte au jus,
Puisque tous ces jours-ci j'eus
La satisfaction grande

Your loyalty to me, for never taking flight.
They'd been counting on my death,
But it wasn't coming fast enough.

Fact is, my endless dying let them down,
Those codgers and their hussies,
In their rush to reach my bedside.
Well, my endless dying let them down!
I went veering, port to starboard,
But I'm alive—and that's what hurts!
Fact is, my endless dying let them down,
Those codgers and their hussies.

Cazals, my friend, I trust you know that come
What may, I love you more than any brother.
Our friendship, with no truce or pause,
Whether a plus, whether a minus,
Belongs to the heart that, if needed,
Furbishes it like a weapon of war.
Cazals, my friend, I trust you know that come
What may, I love you more than any brother.

Eating Song

Our meals this past week
Were perfectly basic: no
Sauces for fish or for shrimp
Or platters excessively rich.

Goodbye to sole in brown butter;
Goodbye to steak in pan drippings!
I had through all these past days
The immense satisfaction

D'être un végétarien
À l'instar de ce poète
Bouchor, ou de cet esthète
Sarcey, critique ancien.

Nous mangeâmes de la soupe
Où lentilles et poireaux
Mêlaient leurs parfums farauds
À celui du pain qu'on coupe.

L'eau coulait dans le cristal
Plus pure que lui, plus claire,
Meilleure que vin ou bière,
Boire idéal et fatal!

C'est dommage que le ventre
Soit un ventre préférant
Encore un bon restaurant
À, Polyphème, ton antre!

Rêve

Je renonce à la poésie!
Je vais être riche demain.
À d'autres je passe la main:
Qui veut, qui veut m'être un Sosie?

Bel emploi, j'en prends à témoin
Les bonnes heures de balade
Où, rimaillant quelque ballade,
Je passais mes nuits tard et loin.

Of dining in vegetarian mode,
As is the fashion of our poet
Bouchor or Sarcey, that esthete
We know for his old-style critiques.

What we ate was a soup
In which lentils and leeks
Combined righteous aromas
With the fragrance of fresh toasted oats.

The water we had as we dined,
Purer, more sparkling than crystal,
Was better than beer, better than wine—
It was ideal, the unavoidable drink!

It's a pity when the belly
Is a belly still craving
A table better than we find
In Polyphemus's cave!

Dream

No more poems; I give up!
I want to be richer tomorrow.
Someone else can take over!
Who'd care to take on my sorrow?

It's a fine job, as I've learned
In all those great walks in the cold
Through long and late nights,
Rhyming this or that sonnet or ode.

Sous la lune lucide et claire
Les ponts luisaient insidieux,
L'eau baignait de flots gracieux
Paris gai comme un cimetière.

Je renonce à tout ce bonheur
Et je lègue aux jeunes ma lyre!
Enfants, héritez mon délire,
Moi j'hérite un sac suborneur.

Réveil

Je reviens à la poésie!
La richesse décidément
Ne veut pas de mon dénûment,
Et c'est un triste dénouement.

À moi la provende choisie,
L'eau claire et pure et ce pain sec
Quotidien non sans, avec,
Un gent petit air de rebec!

À moi le lit problématique
Aux nuits blanches, aux rêves noirs,
À moi les éternels espoirs
Pavanés des matins aux soirs!

À moi l'éthique et l'esthétique!
Je suis le poète fameux
Rimant des vers pharamineux
À l'ombre d'un quinquet fumeux!

In the clear and bright moonlight
The bridges of Paris gleam coldly
As the graceful flow of the Seine
Gives the city a funereal glow.

I'll give up that whole happy craft
And leave youngsters my lyre and lute.
Take this mad mantle, my sons!
I'll trade in my lies for pay and a suit.

Awakening

Poetry's hard to give up—and I won't!
The world of wealth rejects my game
And stripping myself clean of rhyming
For a vague promise of capital gain.

It's for me to elect the diet I want,
Pure water and a dry crust of bread
Every day, along with the trills
And clear notes of an age-old rebec!

It's for me to endure the rough bed
Of nights with no sleep, no untroubled dreams;
It's for me to go on eternally hoping,
Waiting to see what crumbs the day leaves.

It's for me to ponder esthetics and ethics!
I am the poet of notorious fame,
Composing incredibly outlandish verses
In the uncertain light of a wavering flame.

Je suis l'âme par Dieu choisie
Pour charmer mes contemporains
Par tels rares et fins refrains
Chantés à jeun, ô cieux sereins!

Je reviens à la poésie.

I am the soul that God Himself named
To charm my companions and peers
With rare, pure, and first-rate refrains
Sung before food—oh, heavenly cheer!

Poetry's hard to give up—and I won't!

From *Chair* [Flesh]

Autre

Car tu vis en toutes les femmes
Et toutes les femmes c'est toi.
Et tout l'amour qui soit, c'est moi
Brûlant pour toi de mille flammes.

Ton sourire tendre ou moqueur,
Tes yeux, mon Styx ou mon Lignon,
Ton sein opulent ou mignon
Sont les seuls vainqueurs de mon cœur.

Et je mords à ta chevelure
Longue ou frisée, en haut, en bas,
Noire ou rouge et sur l'encolure
Et là ou là—et quels repas!

Et je bois à tes lèvres fines
Ou grosses,—à la Lèvre, toute!
Et quelles ivresses en route,
Diaboliques et divines!

Car toute la femme est en toi
Et ce moi que tu multiplies
T'aime en toute Elle et tu rallies
En toi seule tout l'amour: Moi!

From *Chair* [Flesh]

Other

You live in all women
And all women are you.
And I am all conceivable love,
Burning for you with thousands of flames.

Your smile, whether tender or scornful,
Your eyes, my river Styx or my stream of Lignon,
Your breast, be it full, be it flat,
Are all features that have conquered my heart.

And I bite at your hair, whether straight
Or in curls, on top or below,
Black or red, and the down at your neck
Here and then there—oh, what a meal!

And I drink from your lips, whether thin,
Whether thick—in short, it's the Lip!
And what intoxication as I go,
The work of the devil if it isn't divine!

Yes, Woman herself: that's who you are!
And this self of mine that you heighten
Loves in you all of Her, for you combine
In yourself all the love meant for me!

Les Méfaits de la lune

Sur mon front, mille fois solitaire,
Puisque je dois dormir loin de toi,
La lune déjà maligne en soi,
Ce soir jette un regard délétère.

Il dit ce regard—pût-il se taire!
Mais il ne prétend pas rester coi,—
Qu'il n'est pas sans toi de paix pour moi;
Je le sais bien, pourquoi ce mystère,

Pourquoi ce regard, oui, lui, pourquoi?
Qu'ont de commun la lune et la terre?
Bah, reviens vite, assez de mystère!
Toi, c'est le soleil, luis clair sur moi!

Vers sans rimes

Le bruit de ton aiguille et celui de ma plume
Sont le silence d'or dont on parla d'argent.
Ah! cessons de nous plaindre, insensés que nous fûmes,
Et travaillons tranquillement au nez des gens!

Quant à souffrir, quant à mourir, c'est nos affaires
Ou plutôt celles des toc-tocs et des tic-tacs
De la pendule en garni dont la voix sévère
Voudrait persévérer à nous donner le trac

De mourir le premier ou le dernier. Qu'importe,
Si l'on doit, ô mon Dieu, se revoir à jamais?
Qu'importe la pendule et notre vie, ô Mort?
Ce n'est plus nous que l'ennui de tant vivre effraye!

Misdeeds of the Moon

Upon my brow a thousand-fold lonely,
Since I must sleep far from you,
The moon, more than baleful at heart,
Tonight casts a gaze all too deadly.

The gaze seems to say (Can't it be still!
Can't it ever back off and be quiet?)
That without you I'll never find peace.
Yes, I know. Why this mysterious drill?

Why such a gaze? What's there to see?
What do moon and earth have in common?
Enough! Return soon! Mystery's over!
You are the sun: shine brightly on me!

Poem Without Rhymes

The clicking of your needle and the scratching of my pen
Compose the golden silence behind the talk of money.
Oh, let's stop complaining, crazy as we were,
And go about our quiet work no matter who says what.

All that suffering, all the dying—that's our business
Or it's perhaps the ticking and the tocking
Of the apartment's mantle clock whose unyielding voice
Will never stop, but go on jolting us with fear

Of dying first or second. But what's the difference,
If we're meant—good God!—to be rejoined forever?
What matters the clock? What matters our life, O Death?
No longer is ours the fearful burden of living so long.

Fog!—pour Mme ***

Ce brouillard de Paris est fade,
On dirait même qu'il est clair
Au prix de cette promenade
Que l'on appelle Leicester Square.*

Mais le brouillard de Londres est
Savoureux comme non pas d'autres;
Je vous le dis, et fermes et
Pires les opinions nôtres!

Pourtant dans ce brouillard hagard
Ce qu'il faut retenir quand même
C'est, en dépit de tout hasard,
Que je l'adore et qu'elle m'aime.

* *PRONONCEZ LESTE'SQUÈRE.*

(NOTE DE P. VERLAINE)

Fog!—For Madame ***

The fog in Paris is paltry and thin;
You might even say it's transparent,
If you think of a walk you might take
In the Square that's called Leicester.

In London the fog has a thickness
And savor like no other you know;
That's what I say, and no opinion
Is firmer or surer than ours!

Still, in that untamed and wild fog,
The one thing there is to remember
Is that, whatever may come by chance,
It is she I adore, and I am her love.

From *Biblio-sonnets*

I—Bibliophilie

Le vieux livre qu'on a lu, relu tant de fois!
Brisé, navré, navrant, fait hideux par l'usage,
Soudain le voici frais, pimpant, jeune visage,
Et fin toucher, délice et des yeux et des doigts.

Ce livre cru bien mort, chose d'ombre et d'effrois,
Sa résurrection "ne surprend pas le sage."
Qui sait, ô Relieur, artiste ensemble et mage,
Combien tu fais encore mieux que tu ne dois.

On le reprend, ce livre en sa toute jeunesse,
Comme l'on reprendrait une ancienne maîtresse
Que quelque fée aurait revirginée au point;

On le relit comme on écouterait la Muse
D'antan, voix d'or qu'éraillait l'âge qui nous point:
Claire à nouveau, la revoici qui nous amuse.

12 OCTOBRE 1895.

IV—L'Arrivée du Catalogue

L'Amateur reçoit son courrier! fiévreusement,
Même avant de toucher aux plis qu'il sait intimes,
Il court aux Catalogues et, rapidement,
Non encore rabidement, sans trop de crimes

From *Biblio-sonnets*

I—Bibliophilia

That old book that you've read time and again,
Binding broken and torn, turned grimy with use—
Here it is once again, spruced up, looking new,
Smooth to the touch, a delight to the eyes.

It's a book you thought dead, a shadowy fright;
But resurrection comes as no surprise to the wise.
Who can say, O Binder, wonder-worker of art,
How much better you are than ever supposed?

The book is now here with its youth back in place,
A love rediscovered, like a mistress once prized
Whom some magic had made a virgin once more;

You read it again as you'd attend to the earlier Muse,
A golden voice grown by age strident and coarse
Now again bright and clear and a pleasure to hear.

OCTOBER 12, 1895.

IV—The Catalogue Arrives

The Lover of books receives the day's mail. In a rush,
Before even touching his personal letters,
He attends to the Catalogues' call and rapidly,
Though not rabidly, with no crime on his mind,

Projetés ou conçus pour l'amour de sublimes
Emplettes, et voici qu'il tombe, justement!
Sur celui du libraire aux malices ultimes
Qui ne vend pas trop cher pour vendre sûrement,

Et d'une main fiévreuse, mais honnête, dame,
On est honnête! et comme il a vu tel bouquin,
Qu'il convoite depuis . . . tant d'ans! un vrai béguin!

Il envoie au Négociant un télégramme:
"Gardez-Le-moi."—"C'est fait," répond avant la nuit
Un petit bleu.
                        Le bon Client s'évanouit.

VIII—Les Quais

Quais de Paris! Beaux souvenirs! J'étais agile,
J'étais, sinon bien riche, à mon aise, en ces temps . . .
J'étais jeune et j'avais des goûts très militants,
Tel, un bon iconographobibliophile.

Loin de moi l'orgueil sot de me prétendre habile,
Même alors! Mais c'étaient de précieux instants,
Perdus ou non dans des déboires persistants
Pour les prix . . . et le reste! Et pas la moindre bile!

La Seine s'allongeait—elle s'allonge encor—
Comme un serpent jaspé de vert, de noir et d'or . . .
Le vent frémit toujours . . . L'aimable paysage! . . .

Mais bouquiner, n'y plus songer! De vils pisteurs
Pour les libraires ont exercé leur ravage,
Et les boîtes ont fait la nique aux amateurs.

Whether planned or imagined, for love of sublime
Acquisitions—suddenly spots a long-wanted title
'Mid the wares of the most clever bookseller,
Whose prices are good and good for his sales.

With feverish hand, going at it the right way—
The right way, of course!—now he's seen
This work he's desired forever—a real crush!

He sends the Purveyor a quick telegram:
"Hold It for me." "It's yours!" comes the answer
By the end of the day.
                          The good Client swoons and staggers away.

VIII—The Quais

The quais of Paris! What recollections! I was dapper,
Hardly rich in those days, but comfortable enough . . .
I was young, I was eager, I was ready to fight,
Like the good iconographico-bibliophile that I was!

Not my way, to take pride in a claim to be shrewd—
Even then! But those moments were precious,
Wasted or not in endless disappointments
Over prices—and whatever else! But let's have no fretting!

The Seine was flowing past, as it continues to flow,
A very serpent marbled in green, black, and gold . . .
The wind sighs past, as it's always done . . . What a scene!

But browsing through books is not what it was! Damn touts
For the sellers have done all the damage they could,
And the boxes now mock the men who love books.

Late Uncollected Poems

À Ph . . .

Depuis ces deux semaines
Où j'ai failli mourir,
Ces heures jà lointaines
Qui m'ont tant fait souffrir,

Depuis ce temps, chérie,
Comme d'ailleurs depuis
Si longtemps, je marie
Nos cœurs, mais dès ces nuits

Où tu vis l'agonie
Où j'allais m'enlisant,
Elle semble bénie
À nouveau, l'âme, issant

Du tombeau pour sourire
À ta dive bonté.
Laisse-moi te le dire,
Je t'aime, en vérité,

Comme il me semble, bonne,
Que je n'ai pas aimé . . .
Reçois la fleur d'automne
Que voici. Parfumé

Late Uncollected Poems

To Ph . . .

Since two weeks ago,
When I almost passed away,
Those now distant hours
That caused me such great pain—

Since that time, my dear,
—Just as, besides, for quite
Some time, I've seen our hearts
United—but since that night

When you saw death up close
About to swallow me,
My soul seems blessed anew,
Now coming forth and all

In smiles, from in the grave,
To see your godly caring.
Let me say to you:
I love you truly, with daring,

As I am sure, my dear,
I haven't ever loved . . .
Accept this autumn flower
That now you see in bud,

De peu, le cadeau sombre
Veut être aussi joyeux,
Laisse-m'en suivre l'ombre
Au soleil de tes yeux.

Paris

Paris n'a de beauté qu'en son histoire,
Mais cette histoire est belle tellement!
La Seine est encaissée absurdement,
Mais son vert clair à lui seul vaut la gloire.

Paris n'a de gaîté que son bagout,
Mais ce bagout, encor qu'assez immonde,
Il fait le tour des langages du monde,
Salant un peu ce trop fade ragoût.

Paris n'a de sagesse que le sombre
Flux de son peuple et de ses factions,
Alors qu'il fait des révolutions
Avec l'Ordre embusqué dans la pénombre.

Paris n'a que sa Fille de charmant
Laquelle n'est au prix de l'Exotique
Que torts gentils et vice peu pratique
Et ce quasi désintéressement.

Paris n'a de bonté que sa légère
Ivresse de désir et de plaisir,
Sans rien de trop que le vague désir
De voir son plaisir égayer son frère.

A fragrant, somber gift
Yet joyful too, this prize;
I'll follow its dark shadow
With the sunlight of your eyes.

Paris

Paris is beautiful in its history alone.
But that history's so wonderfully good!
The Seine is absurdly embanked and boxed in,
But its bright flow is alone a glorious gift.

Paris is lively alone in the way that it talks,
But that talk, however foul it may be,
Embraces the world's every tongue,
Adding salt to an otherwise tasteless ragout.

Paris is only prudent and wise in the somber
Ebb and flow of its people and factions,
All the while steeped in small revolutions
With Order lying in wait in the shadows.

Paris has only the charm of its Daughters,
Who betoken, when exotic's at play,
Only nice little wrongs and impractical vice
And, basically, self-disregard.

Paris has only the favor of its ready
Delight in desire and pleasure,
With nothing excessive but an unfocused desire
To see its own pleasure shared by a brother.

Paris n'a rien de triste et de cruel
Que le poëte annuel ou chronique,
Crevant d'ennui sous l'œil d'une clinique
Non loin du vieil ouvrier fraternel.

Vive Paris quand même et son histoire
Et son bagout et sa Fille, naïf
Produit d'un art pervers et primitif,
Et meure son poète expiatoire!

Dernier Espoir

Il est un arbre au cimetière
Poussant en pleine liberté,
Non planté par un deuil dicté,—
Qui flotte au long d'une humble pierre.

Sur cet arbre, été comme hiver,
Un oiseau vient qui chante clair
Sa chanson tristement fidèle.
Cet arbre et cet oiseau c'est nous:

Toi le souvenir, moi l'absence
Que le temps—qui passe—recense . . .
Ah, vivre encore à tes genoux!

Ah, vivre encor! Mais quoi, ma belle,
Le néant est mon froid vainqueur . . .
Du moins, dis, je vis dans ton cœur?

Paris has nothing sad, nothing cruel
But the once-a-year or every-day poet
Bored to death as eyes watch in a clinic
Not far from an old workman and brother.

Long live Paris all the same, along with
Its story, its talk, and its Daughters: primitive
Products of an art perverse and untutored—
And death to a poet who for that wants to atone!

Final Hope

In the graveyard stands a tree
Unstaked and free to grow,
Not planted out of mourning;
Its branches shade a humble stone.

To that tree, in summer as in winter,
Comes a bird that stays there,
Clearly singing a sadly faithful song.
The bird and tree are just like us—

One remembers; one is absent,
As time takes note while passing . . .
Ah, to live again with you!

Ah, to live again! But no, my dear,
The void has come to claim its part . . .
I do, though—no?—still live within your heart . . .

Impression de printemps

Il est des jours—avez-vous remarqué?—
Où l'on se sent plus léger qu'un oiseau,
Plus jeune qu'un enfant, et, vrai! plus gai
Que la même gaieté d'un damoiseau.

L'on se souvient sans bien se rappeler . . .
Évidemment l'on rêve, et non, pourtant.
L'on semble nager et l'on croirait voler.
L'on aime ardemment sans amour cependant

Tant est léger le cœur sous le ciel clair
Et tant l'on va, sûr de soi, plein de foi
Dans les autres, que l'on trompe avec l'air
D'être plutôt trompé gentiment, soi.

La vie est bonne et l'on voudrait mourir,
Bien que n'ayant pas peur du lendemain.
Un désir indécis s'en vient fleurir,
Dirait-on, au cœur plus ou moins qu'humain.

Hélas! faut-il que meure ce bonheur?
Meurent plutôt la vie et son tourment!
Ô dieux cléments, gardez-moi du malheur
D'à jamais perdre un moment si charmant.

1er MAI 1893.

Impression of Spring

There are days—have you noticed?—
When you feel yourself light as a bird,
Young as a boy, more care-free and gay
Than the fanciest beau in the park.

You remember without really recalling . . .
It must be a dream, but no doubt it's not.
Yes, you're swimming, but it feels just like flight:
It's the ardor of love, even when love's not in sight!

Your heart is so light under shimmering skies
And you advance with such trust in yourself
And in others, that you can deceive as you seem
Rather to be sweetly deceived in your turn.

Life is good, and you could happily die,
Though with no fear of whatever might follow.
An unsettled desire here emerges to blossom,
You might say, in a heart very human or even less so.

Alas! is it true that this bliss is certain to die?
Let life die instead, along with its torments!
O merciful gods! Spare me the baleful misfortune
Of losing forever so enchanting a time!

MAY 1, 1893.

Pour le nouvel an—à Saint-Georges de Bouhélier

La vie est de mourir et mourir c'est naître
Psychologiquement tout comme autrement
Et l'année ainsi fait, jour, heure, moment,
Condition *sine qua non*, cause d'être.

L'autre année est morte, et voici la nouvelle
Qui sort d'elle comme un enfant du corps mort
D'une mère mal accouchée, et n'en sort
Qu'aux fins de bientôt mourir mère comme elle.

Pour naître mourons ainsi que l'autre année;
Pour naître, où cela? Quelle terre ou quels cieux
Verront aborder notre envol radieux?

Comme la nouvelle année, en Dieu, parbleu!
Soit sous la figure éternelle incarnée,
Soit en qualité d'ange blanc dans le bleu.

Lamento

> Ma mie est morte,
> Plourez, mes yeux.
> (Vieux poète du XIVe siècle
> dont le nom m'échappe.)

La ville dresse ses hauts toits
Aux mille dentelures folles.
Un bruit de joyeuses paroles
Monte au ciel, rassurante voix.
—Que me fait cette gaîté vile
    De la ville!

For the New Year—To Saint-Georges de Bouhélier

Living is dying, and dying is birth
Psychologically and every which way;
The year gives us a day, an hour, a moment,
The *sine qua non* of our being.

Last year is dead; now here's one that's new,
A child coming out like a dead mother's gift
Once she's delivered—coming out to no end
But to die giving birth in her turn.

To be born we die like the year that's just passed;
Born, yes, but where? What land and what skies
Will witness our resplendent ascent?

Ascent guided by God, yes! like the year that is new!
Led by the Eternal, the figure made flesh,
Led by an angel, white in the heavenly blue.

Lament

> My love is lost.
> Cry tears, my eyes.
> (Old poet of the 14th century
> whose name escapes me.)

The town's roofs rise high
With their thousand jagged edges.
A noise of joyous chatter
Floats up, a voice of reassurance.
—What is it to me, this ugly cheer
    In the town?

Quelle paix vaste règne aux champs!
L'oiseau chante dans le grand chêne,
Les midis font blanche la plaine
Que dorent les soleils couchants.
—Peu m'importe ta gloire pure,
   Ô nature!

Avec les signes de ses flots,
Avec sa plainte solennelle,
La mer immense nous appelle,
Nous tous, rêveurs et matelots.
—Qu'est-ce que tu me veux encore,
   Mer sonore?

—Ah! ni les flots des Océans,
Ni les campagnes et leur ombre,
Ni les cités aux bruits sans nombre,
Qu'édifièrent des géants,
Rien ne réveillera ma mie
   Tant endormie.

Mort!

Les Armes ont tu leurs ordres en attendant
De vibrer à nouveau dans des mains admirables
Ou scélérates, et, tristes, le bras pendant,
Nous allons, mal rêveurs, dans le vague des Fables.

Les Armes ont tu leurs ordres qu'on attendait
Même chez les rêveurs mensongers que nous sommes,
Honteux de notre bras qui pendait et tardait,
Et nous allons, désappointés, parmi les hommes.

Vast peace reigns through the fields!
Birds sing in the great oak tree;
The plain turns white at midday
And then gold with the setting sun.
—Little do I care for pure glory,
    O you, nature!

With the signs in its waves,
With its solemn lament,
The immense sea calls loudly to us,
To us all, dreamers and sailors.
—What more can you ask of me,
    Sonorous sea?

—Ah! not the waves in the ocean,
Nor the long-shadowed countryside,
Nor the countless sounds of cities
That it took giants to build—
Nothing will reawaken my love,
    So deeply asleep.

Dead!

Our Arms have silenced commands as they wait
To shake and rattle anew in hands we admire
Or in villainous hands—and, sad arms hanging loose,
We drift, barely dreaming, into vagueness and fables.

Our Arms have silenced commands long expected
Even by these mendacious dreamers we are,
Ashamed of our arms hanging loose as we wait—
And we drift without bearings midst those still alive.

Armes, vibrez! mains admirables, prenez-les,
Mains scélérates à défaut des admirables!
Prenez-les donc et faites signe aux En-allés
Dans les fables plus incertaines que les sables.

Tirez du rêve notre exode, voulez-vous?
Nous mourons d'être ainsi languides, presque infâmes!
Armes, parlez! Vos ordres vont être pour nous
La vie enfin fleurie au bout, s'il faut, des lames.

La mort que nous aimons, que nous eûmes toujours
Pour but de ce chemin où prospèrent la ronce
Et l'ortie, ô la mort sans plus ces émois lourds,
Délicieuse et dont la victoire est l'annonce!

DÉCEMBRE 1895.

Shake and rattle, you Arms! Take them, hands we admire
Or villainous hands (for want of those we can prize)!
Take them now, as a greeting to the lost we're but seeing
In fables more vague and more shifting than sand.

Our exodus now is no dream—you agree?
We are languid and dying, an unspeakable waste!
Speak for us, Arms! Your commands can now bring
Life's final flower, if needed, at the end of a blade.

The death that we love, that we always considered
The end of this road where nettle and bramble
Grow thick, O death now stripped of worries and pains,
Death, a delight that in winning signals their end!

DECEMBER 1895.

Notes

PREFACE

1. Jules Lemaître, "Paul Verlaine," *Les Contemporains*, vol. 4 (Paris: H. Lecène and H. Oudin, 1889), 104. Our translation.

2. Paul Verlaine, *Les Poètes maudits*, 2nd ed. (Paris: L. Vanier, 1888).

3. See *One Hundred and One Poems by Paul Verlaine*, trans. Norman R. Shapiro (Chicago: University of Chicago Press, 1999), and Paul Verlaine, *Selected Poems*, trans. Martin Sorrell (Oxford: Oxford University Press, 1999).

4. See *Le Parnasse contemporain: Recueil de vers nouveaux*, vol. 1 (Paris: A. Lemerre, 1866).

5. Paul Verlaine, *The Cursed Poets*, trans. Chase Madar (Copenhagen and Los Angeles: Green Integer, 2003), 139.

6. Jules Huret, *Enquête sur l'évolution littéraire* (Paris: Charpentier, 1891), 70–71. Our translation.

7. See the autobiographical volume *Mes Hôpitaux* (Paris: L. Vanier, 1891).

8. See the album *Paul Verlaine chanté par Jean-Marc Versini*, released by Marmottes Productions in 2008.

9. All these names are featured in the recent album by the countertenor Philippe Jaroussky with the Quatuor Ébène and the pianist Jérôme Ducros, *Green: Mélodies françaises sur des poèmes de Verlaine*, released by Erato in 2015.

10. See, for example, the review of *Romances sans paroles* by Émile Blémont in 1874 (but we could quote many recent examples): "It is still music, often bizarre music, always sad, and which seems the echo of mysterious pains." Quoted by Olivier Bivort, ed., *Verlaine* (Paris: Presses de l'Université de Paris-Sorbonne, 1997), 61.

11. Huret, *Enquête sur l'évolution littéraire*, 69. Our translation.

TRANSLATOR'S NOTE

1. I have written elsewhere on the components of musicality in Verlaine and my approach to putting them into English. See Samuel N. Rosenberg, "Remarks on Translating the Poetry of Paul Verlaine into English," *Nouvelle Fribourg* (Summer 2017), http://www.nouvellefribourg.com/universite/remarks-on-translating-the-poetry-of-paul-verlaine-into-english.

PART 1: THE PARNASSIAN YEARS

First Poems

Death—To Victor Hugo (pp. 4–5)

Verlaine's first known poem, written at the age of fourteen, was sent to its dedicatee, the great romantic poet Victor Hugo (1802–1885), on December 12, 1858. "La Mort" is a glowing tribute to the exiled author of *Les Contemplations* (1856), the autobiographical collection of verse whose structuring principle is determined by the death of the poet's daughter Léopoldine Hugo (1824–1843).

To Don Quixote (pp. 6–7)

A manuscript version of this sonnet is dated March 18, 1861, when Verlaine was not yet seventeen years old. A later version is subtitled "Pour mettre en tête des magnifiques illustrations de G. Doré" [To put before the magnificent illustrations by G. Doré], in reference to the translated edition of Miguel de Cervantes's *Don Quichotte*, illustrated by Gustave Doré in 1863. The figure of Don Quixote, with his grotesque and vain pursuits, became a heroic model for romantic and postromantic artists and poets. The sonnet "To Don Quixote" was never published in the course of Verlaine's life, although the poet quotes it in its entirety in his autobiographical *Confessions* (1895).

The Gods (pp. 6–9)

This undated sonnet is among the first poems written by Verlaine in the early 1860s. The postromantic return of the gods—belonging to "heterodox" religions—announced in the sonnet appears deeply influenced by the publication of Leconte de Lisle's *Poèmes barbares* [Barbarous poems] in 1862. The poem was never published during the years of Verlaine's life.

Maid Joan (pp. 8–9)

"La Pucelle" is Joan of Arc (1412–1431), the Maid of Orléans, originally from Lorraine, who led the French army to victory in 1429, preventing England from conquering France. Joan was captured a year later and sentenced as a heretic to the stake by the English, with the complicity of the king of France Charles VII (1403–1461), Jean Dunois (1402–1468), known as "le Bâtard d'Orléans," and Jean Poton de Xaintrailles (1390–1461), her former companions, whom she apostrophizes in the first tercet. Verlaine's sonnet was perhaps composed as early as 1862 and was published in the second volume of *Le Parnasse contemporain* (1869–71), before being included in the collection *Jadis et Naguère* (1884).

The Burial (pp. 8–11)

This sarcastic sonnet was probably written in 1864, although it may have been composed at a later date. It was first published in the journal *L'Écho de Paris* on May 10, 1891, but it was never included in Verlaine's volumes of verse appearing during his life.

From *Poèmes saturniens*

Melancholia I—Resignation (pp. 12–13)

Melancholia, a reference to Albrecht Dürer's engraving *Melencolia I* (illustration 1), is the first section of Verlaine's first volume of verse, *Poèmes saturniens*, published in November 1866. Those "who are born under the sign of Saturn," including the poets, are indeed dominated by black bile, or melancholy. The poem "Resignation" is the first example in Verlaine's corpus of an *inverted sonnet*—that is a pseudo-sonnet in which the order of the quatrains and the tercets is inverted. The same form would later be used by Verlaine in homoerotic poems such as "Sappho" (see pp. 38–39) and "Le Bon

Disciple" (see p. 86). This homoerotic theme cannot be excluded in "Resignation," which proclaims the detestation of "pretty women" and "friends who are wimps."

dreaming of Koh-i-Noor "Koh-i-Noor" is a famous diamond, possibly known since antiquity, which is now one of the British crown jewels.

Heliogabálus and Sardanapálus! Heliogabalus was an eccentric Roman emperor (218–20) and Sardanapalus a legendary king of Assyria, the subject of both a play by Lord Byron (1821) and Eugène Delacroix's painting *The Death of Sardanapalus* (1827).

Melancholia VI—My Familiar Dream (pp. 12–15)

This regular sonnet was first published in the collective volume *Le Parnasse contemporain*, before being included in *Poèmes saturniens*. The poem is an early example of Verlaine's oneiric and undefined poetics, which he would mostly cultivate starting with the "Ariettes oubliées" (1872) of *Romances sans paroles* (see Part 2).

Melancholia VIII—Anguish (pp. 14–15)

This nihilistic sonnet was first published in *Le Parnasse contemporain*. In this poem built on systematic negation, the lyric subject renounces the major themes of classical and romantic poetry. Furthermore, his soul that "is on course for a frightening wreck" seems to announce Rimbaud's "Le Bateau ivre" [The Drunken Boat] (1871).

Etchings II—Nightmare (pp. 16–19)

As in the other sections of *Poèmes saturniens*, the title of the second section, "Eaux-fortes" [Etchings], is a reference to the visual arts. First published in the *Parnasse contemporain*, the six stanzas—each composed of four heptasyllabic lines followed by a tetrasyllable, with the rhyming structure A7A7A7B7B4—of Verlaine's "Cauchemar" [Nightmare] seems primarily inspired by Gottfried August Bürger's German ballad *Lenore* (1774), translated into French by Gérard de Nerval in 1830. But Verlaine's fantastic "etching" also includes symbolic elements drawn from Albrecht Dürer's engraving *Knight, Death and the Devil*, such as the "sword," the "hourglass," and, perhaps, the "teeth" of Death or the Devil.

Etchings III—Seascape (pp. 18–19)

The four pentasyllabic quatrains of this poem, characterized by a jerky rhythm that mimics the movement of the stormy ocean, were first published in the *Parnasse contemporain*.

Dreary Landscapes I—Setting Suns (pp. 18–21)

The title of the third section of *Poèmes saturniens*, "Paysages tristes" [Dreary Landscapes], is another reference to the visual arts in a melancholy tone. The elegiac poem "Coucher de soleils" [Setting Suns] is one of Verlaine's first attempts to create a minimal landscape—one reduced to indeterminate "fields," "shores," and "setting suns" repeated four times in the sixteen pentasyllabic lines of the poem—which is mingled with the undefined melancholy of the lyric subject.

Dreary Landscapes II—Mystical Twilight (pp. 20–21)

Markedly influenced by Baudelaire's "Harmonie du soir" [Evening Harmony], a *pantoum* in which the second and the fourth lines of a quatrain are repeated in the first and third line of the following quatrain, Verlaine's "Crépuscule du soir mystique" is characterized by the repetition of the first line in the last line, which provides a reflexive form to the poem that emphasizes the mirror effect between "memory" and the "twilight sun."

Dreary Landscapes III—Sentimental Stroll (pp. 20–23)
"The setting sun [that] cast its last rays" in this poem seems to refer to Albrecht Dürer's engraving *Melencolia I* (illustration 1) linking it to the general theme of the book. Moreover, the symmetrical repetition—with a few significant variations—of phrases of the first six lines in the last six lines of the poem expresses the circularity of the lyric subject's melancholy wandering, which has no definite goal or purpose.

Dreary Landscapes V—Autumn Song (pp. 22–23)
In the terse lines of this song composed of tetrasyllables and trisyllables, the "dreary landscape" that reflects the melancholy of the lyric subject—himself compared to a "shriveled leaf"—becomes above all a soundscape, dominated by "The long slow sobs / Of violins." This section of *Poèmes saturniens* thus depicts synesthetic landscapes, in which "perfumes, colors, sounds may correspond," to quote Baudelaire's sonnet "Correspondances," in order to express the poet's elusive interiority.

Caprices V—Mister Prude (pp. 24–25)
The first poem published by Verlaine, under the pseudonym "Pablo," in the *Revue du Progrès* in August 1863, "Monsieur Prudhomme" is a satirical sonnet directed against a figure antithetical to the poet: the bourgeois, as embodied by the fictional character Joseph Prudhomme, created by the playwright Henry Monnier (1799–1877) in the 1830s.

Initium (pp. 24–27)
The Latin title *Initium* finds its explanation in the last line of the poem, which describes the *beginning* of love-passion. However, the capital letter that characterizes this "Passion" suggests that it might soon turn into martyrdom . . .

Nevermore (pp. 26–27)
The title and the theme of this poem—the fatal loss of happiness—are borrowed from Edgar Allan Poe's *The Raven* (1845). The symmetrical structure of the four stanzas, in which the first line is repeated in the last line, following the model of Baudelaire's *Réversibilité* [Reversibility], emphasizes the specular dialogue of the lyric subject with his "heart," that is, with himself.

Epilogue (pp. 28–35)
The "Epilogue" of *Poèmes saturniens*, composed of three parts, represents Verlaine's declaration of faith in *Parnassian* poetics. In particular, the rejection of romantic "Inspiration" in favor of "study" and "labor" in the third part, and the poetics of *impassibility* illustrated by the line "Is she, yes or no, made of marble, the Venus de Milo?" pay tribute to the masters of Parnassus Théophile Gautier and Leconte de Lisle, the author of the influential "Vénus de Milo" in *Poèmes antiques* (1852). It is easily observable that impassibility is very far from dominating most pieces of *Poèmes saturniens*, which, on the contrary, exhibit a wide range of inspired sentiments, above all melancholia. Many critics have therefore argued that this "Epilogue" must be ironic and insincere. We

rather believe that it plays a collective and strategic role—emphasized by the pronoun *we* repeated fourteen times in parts II and III—in the postromantic context of publication of the *Parnasse contemporain*, issued the same year (1866) and by the same publisher (Alphonse Lemerre).

Genius speaking with ease and Erato rising   Erato is the Muse of lyric poetry.

Gabriel with his lute and Apollo with his lyre   The archangel Gabriel is the heavenly messenger in the Judaic and Christian traditions. Apollo is the god of the arts and the leader of the Muses in Greco-Roman mythology. The poet here brings together, in a somewhat blasphemous manner, Judeo-Christian and pagan references.

For whom no Beatrice has come to guide our steps   Beatrice is Dante's guide in "Paradiso" of *The Divine Comedy* (fourteenth century).

Groups wrapt in the trap of lake banks   The word *lac* [lake], emphasized by italics in the original text, alludes to the most famous French romantic poem: Alphonse de Lamartine's "Le Lac" (1820).

It is Faust in old prints   Doctor Faustus, the subject of Christopher Marlowe's tragedy (1604) and Rembrandt's etching (1652), among other works, is the figure of the learned man who makes a pact with the devil in order to learn magic.

The untouched block of the Beautiful, pure Paros   Paros, a Greek island of the Cyclades, lends its name, through a metonymy, to the immaculate white marble of which the island is mainly composed. Théophile Gautier's famous 1849 "Le Poème de la femme" [The Poem of Woman] is subtitled "Marbre de Paros" [Marble of Paros].

The serene masterwork, our successor to Memnon   Memnon does not refer here to the Trojan hero, son of Tithonus and Eos (Dawn) who was slain by Achilles, but to the two colossal statues, named after him, near Luxor in Egypt, which were believed to sing when touched at dawn by the rays of the rising sun.

From *Les Amies* *(pp. 36–39)*

Les Amies [Girlfriends] is a collection of six Sapphic sonnets, clandestinely published in Belgium at the end of 1867, under the pseudonym Pablo de Herlagnez, and later reissued in *Parallèlement* (1889). The lesbian theme of the series is underlined, at the formal level, by the exclusive use of feminine rhymes, which contradicts the rule of alternating masculine and feminine rhymes in French prosody, and by the inversion of the quatrains and the tercets in "Sappho," the last pseudo-sonnet of the series; a feature that characterizes other homoerotic pseudo-sonnets in Verlaine's works (see note to "Melancholia I"). But if Verlaine's Sapphic sonnets challenge the heteronormative literary tradition, it is also because, on the level of content, Sappho's love is not exclusively homosexual or heterosexual, as the legend of Phaon mentioned in the last poem shows (see next note); a bisexuality that Verlaine had himself experienced.

VI—*Sappho* *(pp. 38–39)*

Sappho (sixth century BC) was a Greek lyric poet from the island of Lesbos, whence the word *lesbian*. According to a legend, Sappho committed suicide by leaping into the sea from the cliff of Leucas because of her desperate love for the sailor Phaon. Selene is the goddess of the moon.

From *Fêtes galantes*

Moonlight (pp. 40–41)

This poem was first published in *La Gazette rimée* on February 20, 1867, under the title "Fêtes galantes" [Gallant Festivities], which later became the title of the 1869 volume that it opens. The "landscape" depicted in the poem is a metaphor of the addressee's soul ("Your soul"), which reveals its sadness disguised under fancy dress. More generally, the poet focuses on the melancholy that hides behind the masks of the *Fêtes galantes*.

Where masks and bergamasks go casting their spells A *bergomask dance* is "a rustic dance, framed in imitation of the people of Bergamo (a province in the state of Venice), ridiculed as clownish in their manners and dialect" (*OED*).

As We Stroll (pp. 40–43)

First published in the journal *L'Artiste* on July 1, 1868, this poem, with its attention to the pictorial details of the landscape and the playful attitudes of the characters, could well be a description—in literary terms: an *ekphrasis*—of a painting by Watteau, for instance the *Assembly in the Park* (1716–17) held by the Louvre.

The Artless (pp. 42–43)

This poem, expressive of a subtle eroticism, was first published in the journal *L'Artiste* on July 1, 1868.

Seashells (pp. 44–45)

"Les Coquillages" is composed in the tradition of the *Blasons anatomiques du corps féminin* (1543), which celebrate—or denigrate—the female body parts through a series of metaphors and similes. In this connection, the "confounding" seashell, emblem of Venus, that concludes the poem alludes to the woman's genitalia.

The Faun (pp. 44–45)

The Faun is a mythological figure, part human and part goat, which symbolizes lust. Verlaine's poem, a variation on the classical theme of fleeting time, is marked by a melancholy tension between the immobility of the statue of the Faun and the ephemeral nature of human love.

Resounds with the tambourins' beat The *tambourin*, "the long narrow drum or tabor used in Provence" (*OED*), should not be confused with the *tambourine*.

Mandolin (pp. 46–47)

First published in *La Gazette rimée* on February 20, 1867, this poem depicts a pastoral scene, once more inspired by Watteau's paintings, in which classical characters of shepherds and lovers (Tircis and Aminta from Torquato Tasso's *Aminta* [1573], Clitander and Damis from comedies by Molière and Marivaux) compose verse and play music for beautiful female listeners ("les belles écouteuses"). An ironic tone is, however, perceptible in the poem, specifically in phrases such as "donneurs de sérénades" [serenaders], "propos fades" [dull chat], "l'éternel Clitandre" [inescapable Clitander], and "la mandoline jase" [the mandolin chatters].

To Clymene *(pp. 46–49)*

This poem was first published in the journal *L'Artiste* on July 1, 1868. The dedication "To Clymene" situates this love poem—or rather this love prayer—in an unspecified mythological context. A "barcarole" is a song sung by Venetian *barcaruoli* as they row their gondolas. The "romances sans paroles" [songs without words] in the second line alludes to Felix Mendelssohn's works for piano *Lieder ohne Worte* and provides the paradoxical title of Verlaine's 1874 collection of verse (see below). The *correspondances* of the last stanza refers to Baudelaire's famous sonnet (see note to "Dreary Landscapes V," p. 340), to the extent that these correspondences are based on a synesthetic perception of reality (the "mirage" of the "voice," the "aroma" of the "pallor," the "white" of the "scent," etc.).

Muted *(pp. 48–51)*

The title "En sourdine" [Muted, that is, "softened or deadened in volume or tone," according to *OED*], gives the poem a musical connotation, emphasized by the nightingale's song. This love poem may also be considered a funeral poem, for the "evening" that "descends from the tall black oaks," accompanied by the nightingale's song, seems to allude to the evening of life. Indeed, in the literary tradition going back to the myth of Philomela, the nightly song of the nightingale is often considered a mourning lament. Moreover, the poet asks his lover to take the posture of a dead body, lying with the "eyes almost closed" and the arms crossed on the breast.

Lovers' Conversation *(pp. 50–51)*

In the final poem of *Fêtes galantes*, first published in the journal *L'Artiste* on July 1, 1868, the warm and animated landscapes of the collection are replaced by an "old park unattended and cold," and the playful talk of young lovers by the nostalgic conversation of "two specters." This poem from beyond the grave truly marks the end of the "gallant festivities."

Poems Contemporaneous with *Poèmes saturniens*, *Les Amies*, and *Fêtes galantes*

Circumspection *(pp. 52–53)*

This sonnet was first published in the journal *Le Hanneton* on July 25, 1867, and later included in the volume *Jadis et Naguère* (1884), with a dedication to the bohemian poet Gaston Sénéchal (1858–1914).

Allegory I *(pp. 52–55)*

First published in the journal *Le Hanneton* on September 26, 1867, and later included in the collection *Parallèlement* (1889), this sonnet may be a poetic transposition (that is, an *ekphrasis*) of a mythological landscape depicted on an old tapestry. In any case, the sonnet highlights the decline of mythological themes in poetry, after their brief revival in the 1850s, notably with Leconte de Lisle's *Poèmes antiques* (1852).

Interior *(pp. 54–55)*

A manifest tribute to Baudelaire's *Fleurs du Mal*, this sonnet was first published in the journal *Le Hanneton* on October 3, 1867, a month after Baudelaire's death on August 31, and later included in the volume *Jadis et Naguère* (1884).

Allegory II (pp. 56–57)

This second sonnet called "Allegory" was first published in the journal *Le Hanneton* on March 5, 1868, and later included in the volume *Jadis et Naguère* (1884), with a dedication to the painter Jules Valadon (1826–1900), who painted a portrait of Verlaine in 1883. If spring is the season of love and rebirth (see "Green," p. 115), summer, for Verlaine, is the season of lethargy, if not death.

The Vanquished (pp. 56–63)

The first two sections of "Les Vaincus" were published in the journal *La Gazette rimée*, under the title "Les Poëtes" [The Poets], on May 20, 1867, and in the second volume of *Le Parnasse contemporain* (1869–71). Verlaine's plan was to compose a whole collection of verse entitled *Les Vaincus*; but after France's defeat in the Franco-Prussian War in 1870 and the bloody suppression of the Paris Commune in May 1871, the seditious verse of "Les Vaincus" must have been considered too revolutionary, so no publisher dared to print it. The last three sections of the poem were probably written in London in 1872, alongside exiled Communards such as Eugène Vermersch (1845–1878), and the whole poem was published in the volume *Jadis et Naguère* in 1884, with a dedication to the progressive writer Louis-Xavier de Ricard (1843–1911), at a time when Verlaine had definitively renounced the socialist and revolutionary fervor of his youth.

From *La Bonne Chanson*

IV (pp. 64–67)

According to Mathilde Mauté, Verlaine's fiancée to whom the volume *La Bonne Chanson* [The Good Song] is dedicated, this poem is the response to the first encouraging letter that the poet received from her in August 1869. The hope for a happy love and, possibly, marriage prompts the poet to renounce irony, alcohol, and violence, so as to "walk straight" (an adverb that can also be interpreted in sexual terms). Wishful thinking?

V (pp. 66–67)

This poem is characterized by the progressive intertwining of two themes in each of its five stanzas: a celestial and spiritual theme in the first part of the stanza, and a terrestrial and naturalistic theme in the second part.

VII (pp. 68–71)

This is one of the first poems in French literature to describe the modernist perception of a flying landscape as seen from a train in motion. The "beautiful Name" is, of course, that of Mathilde, the poet's fiancée, a "name" that is also the subject of the following poem.

VIII (pp. 70–71)

Mathilde Mauté allegedly received this medievalizing poem from Verlaine during her stay at the Château de Bouëlle, in Normandy, in September 1869 (hence the "Chatelaine in her tower"). The "Carolingian name" of the "Saint in her halo" seems to refer to Saint Matilda (or Maud) of Ringelheim, Queen of the Franks from 919, although she did not belong to the Carolingian dynasty, which ruled France from Pippin the Short (751) to Louis V (987).

And the blush of a wife-like child   Mathilde Mauté was sixteen years old in September 1869.

XIII   *(pp. 72–73)*

This poem was written after Verlaine's first visit at Mathilde's house, in the presence of her parents, in October 1869.

XIV   *(pp. 72–75)*

The poetics of domestic happiness characterizing this poem seems inspired by the *dizains* (ten-line poems) of *Promenades et Intérieurs* (1870) by François Coppée. Verlaine's marriage proposal was—reluctantly—accepted by Mathilde Mauté's father in October 1869; but the marriage itself was repeatedly postponed, until it took place on August 11, 1870.

XV   *(pp. 74–77)*

In this poem, described by Verlaine as a "madrigal," the poet seems to foresee the "dark" future, "filled with fears," which would follow his marriage. The last line of the poem is notable for its transition from the formal *vous* for "you" to the familiar *tu*, which signals a greater intimacy between the fiancés.

XVII   *(pp. 76–77)*

This poem is written in *terza rima* (a form of interlocking tercets: *aba, bcb, cdc*, etc.), the form used by Dante in *The Divine Comedy*. In this connection, the themes of the "dark forest" (the "*selva oscura*" of *Inferno* I), the "path as directed by Hope," and the journey traveled with the Muse vaguely evoke Dante's journey. See also, below, poem XX.

XVIII   *(pp. 78–79)*

This is the only poem in *La Bonne Chanson* in which Verlaine (covertly) expresses his republican and revolutionary position—which he would later renounce—at the time of the decline of the Second Empire, which would fall this very year after the defeat of France in the Franco-Prussian war in September 1870. The mention of the "customs austere of the just" alludes to Victor Hugo's 1853 anti-Napoleonic volume of verse *Châtiments* [Punishments].

XX   *(pp. 78–81)*

See note to XVII. In this instance, Mathilde becomes Verlaine's Beatrice.

XXI   *(pp. 80–81)*

The final poem of *La Bonne Chanson*, set in the spring—the season of love and rejuvenation in the literary tradition—announces Verlaine's marriage to Mathilde in the summer of 1870 ("Let summer now come!"), a year after their meeting ("For a year now I have felt in my soul") in June 1869. The collection therefore covers a year in the poet's love life.

PART 2: UNDER THE SPELL OF RIMBAUD

First Encounters (1871–72)

The Good Disciple (pp. 86–87)

The manuscript of this inverted sonnet (see note to "Melancholia I," p. 338) was found by the Belgian police in Rimbaud's wallet after Verlaine had shot him in Brussels on July 10, 1873, which strongly suggests that the author dedicated this blasphemous pseudo-sonnet to the younger poet. The antithetical structure of the poem, evident in its first line "I am blessed! I am damned!" is characteristic of ecstatic poetry, be it mystical or orgasmic, or both as in this instance. "Le Bon Disciple" was first published in Verlaine's *Œuvres posthumes* [Posthumous Works] in 1929.

Libelous Lines (pp. 86–89)

This sonnet was first published in *La Revue critique* on March 28, 1884, and was included the same year in the volume *Jadis et Naguère*; but it had most likely been composed in 1872, when Verlaine was living and traveling with Rimbaud. The title of the sonnet, its content and its prosody (Sapphic hendecasyllables with predominance of masculine rhymes) suggest that the poet's "frail love" is none other than Rimbaud.

Poet and Muse (pp. 88–89)

A note written by Verlaine in the manuscript of this sonnet, composed in prison in 1874, specifies: "About a room in the rue Campagne-Première, in Paris, in January 1872." This is precisely the "Room" where Verlaine and Rimbaud were staying most nights at the beginning of 1872. These nights are described in the poem as "Herculean," by reference to the mythological hero Hercules who, according to Alfred Delvau's *Dictionnaire érotique moderne* [Modern Erotic Dictionary], is a "fucker capable of performing the twelve labors, or even somewhat fewer, which is not bad" (our translation). The undue denial in the first tercet seems to confirm the homosexual interpretation of the sonnet, which was published in *Jadis et Naguère* (1884).

Explanation (pp. 90–91)

The title of this sonnet seems to refer to the epigraph that quotes the previous sonnet "Le Poète et la Muse," and therefore to its homoerotic content. In the collection *Parallèlement* (1889), this "Explanation" appears in the section "Lunes" [Moons], a title that, given the sexual content of the poems it introduces, needs to be interpreted in its metaphorical sense: "fesses" in French, "buttocks" in English.

From *Album zutique*

The Death of Pigs (pp. 92–93)

This sonnet is an obscene parody, handwritten by Verlaine in collaboration with Léon Valade (1842–1884) in the *Album zutique* in 1871, of the famous sonnet "La Mort des amants" [The Death of Lovers] by Charles Baudelaire. The parody suggests that Baudelaire's sonnet could be interpreted in a homosexual sense, since the gender of the "lovers" is not specified.

Sonnet on the Asshole (pp. 94–95)

This sonnet is the only poem known to have been composed in collaboration with Rimbaud. According to Verlaine, he himself wrote the quatrains and Rimbaud wrote the tercets. The sonnet is an obscene parody of *L'Idole* [The Idol] by Albert Mérat (Paris: Lemerre, 1869), a collection of twenty sonnets, each devoted to a female body part, in the tradition of the *Blasons anatomiques du corps féminin* [Anatomical blazons of the female body], published in 1543. The sonnet by Verlaine and Rimbaud, however, alludes to sodomy, thus subverting the traditional heteronormative relationship between the poet and his muse. It was handwritten in the *Album zutique* in 1871 and clandestinely published in the posthumous, Spanish-titled pornographic collection *Hombres* [Men] in 1904.

From *Romances sans paroles*

Forgotten Ariettas I   (*pp. 96–97*)
The first "Ariette oubliée" was published in the journal *La Renaissance littéraire et artistique* on May 18, 1872, under the title "Romances sans paroles," which would later be selected by Verlaine as the title of his collection of verse printed in 1874. Rimbaud had sent to Verlaine an "Ariette oubliée" composed by Charles-Simon Favart (1710–1792) and quoted in the epigraph. Moreover, Verlaine was planning to dedicate his volume to Rimbaud. "The soul that mourns" in the third stanza of the poem thus appears to be that of the two poets.

Forgotten Ariettas III   (*pp. 98–99*)
The octosyllable attributed to Rimbaud in the epigraph of the third "Ariette oubliée" is apocryphal ("of unestablished authenticity" [*OED*]). This "arietta" is perhaps the most emblematic example of Verlaine's "languor" and poetics of vagueness.

Forgotten Ariettas IV   (*pp. 100–101*)
In the fourth "Ariette oubliée," the poet seems to be intentionally blurring the identities and gender roles of the speaker and addressee, who are successively likened to "sistersouls," "two children," and "two girls" who wander "far from women and men." This is the first poem that Verlaine is known to have written in hendecasyllables (elevensyllable lines), a meter originating in Sapphic poetry and uncommon in the French tradition.

Forgotten Ariettas VII   (*pp. 100–103*)
This is the only poem in the series of "Ariettes oubliées," dominated by the figure of Rimbaud, in which Verlaine laments his desertion—psychological before physical—of his wife, Mathilde, whom he had married two years earlier, in August 1870, and with whom he had a son, Georges, born on October 30, 1871.

Forgotten Ariettas VIII   (*pp. 102–5*)
The eighth "arietta" depicts an impressionist winter landscape that is inextricably interwoven—as was already true of "Paysages tristes" [Sad Landscapes] in *Poèmes saturniens*—with the poet's mood of gloominess.

Forgotten Ariettas IX   (*pp. 104–5*)
The epigraph is a quotation from "Sur l'ombre que faisaient des arbres dans l'eau" [On the shadow left by trees in the water] by Cyrano de Bergerac (1619–1655). In this last "arietta," the poet establishes an analogy between the "trees" and the "turtle-doves" in the first stanza, and the "traveler" and his "hopes" in the second stanza. The date "May, June 72" refers to the composition of the whole series of "Ariettes oubliées."

Brussels—Merry-Go-Round   *(pp. 106–9)*

This poem, which is part of the section "Paysages belges" [Belgian Landscapes] of *Romances sans paroles*, was composed while Verlaine was wandering through Belgium with Rimbaud, after abandoning his wife and baby son in Paris on July 7, 1872. The epigraph is a quotation from *Odes et Ballades* (1828) by Victor Hugo. Saint-Gilles is a municipality of Brussels.

Birds in the Night   *(pp. 108–15)*

This long poem expresses the memory of the last night of love, on July 22, 1873, between Verlaine and his wife, Mathilde, who came to Brussels to try to win back her husband but found herself abandoned anew as he fled again with Rimbaud. Verlaine had titled an early version of the poem "La Mauvaise Chanson" [The Bad Song], by way of contrast with the epithalamic book *La Bonne Chanson* [The good song], which, merely three years earlier, had celebrated the couple's engagement. The last section of the poem (its final three stanzas) resonates, retrospectively, with Rimbaud's "Le Bateau ivre" [The Drunken Boat], insofar as the poet figures himself as "the Poor Ship / That unmasted sails ahead through the storm," while it announces, prospectively, Rimbaud's *Une saison en enfer* [A Season in Hell], where "the Sinner / [. . .] / Writhes through Hell," probably for committing adultery with a man. The English title "Birds in the Night" is borrowed from a lullaby composed by Arthur Sullivan (1842–1900) in 1869.

Green   *(pp. 114–17)*

The choice of the English title "Green" for this poem, which opens the section "Aquarelles" [Watercolors] of *Romances sans paroles*, seems inspired by the etymological sense of the word (see *to grow*): "flourishing, fresh, new, immature" (*OED*).

Spleen   *(pp. 116–17)*

This poem, whose English title alludes to Baudelaire's *Fleurs du Mal*, where it refers to a spiritual form of melancholy, provides a key for interpreting the title of the section "Aquarelles" [Watercolors] in *Romance sans paroles*, as well as a major aspect of Verlaine's poetics (see "Art of poetry," p. 153): the rejection of "glossy" and "shiny" colors in favor of the washed-out tones of watercolor. The translated distichs all show rhyme or assonance.

Streets I   *(pp. 118–19)*

This poem, composed, according to Verlaine, in a pub at the junction of Old Compton Street and Greek Street in the Soho district of London, is characterized by the dynamic tension between the cheerful refrain "Let's dance a jig!" and the nostalgic memory of the abandoned wife in all the three-line stanzas. The translated stanzas all show rhyme or assonance.

A Poor Young Shepherd   *(pp. 120–21)*

The English title "A poor young shepherd" designates the poet himself, by reference to classical bucolic poetry, where shepherds pine with love for shepherdesses. In this poem the pastoral context is transposed into modern-day England. Note the play of repetition, rhyme, and assonance in the translation.

Beams *(pp. 122–23)*

The English title "Beams" refers first of all to the rays of light emitted by the sun or a lighthouse; but it may also, in a poetic context, refer to ships. Who is this *woman* whose "choice [is] to sail out on the sea"? A woman met on the ship? The ship itself, named "Comtesse-de Flandre" [Countess of Flanders]? A mask of Rimbaud? All of the above? We do not know. In any event, on April 4, 1873, Verlaine and Rimbaud went back to the continent after spending eight months in London. They would embark again for England the following month, on May 27. This is the final poem of *Romances sans paroles*.

Poems Contemporaneous with *Romances sans paroles*

"The sound of the horn . . ." *(pp. 124–25)*

This sonnet, composed in Jehonville (Belgium) in the spring of 1873, is described, in the manuscript, as a "memory of Charleville," Rimbaud's hometown, where the poets had met in December 1871. The sentimental "landscape" (and soundscape) of the poem is reminiscent of the tale in verse "Le Cor" [The Horn] (1825) by Alfred de Vigny (1797–1863). Verlaine's sonnet was first published in the volume *Sagesse* [Wisdom] (III. ix) in 1880.

"The wintry wind blasts . . ." *(pp. 124–27)*

This poem is dated "Jehonville, May 1873, across the fields." Composed a few weeks before the Brussels affair, on July 10, and the subsequent imprisonment of Verlaine, the poem celebrates the coming of spring and is still full of "hope." An early version of the poem is included, as a sonnet that ends at line 14 ("J'ai des fourmis plein les talons"), in the manuscript of *Cellulairement*, and the full version was published in *Sagesse* (III.xi).

After the Shooting

Harvesting Grapes *(pp. 128–29)*

This Bacchic sonnet was composed in prison in September 1873. It is included in the manuscript of *Cellulairement* and was published in the collection *Jadis et Naguère* (1884), with a dedication to the obscure journalist Georges Rall (born in 1858).

Limping Sonnet *(pp. 128–31)*

This sonnet was composed, according to the manuscript of *Cellulairement*, in prison in September 1873, and was probably inspired by the dramatic conclusion of the romance between Verlaine and Rimbaud in London two months earlier. The adjective "limping" refers to the prosody of the sonnet, which is written in supernumerary thirteen-syllable lines (compared to the traditional twelve-syllable alexandrines), with no regular rhyme scheme (cf. the sonnet "À la louange . . ." p. 180). The poem was published, with its current title and a dedication to Ernest Delahaye (1853–1930), a friend and former class-mate of Rimbaud's, in *Jadis et Naguère* (1884).

On a Statue of Ganymede *(pp. 130–31)*

In Greek mythology, the young Trojan hero Ganymede was abducted by Zeus, dis-guised as an eagle, because of his exceptional beauty. The bronze statue of *Ganymede* by Jean Turcan (1846–1895) that Verlaine describes in this sonnet was located in the park of the Thermes at Aix-les-Bains until World War II, when it was removed and melted down. Revard is a mountain near Aix-les-Bains, where the poet spent the summer of 1889. The sonnet was first published in the journal *Le Courrier français* on July 12, 1891, and later included in the second edition of *Parallèlement* (1894) as well as in the licentious collection *Hombres* (1904), which highlights its homoerotic nature.

To Arthur Rimbaud (pp. 132–33)

This late sonnet was first published in the journal *Le Chat noir* on August 17, 1889, almost fifteen years after Verlaine had seen Rimbaud possibly for the last time, in Stuttgart, in January 1875. The first hemistich "Mortal, angel AND demon" is a variation, highlighted by the capital letters, of a poem by Alphonse de Lamartine dedicated "To Lord Byron": "Mortal, angel or demon." Verlaine's sonnet is included in the second edition of *Dédicaces* (1894).

To Arthur Rimbaud—On a Sketch of Him by His Sister (pp. 132–35)

Rimbaud died of cancer in Marseille on November 10, 1891. His sister Isabelle made several sketches of him on his deathbed at the Hospital of the Conception. Before being included in the second edition of *Dédicaces* in 1894, this sonnet had been published in the journal *La Plume* on February 15, 1893, with an epigraph from Rimbaud's *Une saison en enfer* (1873): "Des climats perdus me tanneront" [lost climates will tan me]. In fact, before going back to France in 1891, Rimbaud had spent more than ten years, from 1880, in Abyssinia (Ethiopia) and on the Gulf of Aden. The Latin prayer in the last line of the sonnet, "*pax tecum sit, Dominus sit cum te,*" means "peace be with you, the Lord be with you."

To a Passerby (pp. 134–35)

The identity of this "dear child" is not disclosed in the sonnet, which seems to memorialize both Rimbaud and Lucien Létinois (on the latter, see note to "Lucien Létinois," p. 356). The sonnet was first published in the journal *La Plume* on January 15, 1893, and included the following year in the second edition of *Dédicaces*.

PART 3: FROM PRISON TO CONVERSION

In Prison (Poems from *Cellulairement* and Other Poems)

To the Reader (pp. 140–43)

This poem serves as the prologue to *Cellulairement* [Cellularly], the collection of verse that Verlaine composed in prison, from July 1873 until his release in January 1875. Unpublished as a book during Verlaine's life, the poems were scattered through other collections. "Au lecteur" was published in *Parallèlement* (1889) under the title "Prologue d'un livre dont il ne paraîtra que les extraits ci-après" [Prologue of a book of which only the following excerpts will ever be published].

False Impression (pp. 142–45)

This poem was allegedly composed on the day of Verlaine's imprisonment, after he shot Rimbaud on July 10, 1873, in Brussels. The poem is included in the manuscript of *Cellulairement* and was published in the collection *Parallèlement* (1889).

Upon the Waters   *(pp. 144–46)*
"Upon the waters," one of the first poems composed in prison in July 1873, implies a
striking contrast between the poet's imprisoned body and his "bitter spirit," which
"takes flight across the sea." The metaphor of the "gull" in the second stanza recalls the
"gull" of "Puisque le juste est dans l'abîme" [Since the righteous man is in the abyss] by
Victor Hugo, a poem in the collection *Châtiments* [Punishments] composed in exile in
Jersey in 1852. Verlaine's poem is included in the manuscript of *Cellulairement* and was
first published in *Sagesse* (III.vii).

Lullaby   *(pp. 146–49)*
This "Lullaby" of despair was composed by Verlaine on August 8, 1873, the very day that
the poet was sentenced to two years of imprisonment in Belgium. The epigraph is a
quotation from the Italian collection of verse *Rime* [Rhymes] by the artist Michelangelo
Buonarroti (1475–1564). Verlaine's poem is included in the manuscript of *Cellulairement*
and was first published in *Sagesse* (III.v).

"The sky is, above the rooftop"   *(pp. 148–49)*
One of the most famous poems by Verlaine, "The sky is, above the rooftop" was com-
posed in September 1873. The poet describes the circumstances of its composition in
his autobiographical volume *Mes Prisons* [My Prisons]. The poem is included in *Sagesse*
(III.vi).

Ten Lines on 1830   *(pp. 150–51)*
This poem, composed in 1874, is part of the series "Vieux coppées" in the manuscript of
Cellulairement, consisting of ten parodic *dizains* (ten-line poems) that mock the prosaic
style of François Coppée's poetry. 1830 is the year of the famous "battle of Hernani,"
named after the title of Victor Hugo's Spanish drama that opened at the Comédie-
Française (the main state theater in France) on February 25, 1830; a "battle" fought by
the young avant-garde of romantic writers and artists against the old classical order.
Verlaine's *dizain* was published in the collection *Jadis et Naguère* (1884).

Hard to Believe, but True   *(pp. 150–51)*
This *dizain* was composed in 1874. In a note added to the manuscript of the poem,
Verlaine explains that the sonnet "Don Quichotte" in the collection *À mi-côté* by Léon
Valade (one of the poet's "brave friends"), published by Alphonse Lemerre in 1874, is
dedicated to "Paul V***," a censoring of his name for which he holds his former pub-
lisher responsible.

The Last Ten Lines   *(pp. 150–53)*
This last *dizain*, followed by the date "Brussels, August 1873—Mons, January 1875" in the
collection *Parallèlement*, is the poem of Verlaine's that most explicitly refers to his im-
prisonment in Belgium. The expression in the last line "c'est bon pour une fois, sais-tu!"
is typically—and mockingly—Belgian.

Art of Poetry   *(pp. 152–55)*
One of the most discussed of Verlaine's poems, "Art poétique" was composed in prison
in April 1874. Verlaine's poetics, as presented in this poem, contrasts in particular with
the classical "Art poétique" (1674) by Nicolas Boileau (1636–1711) and its famous couplet

"Ce que l'on conçoit bien s'énonce clairement, / Et les mots pour le dire arrivent aisément" [Whatever is well conceived is clearly said, / And the words to say it flow with ease]. For his part, Verlaine favors the musicality of verse, the vagueness of meaning, and the indistinctness of color; to the point where this "Art of poetry" has often been considered a manifesto of impressionist poetics, although Verlaine did not always follow its principles. The *Impair* of the second line refers to the odd meter that Verlaine often favors in his verse (in this case nine-syllable lines), to make it closer to popular song. The poem was first published in the journal *Paris moderne* in November 1882, and later included in the volume *Jadis et Naguère*, with a dedication to Charles Morice (1860–1919).

After the Conversion (Poems from *Sagesse* and Other Poems)

"Jesus just told me . . ." (pp. 156–57)

This is the first of the ten dialogical sonnets that constitute the "Final" section of *Cellulairement*, in which the poet converses with Jesus soon after his conversion. The section is dated "January 16, 1875," the day Verlaine was released from prison, but it was certainly composed, in prison, before September 1874. The ten sonnets are included, with a few variants, in *Sagesse* (II.iv).

"O my God . . ." (pp. 158–61)

This litany in verse is dated "August 15, 1874," the very day Verlaine received Communion for the first time after his conversion, but it was probably composed a year later (the manuscript is dated "July 75"). The poem, which opens the second section of *Sagesse* (II.i), can be considered a contradictory response to the (in)famous "Litanies de Satan" [Satan's Litanies] by Baudelaire.

"Beauty of women . . ." (pp. 162–63)

This sonnet was probably composed in September 1875. Verlaine was hoping that it would appear in the third volume of *Le Parnasse contemporain* in 1876, but Anatole France, co-director of the *Parnasse*, refused to publish it, arguing that "the author is disgraceful and the verses are the worst we have seen." The sonnet was later included in the collection *Sagesse* (I.v).

"A humble life . . ." (pp. 162–65)

This sonnet is dated October 1875. Following up on his conversion to Catholicism, the poet is trying to adapt to the strict life of a penitent by repressing his pride. The sonnet is included in the collection *Sagesse* (I.viii).

"Hedges ranged . . ." (pp. 164–65)

Verlaine recounts the circumstances of composition of this poem, inspired by his discovery of the Lincolnshire landscape in March 1875, in his "Notes on England: Myself as a French Master": "Twilight was about to fall on the scenery in front of us. [. . .] Both sides of the road, which was fringed with fine quickset hedges, were studded, so to speak, with big sheep and nimble colts roaming free. I made a sketch of the scene in these few verses, which are taken from my book *Sagesse* [III.xiii]." *Fortnightly Review* 56, no. 331 (July 1894): 71.

London (pp. 166–69)

This poem was probably composed in the summer of 1876. The epigraph quotes Victor Hugo's poem "France et Âme" [France and Soul], included in the second series of *La Légende des siècles* [The Legend of the Centuries], the "grave Englishman" being none other than Charles Darwin. Verlaine's poem was published in the journal *La Revue blanche* in December 1893, and not collected in any volume during the poet's life.

"The immensity . . ." (pp. 168–69)

In the context of the historical rivalry between France and England, the laudatory poem "The immensity . . ." in honor of London and its "civilized" inhabitants could have been considered provocative by a French reader. In the last stanza, the poet suggests that the English subjects are ready to come back to the Catholic Church. The poem was published in *Sagesse* (III.xiv).

"'Big city' . . ." (pp. 170–71)

Verlaine came back to France in 1877, after two years spent in England. As opposed to "civilized" London, Paris is presented in the poem as the "Big city" of corruption and vanity, where the converted "Sage" (the poet himself) nevertheless pledges to find his *Thébaïde*: his retreat in the desert. The "two parts of his soul [that] shed tears" in the last line are his wife and his son. The poem is included in *Sagesse* (III.xvi).

"Once more I have seen my sole child . . ." (pp. 170–73)

Verlaine wrote this sonnet in July 1876, following a brief meeting with his son, Georges (born on October 30, 1871), whom he had not seen in four years. The sonnet is included in *Sagesse* (I.xviii).

A Widower Speaks (pp. 172–75)

This poem, dated 1878, is a maritime invocation of Verlaine's wife, Mathilde, from whom he had been legally separated in April 1874, and their son Georges, born in 1871. The poet recommends them to God, in accordance with his new Catholicism. The poem was first published in the journal *La Revue critique* on April 27, 1884, and included in the Catholic collection *Amour* in 1888.

"Born the child . . ." (pp. 174–75)

This prayer in verse was composed before September 1878. It is included in *Sagesse* (I.xxiii). See the sonnet "A humble life . . ." (p. 163).

"Prince brought down . . ." (pp. 176–79)

This eulogistic poem was composed by Verlaine after the death of Prince Napoléon Eugène Louis Bonaparte (1856–1879), the sole child of the former Emperor Napoléon III, in South Africa on June 1, 1879. The chauvinism ("Glory to your death as a Frenchman!") and the royalism ("I pronounce my ultimate tribute / Before Louis Sixteenth") shown in this poem are far removed from the republican and socialist fervor of Verlaine's youth.

Prologue of "Long Ago" (pp. 178–81)

The "Prologue" of the section "Jadis" of the retrospective volume *Jadis et Naguère* [Long Ago and Yesterday] (1884) was initially meant to introduce a selection of poems written in prison in the journal *Le Progrès artistique* in 1881 (a project that failed). The "wicked band," "rudderless children," "little bits of despair," "bitter dreams" etc. thus refer to the poems composed before Verlaine's conversion, poems that he paradoxically disowns while introducing them with this palinodic prologue.

Prologue of "Yesterday" (pp. 180–81)
The "Prologue" of the second part of *Jadis et Naguère* allegedly introduces poems composed recently, but in fact written ten years earlier, in prison, in the summer of 1873, before the poet's conversion. These long poems, namely "Crimen amoris" [Crime of Love], "La Grâce" [Grace], "L'Impénitence finale" [Final Impenitence], "Don Juan pipé" [Don Juan Caught], and "Amoureuse du Diable" [In Love with the Devil] were described by Verlaine as "more or less diabolical stories."

In Praise of Laura and Petrarch (pp. 180–83)
The sonnet "In Praise of Laura and Petrarch," opening the section "Sonnets and other verses" in *Jadis et Naguère*, is really a sonnet in praise of the sonnet itself, which is apostrophized in the second quatrain. In fact, the form of the sonnet was not invented by Francesco Petrarca (1304–1374) in his famous *Canzoniere* [Songbook] inspired by his muse Laura, but by poets of the Sicilian School at the beginning of the thirteenth century. The mention of "Saint Peter of Verse" is an allusion to the architecture of St. Peter's Basilica in the Vatican, which is considered the matrix of all churches, just as the Italian sonnet is the matrix of all sonnets in other languages. Verlaine's sonnet is a hybrid of an Italian sonnet, composed of hendecasyllables (eleven-syllable lines), and a French sonnet with its traditional rhyme scheme ABBA ABBA CCD EDE (a scheme preserved in the English translation). The coined adjectives *edmondschéresque* and *francisquesarceyse* refer to the conservative literary critics Edmond Schérer (1815–1889) and Francisque Sarcey (1827–1899).

From *Amour* and Other Poems

About a Calderón Centenary (pp. 184–85)
Verlaine was a great admirer of the Spanish Golden Age playwright Pedro Calderón de la Barca (1600–1681) who, in this instance, serves his Catholic agenda. This sonnet, composed in May 1881, two hundred years after Calderón's death, was first published in the journal *Lutèce* in January 1886, and later included in the volume *Amour*, with a dedication to the French-Spanish poet José-Maria de Heredia (1842–1905).

To Victor Hugo, upon Sending Him "Sagesse" (pp. 184–87)
This sonnet, composed at the end of 1880, when Victor Hugo (1802–1885) was at the height of his literary glory in France, highlights the divergence between the secular republicanism of the great romantic poet ("I abhor, in your verse the Serpent I see there") and the strict Catholicism of the newly converted Verlaine ("I have changed"), whose collection *Sagesse* offers the first public account of his conversion. The last line recalls that Hugo had interceded on Verlaine's behalf while the latter was in prison, in July 1873. The sonnet was first published in the journal *Lutèce* in January 1886, less than a year after Hugo's death.

I have changed. As have you. But not the same way.   Victor Hugo recounts his evolu-
tion from the royalist Catholicism of his youth to his secular republicanism—an

opposite path to Verlaine's—in the poem "Écrit en 1846" [Written in 1846] of *Les Contemplations* (1856).

To Ernest Delahaye *(pp. 186–87)*

Ernest Delahaye (1853–1930), a friend of Rimbaud and Verlaine, wrote several biographical books on the two poets at the beginning of the twentieth century (see, for example, *Verlaine* [Paris: Messein, 1919] and *Rimbaud* [Paris: Messein, 1923]). Verlaine's sonnet, dated February 1882, was first published in the journal *Paris moderne* on March 25, 1883.

Languor *(pp. 188–89)*

This sonnet, published in the journal *Le Chat noir* on May 26, 1883, and included the following year in the volume *Jadis et Naguère*, was immediately considered one of the emblems of the Decadent movement in literature at the end of the nineteenth century—a movement in which Verlaine was himself considered the leading poet. The first line of the sonnet refers to the decline of the Roman Empire in the fourth and fifth centuries.

While I sit composing indifferent acrostics An *acrostic* is a poem "in which the initial letters of the lines, taken in order, spell a word, phrase, or sentence" (*OED*).

Ah! it's all drunk! is your laughing, Bathyllus, now done? Bathyllus was a comic pantomime active in Rome in the first century BC.

Parsifal *(pp. 188–91)*

This sonnet is inspired by Richard Wagner's opera *Parsifal*, first performed at Bayreuth on July 26, 1882. Wagner's music drama was itself inspired by the German epic poem *Parzival* (1200–10) by Wolfram von Eschenbach, and the French romance *Perceval, ou le Conte du Graal* (1180 or 1190), which recounts the Arthurian legend of the knight Parsifal in his quest for the Holy Grail, subsequently identified with the vessel used to catch the blood flowing from Christ's wounds. Verlaine's sonnet was commissioned by Édouard Dujardin for his *Revue wagnérienne*, where it was first published on January 8, 1886.

Ballade—About Two Elms That He Had *(pp. 190–93)*

A French *ballade* is a medieval fixed-form poem, going back to the thirteenth century, consisting of three stanzas of eight lines rhyming ABABBCBC, followed by a four-line envoy rhyming BCBC, with the repetition of the final line (called "refrain") in each stanza and the envoy. Verlaine's "Ballade" was first published in *La Petite Revue de littérature et d'art* in January 1888.

Sappho Ballade *(pp. 192–95)*

The "Ballade Sappho" (on the versification of the French *ballade*, see previous note) is characterized by an ambiguity between heterosexual and homosexual desire, which also distinguishes the legendary character of Sappho (see note to *Les Amies*, p. 341). In the manuscript, the poem is titled "Ballade horrifique, dédiée à S. M. M. M." [Horrific ballade, dedicated to S. M. M. M.] (the initials of Verlaine's wife, Sophie Marie Mathilde Mauté), obviously with an insulting intent. The ballade was published in the journal *Le Décadent* on September 18, 1886, and included in the volume *Parallèlement*.

Guitar   *(pp. 194–97)*

In this poem Verlaine recounts his own version of the break-up with his wife, Mathilde, who would relate a completely different version of this same event in her posthumous memoirs (Mme Paul Verlaine [Mathilde Mauté], *Mémoires de ma vie* [Paris: Flammarion, 1935], 253–54). The name "Pierre Duchatelet" refers to Verlaine's autobiographical short story published in the volume *Louise Leclercq* (Paris: Vanier, 1886). The poem "Guitare" was first published in the journal *La Plume* on June 1, 1889, and included the same year in the collection *Parallèlement*.

Cheerful and Glad   *(pp. 196–97)*

The title "Gais et contents" quotes the first line of the popular song "En revenant de la revue" [Returning from the parade], composed on the occasion of the restoration of the military parade on Bastille Day, July 14, 1886, by the nationalist General Georges Boulanger (1837–1891). Verlaine was himself an occasional supporter of Boulanger, nicknamed "Général Revanche," to whom the fourth stanza alludes. The poem, dated July 1887 in the manuscript, was first published in *La Revue littéraire septentrionale* in March–July 1888.

To Emmanuel Chabrier   *(pp. 198–99)*

Verlaine had known the composer Emmanuel Chabrier (1841–1894) since 1864. They had collaborated on a few projects, including the unfinished opera buffa *Vaucochard et fils Ier*, written with Lucien Viotti (the "dear friend of mine" mentioned in the first line), and possibly on Chabrier's opera *L'Étoile* [The star] (1877). Verlaine's sonnet was composed in June 1887 (a year after his mother's death), and first published in the journal *Les Chroniques* in August 1887.

To Fernand Langlois   *(pp. 198–203)*

The painter Fernand Langlois was one of Verlaine's closest friends, and a next-door patient at Broussais Hospital in Paris, where the poet was housed numerous times in the last ten years of his life (see the autobiographical volume *Mes Hôpitaux* [My Hospitals]), and where he composed, in extreme poverty, this poem in September 1887. The Latin biblical phrase *Surrexit hodie* means "He is risen today," *de profundis* means "from the depths," and *fiat!* means "so be it!"

Lucien Létinois   *(pp. 202–7)*

The series of twenty-five poems that constitute the section dedicated to Lucien Létinois (1860–1883) in the collection *Amour* recounts the filial—and probably romantic—relationship between Verlaine and his pupil Lucien, from 1877 to the sudden death of the latter on April 7, 1883, which deeply and lastingly affected the poet.
   Of him as my son, since the actual fruit of my loins Verlaine's son Georges. In the following lines, the poet evokes his flight with Rimbaud in July 1872 (see Part 2).
   Enough to send Ms. Oh-So-Proper into a spin! "Madame Prudhomme," here translated as "Ms. Oh-So-Proper," scornfully designates Verlaine's wife, Mathilde.

To Georges Verlaine   *(pp. 208–9)*

With this final poem of *Amour*, dated May 1887, Verlaine dedicates the entire collection to his son Georges, born in 1871, from whom he had been separated since 1872 (see note to "Hard to Believe, but True," p. 351). The first stanza alludes to Ovid's *Tristia*

[Sorrows] (I.i): "*Parve—nec invideo—sine me, liber, ibis in urbem, / ei mihi, quo domino non licet ire tuo!*" [Little book, you will go without me—and I grudge it not—to the city, whither alas your master is not allowed to go!] (Ovid, *Tristia; Ex Ponto*, trans. A. L. Wheeler, Loeb Classical Library [Cambridge, MA: Harvard University Press, 1924], 3).

From *Bonheur*

Christmas—To Rodolphe Salis (pp. 210–13)

Verlaine spent the fall and winter of 1889 at Broussais Hospital. Rodolphe Salis (1851–1897) was the creator and director of the cabaret and journal *Le Chat noir* [The Black Cat], where this sonnet was first published on December 21, 1889, before being included, without title, dedication, and date, in the Catholic collection *Bonheur* [Happiness] in 1891.

XX (pp. 212–17)

This triptych of sonnets, composed at Broussais Hospital in 1889, depicts a hypothetical and reasonable union with a woman, signaled by the conditional tense of the verbs ("I would like . . ."), which highlights the unreality, or even the impossibility for the poet of such a union. The last stanza of the third sonnet expresses the poet's nostalgic longing for his marriage to Mathilde twenty years earlier, which was announced by the prenuptial book *La Bonne Chanson* (see Part 1).

XXXIII (pp. 216–19)

This poem, concluding the collection *Bonheur*, was composed by Verlaine at Broussais Hospital in February 1888.

From *Liturgies intimes*

To Charles Baudelaire (pp. 220–21)

This palinodic sonnet, in which Verlaine compares his own fate as sinful poet to that of Baudelaire, serves as a prologue to the Catholic collection *Liturgies intimes*, published in 1892, although the sonnet was probably composed in 1890 and initially intended for *Dédicaces*.

Kings (pp. 220–23)

The Epiphany, or Three Kings' Day, is observed on January 6, the twelfth day after Christmas.

Gloria in excelsis (pp. 224–27)

In this poem Verlaine rephrases the early Christian hymn *Gloria in excelsis Deo* [Glory to God in the highest].

Credo (pp. 226–27)

In this poem Verlaine provides his personal, Catholic version of the Apostles' Creed, the statement of faith used in the Christian liturgy.

Agnus Dei (pp. 228–29)

The *Agnus Dei* [Lamb of God] designates Jesus Christ in the Christian liturgy, based on the exclamation of John the Baptist: "Behold the Lamb of God who takes away the sin of the world" (John 1:29). The four stanzas of Verlaine's poem present an iconic pyramidal (trinitarian) structure: a nine-syllable line, followed by an eleven-syllable line, followed by a thirteen-syllable line. The poem was first published in the journal *Le Zig-zag* on September 13, 1885.

PART 4: THE LAST YEARS

From *Dédicaces*

To Jules Tellier   *(pp. 234–35)*

Jules Tellier (1863–1889), a poet and literary critic, was a close friend of Verlaine, who dedicated several poems to him, including "Parsifal" (see Part 3, pp. 188–91). This sonnet was first published, under the title "Les Amis" [Friends], in the journal *La Cravache* on January 5, 1889. Tellier died a few months after the sonnet was composed, on May 26, 1889, at the age of twenty-six.

To Villiers de L'Isle-Adam   *(pp. 234–37)*

This sonnet, published in the journal *Le Chat noir* on September 7, 1889, is a eulogistic poem dedicated to Auguste de Villiers de L'Isle-Adam (1838–1889), the author of the early science fiction novel *L'Éve future* [Tomorrow's Eve] and of *Contes cruels* [Cruel Tales], who died on August 18, 1889. Verlaine had known Villiers, whom he included in the second edition of his critical anthology *Les Poètes maudits* [The Accursed Poets] (1888), since 1863.

To Germain Nouveau   *(pp. 236–37)*

Verlaine met the poet and friend of Rimbaud Germain Nouveau (1851–1920) in London in the summer of 1875. This sonnet was first published in the journal *Le Chat noir* on August 24, 1889.

To François Coppée   *(pp. 238–39)*

In this sonnet dedicated to his former friend and rival, the poet François Coppée (1842–1908), Verlaine recalls the Parnassian years (see Part 1), when Coppée composed his first collection *Le Reliquaire* [The Reliquary] and Verlaine his *Poèmes saturniens*, both published in 1866 by Alphonse Lemerre, located in the Passage Choiseul in Paris. In the meantime, Coppée achieved great literary success, crowned by his election to the French Academy in 1884, while Verlaine's poetry barely attained critical and public recognition. Only in the twentieth century were their literary fates reversed, so much so that Coppée's poetry is almost forgotten today. This sonnet, first published in the journal *Le Chat noir* on December 7, is one of the few poems in which Verlaine confesses his alcoholism, fueled by absinthe, the "green drink."

To Stéphane Mallarmé   *(pp. 238–41)*

Verlaine and Stéphane Mallarmé (1842–1898) were considered the two leading figures of the French poetic avant-garde from the mid-1880s, the first as the master of the Decadent movement and the second as the master of Symbolism. In the last stanza, the phrase "*vers les n . . .*" [toward the n . . .] is a pun on the name of Verlaine, the phrase "*mal armé*" [poorly armed] a pun on the name of Mallarmé, and "Prud'homme" [valiant man, member of a tribunal] a pun on the name of the Parnassian poet Sully Prudhomme (1839–1902), member of the French Academy and first winner of the Nobel Prize in Literature in 1901. Contrary to Sully Prudhomme, Verlaine and Mallarmé did not achieve critical and popular success in the course of their lives. This sonnet was first published in the journal *Le Chat noir* on December 14, 1889.

Fernand L'Anglois *(pp. 240–41)*
On Fernand L'Anglois, or Langlois, see note (p. 356) on "To Fernand Langlois."

On a Bust of Me—For My Friend Niederhausern *(pp. 240–43)*
The first maquette of the bust of Verlaine carved by the Swiss sculptor Auguste de Niederhäusern, also known as Rodo (1863–1913), was exhibited at the first Salon of the Rose+Croix in 1892, and later served as a model for the *Monument to Paul Verlaine* erected at the Luxembourg Garden in Paris in 1911. This sonnet is included in the second edition of *Dédicaces* (1894).

To G... *(pp. 242–43)*
This poem was first published in the journal *La Plume* on May 15, 1893, and included the following year in the second edition of *Dédicaces*. We do not know the identity of G . . .

Birthday—To William Rothenstein *(pp. 244–45)*
The English painter William Rothenstein (1872–1945) visited Verlaine at Broussais Hospital in the summer of 1893, drawing a few portraits of the sick poet, and invited him to give several lectures in England in November and December of the same year. Back in Paris, Rothenstein visited Verlaine again on March 30, 1894, the day of his fiftieth birthday, when the poem was allegedly composed. The reference to the "Blue Bird" is not clear (it seems to be an inside joke), although the most famous *Blue Bird* is a 1697 fairy tale by Marie-Catherine d'Aulnoy, in which King Charming is turned into a Blue Bird that sings his love for Princess Florine. The poem was first published in the London journal *The New Review* in May 1894 and included in the second edition of *Dédicaces*.

To Edmond Lepelletier *(pp. 246–47)*
The writer and journalist Edmond Lepelletier (1846–1913) was a longtime friend of Verlaine's and one of his first biographers (*Paul Verlaine: sa vie, son œuvre* [Paris: Mercure de France, 1907]). This sonnet is included in the second edition of *Dédicaces*.

From *Chansons pour Elle* *(pp. 248–59)*
The twenty-five erotic poems that constitute the collection *Chansons pour Elle* [Songs for Her], published in December 1891, were in part inspired by Philomène Boudin, with whom Verlaine had a liaison from the late 1880s, and for the most part by the former dancer Eugénie Krantz, who was the poet's lover until his death on January 8, 1896, or even by both women, as poem XIII "Are you blonde or brunette? . . ." suggests. In addition, an autograph manuscript of poem XVIII ("If it's all right with you . . .") is dedicated to Rachilde (pseud. of Marguerite Eymery, 1860–1953), the author of the novel *Monsieur Vénus* (1884), who had hosted Verlaine in her apartment in Paris in November 1886.

From *Odes en son honneur* and *Élégies* *(pp. 261–69)*

If the collection *Chansons pour Elle* is mostly inspired by Eugénie Krantz, the nineteen erotic poems of *Odes en son honneur* and the twelve chaste poems of *Élégies* are dominated by the figure of Philomène Boudin, who, in the meantime, had won back Verlaine. The two volumes, composed between 1891 and 1892, were published simultaneously in May 1893.

XIII *(pp. 264–65)*

She clearly outdoes in that way the late Tragaldabas Tragaldabas is the eponymous character of the buffo drama by Auguste Vacquerie, premiered in 1848. In the second actof the drama, Tragaldabas complains: "I am sick. / I repent having eaten salad."

XIX *(pp. 266–67)*

"Love me or not, I'm in love with you!" The line "Si tu ne m'aimes pas, je t'aime" is a quotation from the famous "Habanera" in the first act of Georges Bizet's opera *Carmen* (1875).

Elegies IV *(pp. 268–69)*

An *elegy* is a poem of lamentation.

From *Dans les limbes* *(pp. 270–79)*

The seventeen poems of *Dans les limbes* [In Limbo], published in July 1894, were composed at Broussais Hospital (the "limbo") between December 1892 and January 1893, and inspired by Philomène Boudin, who came regularly to visit her sick lover. The *limbo* is "a region supposed to exist on the border of Hell as the abode of the just who died before Christ's coming, and of unbaptized infants" (*OED*).

IX *(pp. 272–73)*

Honest Iagos, go on your way. Iago is the intriguing villain of Shakespeare's tragedy of *Othello* (1603–4).

X *(pp. 272–75)*

"Life is out there, quiet and simple." Quotation from Verlaine's own poem "The sky is, above the rooftop . . ." (see Part 3, p. 149).

XIII *(pp. 276–79)*

(The Good Song.) See Part 1, p. 65.

And he runs from the realm of the dead. This stanza paraphrases Victor Hugo's "La Chanson de Sophocle à Salamine" [The song of Sophocles at Salamis] in the second series of *La Légende des siècles* (1877).

In England (1893)

Memory of November 19, 1893 (Dieppe–Newhaven) *(pp. 280–83)*

Verlaine traveled to England for the last time in November and December 1893, to give lectures in London, Oxford, and Manchester, at the invitation of several young English writers, clergymen, and artists, including Arthur Symons, Ernest Dowson, Theodore

C. London, and William Rothenstein. The woman ("my queen") whom Verlaine left in France is Philomène Boudin, to whom he had promised to come back rich, or even to marry her. The poem was published in the journal *La Revue blanche* in April 1894 and included in the first volume of *Œuvres posthumes* [Posthumous Works] in 1903.

Paul Verlaine's Lecture at Barnard's Inn (pp. 282–85)

Barnard's Inn in the neighborhood of Holborn in London, where Verlaine gave his lecture on contemporary French poetry (see "Conférence sur les poètes contemporains" in *Œuvres posthumes*, II, 381–90), is a former Inn of Chancery (a "place of residence and study for students and apprentices of law" [*OED*]) dating back to the thirteenth century. The quotation in the fifth stanza "Bien dire et bien faire" [Say-well and do-well] is a French transposition of Cato the Elder's definition of the orator: "*Vir bonus dicendi peritus*" [a good man, skilled in speaking]. Verlaine's poem was published in the London journal *The Athenæum* on May 12, 1894 and not included in any volume during the poet's life.

Oxford (pp. 284–87)

Verlaine gave the same lecture on contemporary French poetry (see previous note) in Oxford on November 23, 1893. The poem was published, with illustrations, in *The Pall Mall Magazine* in May 1894, and not included in any volume during Verlaine's life.

Memory of Manchester—To Theodore C. London (pp. 286–89)

Verlaine gave the same lecture on contemporary French poetry (see previous note) in Manchester on December 1, 1893. Theodore C. London was a young clergyman who was particularly enthusiastic about Verlaine's talk. Salford is an industrial city adjacent to Manchester. The poem was first published in the journal *La Plume* on February 15, 1894, and included the same year in the second edition of *Dédicaces*.

Than of that other oh! so intellectual place   The "intellectual place" refers to Oxford, where Verlaine had spoken a week earlier, on November 23.

Their French guest Verlaine as the author of Esther   The author of the tragedy of *Esther* (1689) is the French playwright Jean Racine (1639–1699).

From *Épigrammes* (pp. 290–97)

The collection *Épigrammes* [Epigrams], published in December 1894, was mostly composed during the first half of the year. In it Verlaine playfully revisits the poetic principles of his youth, in particular the Parnassian poetry of *Poèmes saturniens* and *Fêtes galantes* (see Part 1), prior to the autobiographical vein of his later collections. An *epigram* is "a short poem ending in a witty or ingenious turn of thought" (*OED*).

III—To Edmond de Goncourt (pp. 290–91)

This poem is a tribute to *japonisme*, the vogue of Japanese art in France at the end of the nineteenth century, which the novelist and art critic Edmond de Goncourt (1822–1896) contributed to fuel, notably with his monograph on Utamaro and eighteenth-century Japanese art, published in 1891. The last line of the poem contains seventeen syllables, as opposed to the regular eleven-syllable lines of the rest: a way for Verlaine to mock the emergence of free verse in French poetry at the end of the century, which he vehemently opposed.

For his arms chose a swan instead of a rat   The French classical playwright Jean Racine did indeed remove the rat from the coat of arms of his family (*rat-cygne*) to keep only the swan (*cygne*).

VII—To Francis Poictevin   (pp. 290–93)

Francis Poictevin (1854–1904) was a French Symbolist writer. The contrast between the "flute," as a symbol of melody and lyric poetry, and the "horn" or "trumpet," as symbols of monotony and epic poetry, is recurrent in Verlaine's works (see, for example, "Art of poetry," Part 3, p. 153).

XI—To François Coppée   (pp. 292–93)

On François Coppée, see multiple notes above, especially on the other "To François Coppée" in Part 4. The "city" referred to in this poem is Arras, in the north of France, where the military engineer Sébastien Le Prestre de Vauban (1633–1707) had constructed fortifications during the reign of Louis XIV.

XVI.vii—Birth of Venus (Botticelli)   (pp. 294–95)

This poem is a literary description, an *ekphrasis*, of the painting *The Birth of Venus* by Sandro Botticelli (1445–1510).

XXII—To Sully Prudhomme   (pp. 296–97)

On Sully Prudhomme, see note on "To Stéphane Mallarmé," p. 358. In this poem Verlaine distances himself from the vogues of Arthur Schopenhauer's (1788–1860) pessimistic philosophy and Henrik Ibsen's (1828–1906) naturalist drama in France at the end of the nineteenth century.

XXVIII—On a Copy of The Flowers of Evil (*First Edition*)   (pp. 296–97)

The first edition of Charles Baudelaire's collection of verse *Les Fleurs du Mal*, published in 1857, was censored in part soon after its publication because of the alleged obscenity of six of its poems. The French writer Donatien Alphonse François de Sade (1740–1814) is famous for the sexual violence (whence the word *sadism*) of his novels and essays.

From *Invectives*

Academic Portrait   (pp. 298–99)

The subject of this "academic portrait," which was never published in the course of Verlaine's life, but included in the posthumous—and polemical—collection *Invectives* in 1896, is the Parnassian poet Leconte de Lisle (1818–1894), whose name (which is in fact his real family name) is revealed in the author's note that quotes the first act of Molière's comedy *L'École des femmes* [The School for Wives, 1662]. During the Parnassian years, Verlaine considered himself a disciple of Leconte de Lisle (see Part 1), but the two poets came to hate each other, for personal as well as political reasons, following the Paris Commune in 1871, which Verlaine supported and Leconte de Lisle vigorously opposed. The poem was certainly written after 1886, the year of Leconte de Lisle's election to the French Academy (whence the title of the poem).

Which would put Vadius and Trissotin to shame.   Vadius and Trissotin are two pedantic characters in Molière's comedy *Les Femmes savantes* [The Learnèd Ladies, 1672].

Sonnet for Weeping *(pp. 300–301)*

The identity of this judge is unknown, as is the date of composition of the sonnet. It may be that the name of the judge (which Verlaine *proves* he did not forget) is actually the same as the title of the sonnet: *larmoyer* [weeping]. In fact, a certain M. Larmoyer was appointed judge of the canton of Attigny, in the Ardennes, in April 1879, where Verlaine was living, in Rethel from October 1878 to July 1879, and in Juniville from March 1880 to the beginning of 1882.

Grievances *(pp. 300–303)*

This poem was most likely composed in 1894, when Verlaine was fifty years old.

To F.-A. Cazals *(pp. 302–5)*

The illustrator and writer Frédéric-Auguste Cazals (1865–1941) was one of Verlaine's closest friends until the poet's death in 1896. Verlaine had almost died of a leg infection at Broussais Hospital in June 1893, when this poem was composed. Several drawings by Cazals of Verlaine at the hospital are reproduced in *Les Derniers Jours de Paul Verlaine*. The poem was first published in the journal *La Plume* on August 1, 1893.

Those codgers and their hussies. Verlaine is probably referring to Eugénie Krantz, who was having an affair with a hairdresser while he was "dying" at the hospital.

Eating Song *(pp. 304–7)*

This poem, first published in *La Revue blanche* on November 1, 1895, was composed by Verlaine a few months before passing away, while he was living in poverty with Eugénie Krantz. Nicolas Marguery (1834–1910) was a chef famous for the "sole Marguery." The poet Maurice Bouchor (1855–1929) and the literary critic Francisque Sarcey (1827–1899) were two well-known vegetarians. The last line of the poem alludes to the episode of Polyphemus's cave in Book 9 of Homer's *Odyssey*, where Odysseus and his companions find an abundance of provisions, taking the risk of being eaten themselves by the Cyclops.

Dream and *Awakening* *(pp. 306–11)*

The diptych of poems "Rêve" [Dream] and "Réveil" [Awakening] was published in *La Revue blanche* on November 1, 1895.

From *Chair* [Flesh] **(pp. 312–17)**

The collection *Chair*, published, with a frontispiece by Félicien Rops, in February 1896, a few weeks after Verlaine's death, includes mildly erotic poems, composed between 1893 and 1895, and inspired by the poet's last lovers: Eugénie Krantz, Philomène Boudin, and a few others.

Other *(pp. 312–13)*

Your eyes, my river Styx or my stream of Lignon The Styx is, in Greek mythology, one of the rivers of the underworld, and therefore a symbol of death; the Lignon is a river in France, popularized by Honoré d'Urfé's pastoral novel *L'Astrée* (1607–27), and therefore a symbol of love.

Poem Without Rhymes (pp. 314–15)

This title finds its explanation in the fact that, according to the traditional rules of French prosody, it is not acceptable for a word in the singular (e.g., *argent*) to rhyme with a word in the plural (e.g., *gens*), nor for a word that ends with a mute syllable (e.g., *effraye*) to rhyme with a voiced syllable (e.g., *jamais*).

Fog!—For Madame *** (pp. 316–17)

We do not know who this Madame *** is, nor when the poem was composed. The last time Verlaine went to London was in December 1893.

From *Biblio-sonnets* (pp. 318–21)

The *Biblio-sonnets* and their subjects were commissioned in 1895 by Pierre Dauze, the director of the *Revue biblio-iconographique*, where five of these bibliophilic poems were published from October to December 1895. The complete series was supposed to add up to twenty-four sonnets, but Verlaine had written only thirteen at the time of his death. The unfinished collection was published in 1913.

I—Bibliophilia (pp. 318–19)

But resurrection comes as no surprise to the wise. "La Mort ne surprend point le sage"
    [Death is no surprise to the wise] is the first line of the fable "La Mort et le Mou-
    rant" [Death and the Dying] (1678) by Jean de La Fontaine.

VIII—The Quais (pp. 320–21)

Since the seventeenth century, the "quais de la Seine" [the banks of the Seine] in Paris have been the traditional location of the *bouquinistes*, booksellers of used and rare books.

Late Uncollected Poems

To Ph . . . (pp. 322–25)

"Ph . . ." refers to Philomène Boudin, who was visiting Verlaine at Broussais Hospital after he almost died in June 1893. The poem is indeed dated "July 6, 1893" in one manuscript (the likely date), and "End of August 1893, Broussais Hospital" in another.

Paris (pp. 324–27)

This poetic tribute to Paris, published in *La Revue blanche* in October 1893, was probably written at Broussais Hospital, where Verlaine had almost died of a leg infection in the summer. In this connection, the last two stanzas appear autobiographical. As for the "Fille" [Daughter or Girl] of Paris in the fourth stanza, she is most likely a *fille de joie* [a prostitute].

Final Hope (pp. 326–27)

This sonnet was probably inspired by Philomène Boudin. It was first published in the journal *Fin de Siècle* on May 1, 1893, and intended to be part of a projected volume of verse, *Le Livre posthume* [The Posthumous Book], which was never completed.

Impression of Spring (pp. 328–29)

This poem was published in the journal *La Plume* on June 15, 1893.

For the New Year—To Saint-Georges de Bouhélier   *(pp. 330–31)*
Saint-Georges de Bouhélier (1876–1947), the son of Verlaine's friend Edmond Lepelletier
(see note on p. 359), was a poet and a playwright. Verlaine's poem was published in
January 1895 in *Le Rêve et l'Idée*, a journal co-founded by Bouhélier the previous year.

Lament   *(pp. 330–33)*
The undated poem *"Lamento"* ["Lament" in Italian] was published in the journal *La
Revue blanche* in April 1896, three months after Verlaine's death, with this note by the
author: "Unpublished poem that will remain so." The anonymous fourteenth-century
"old poet" to whom Verlaine attributes the epigraph is unknown. The closest possible
source that we were able to find is the "Air de M. de Mollier" in *Recueil des plus beaux
vers mis en chant* (Paris: Ballard, 1667), the first line of which reads: "Pleurez, pleurez,
mes yeux, Amarante n'est plus" [Cry, cry, my eyes, Amaranth is no longer].

Dead!   *(pp. 332–35)*
This is possibly the last poem written by Verlaine, a few days before his death on Jan-
uary 8, 1896. In this testamentary poem, published the same month in the socialist
journal *La Revue rouge*, Verlaine regains the insurrectionary inspiration of his youth,
as exemplified in the 1867 poem "Les Vaincus" (see note to "The Vanquished," p. 344),
which he abandoned in the following years.

Selected Bibliography

ORIGINAL EDITIONS AND ENGLISH TRANSLATIONS

Poetry

Verlaine, Paul. *Poëmes saturniens*. Paris: Lemerre, 1867 [1866]. Translated by Karl Kirchwey as *Poems Under Saturn* (Princeton: Princeton University Press, 2011).

———. *Les Amies: Sonnets, par le licencié Pablo de Herlagnez*. Ségovie [Bruxelles: Poulet-Malassis], 1868.

———. *Fêtes galantes*. Paris: Lemerre, 1869.

———. *La Bonne Chanson*. Paris: Lemerre, 1870.

———. *Romances sans paroles*. Sens: L'Hermitte, 1874. Translated by Donald Revel as *Songs Without Words* (Richmond, CA: Omnidawn, 2013).

———. *Sagesse*. Paris: Société générale de librairie catholique, 1881 [1880].

———. *Jadis et Naguère: Poésies*. Paris: Vanier, 1884.

———. *Amour*. Paris: Vanier, 1888.

———. *Parallèlement*. Paris: Vanier, 1889.

———. *Dédicaces*. Paris: Vanier, 1890 [2nd ed. 1894].

———. *Femmes*. Imprimé sous le manteau et ne se vend nulle part [Bruxelles: Kistemaeckers], 1890. Translated by Alistair Elliot as *Femmes/Hombres, Women/Men* (London: Anvil Press, 1979).

———. *Bonheur*. Paris: Vanier, 1891.

———. *Chansons pour Elle*. Paris: Vanier, 1891.

———. *Liturgies intimes*. Paris: Bibliothèque du Saint-Graal, 1892.

———. *Élégies*. Paris: Vanier, 1893.

———. *Odes en son honneur*. Paris: Vanier, 1893.

———. *Dans les limbes*. Paris: Vanier, 1894.

———. *Épigrammes*. Paris: Bibliothèque artistique et littéraire, 1894.

———. *Chair*. Paris: Bibliothèque artistique et littéraire, 1896.

———. *Invectives*. Paris: Vanier, 1896.

———. *Œuvres posthumes*. 2nd ed. 2 vols. Paris: Messein, 1911–13.

———. *Hombres (hommes)*. Imprimé sous le manteau et ne se vend nulle part [Paris: Messein, 1903/1904]. Translated by Alistair Elliot as *Femmes/Hombres, Women/Men* (London: Anvil Press, 1979).

———. *Biblio-sonnets*. Paris: Floury, 1913.

Prose

Verlaine, Paul. *Les Poètes maudits: Tristan Corbière, Arthur Rimbaud, Stéphane Mallarmé*. Paris: Vanier, 1884 [2nd ed. 1888]. Translated by Chase Madar as *The Cursed Poets* (Copenhagen and Los Angeles: Green Integer, 2003).

——. *Les Mémoires d'un veuf*. Paris: Vanier, 1886.

——. *Louise Leclercq*. Paris: Vanier, 1886.

——. *Mes Hôpitaux*. Paris: Vanier, 1891.

——. *Mes Prisons*. Paris: Vanier, 1893.

——. *Quinze Jours en Hollande*. Paris: Vanier, [1893].

——. *Confessions: Notes autobiographiques*. Paris: Fin de siècle, 1895. Translated by Karl Kirchwey as *Confessions of a Poet* (New York: Philosophical Library, 1950).

MODERN EDITIONS

Verlaine, Paul. *Œuvres complètes*. Edited by Henry de Bouillane de Lacoste and Jacques Borel. 2 vols. Paris: Club du meilleur livre, 1959–60.

——. *Œuvres poétiques complètes*. Edited by Yves-Gérard Le Dantec and Jacques Borel. Paris: Gallimard, 1962 and 1989.

——. *Œuvres poétiques*. Edited by Jacques Robichez. Paris: Classiques Garnier, 1969.

——. *Œuvres en prose complètes*. Edited by Jacques Borel. Paris: Gallimard, 1972.

——. *Œuvres poétiques complètes*. Edited by Yves-Alain Favre. Paris: Laffont, 1992.

Rimbaud, Arthur, and Paul Verlaine. *Un concert d'enfers: Vies et poésies*. Edited by Solenn Dupas, Yann Frémy, and Henri Scepi. Paris: Gallimard, 2017.

TRANSLATED EDITIONS

Verlaine, Paul. *Poems*. Translated by Gertrude Hall Brownell. Chicago: Stone & Kimball, 1895.

——. *Forty Poems*. Translated by Roland Gant and Claude Apcher. London: Falcon Press, 1948.

——. *Selected Poems*. Translated by Carlyle Ferren MacIntyre. Berkeley: University of California Press, 1948.

——. *Poems*. Translated by Jacques Leclercq. Mount Vernon, NY: Peter Pauper Press, 1961.

——. *Selected Verse*. Translated by Doris-Jeanne Gourévitch. Waltham, MA: Blaisdell Publishing, 1970.

——. *Selected Poems*. Translated by Joanna Richardson. Harmondsworth: Penguin, 1974.

——. *One Hundred and One Poems by Paul Verlaine: A Bilingual Edition*. Translated by Norman R. Shapiro. Chicago: University of Chicago Press, 1999.

——. *Selected Poems*. Translated by Martin Sorrell. Oxford: Oxford University Press, 1999.

CORRESPONDENCE

Verlaine, Paul. *Correspondance de Paul Verlaine: Publiée sur les manuscrits originaux*. Edited by Adolphe Van Bever. 3 vols. Paris: Messein, 1922–29 (Geneva: Slatkine Reprint, 1983).

——. *Correspondance générale*. Edited by Michael Pakenham. Vol. 1 (1857–85). Paris: Fayard, 2005.

——. *Lettres inédites de Verlaine à Cazals*. Edited by Georges Zayed. Geneva: Droz, 1957.

———. *Lettres inédites à Charles Morice*. Edited by Georges Zayed. Geneva: Droz, 1964.

———. *Lettres inédites à divers correspondants*. Edited by Georges Zayed. Geneva: Droz, 1976.

BIOGRAPHIES

Buisine, Alain. *Paul Verlaine: Histoire d'un corps*. Paris: Tallandier, 1995.

Cazals, Frédéric-Auguste, and Gustave Le Rouge. *Les Derniers Jours de Paul Verlaine*. Paris: Mercure de France, 1911.

Delahaye, Ernest. *Verlaine*. Paris: Messein, 1919.

Lepelletier, Edmond. *Paul Verlaine: His Life, His Work*. Translated by Elsie M. Lang. New York: AMS Press, 1970 [1907].

Petitfils, Pierre. *Verlaine*. Paris: Julliard, 1981.

Richardson, Joanna. *Verlaine*. London: Weidenfeld & Nicolson, 1971.

Verlaine, Madame Paul (Mathilde Mauté). *Mémoires de ma vie*. Seyssel: Champ Vallon, 1992 [1935].

ICONOGRAPHY

Cazals, Frédéric-Auguste. *Paul Verlaine: Ses portraits*. Paris: Bibliothèque de l'Association, 1896.

Petitfils, Pierre. *Album Verlaine: Iconographie*. Paris: Gallimard, 1981.

Ruchon, François. *Verlaine: Documents iconographiques*. Geneva: Cailler, 1947.

DISCOGRAPHY

Debussy, Claude. *L'Intégrale des mélodies*. Jean-Louis Haguenauer, pianist, and various vocalists. Ligia, 2014. 4 compact discs.

Ensemble Kadéléis. *Verlaine ou la musique des mots*. Various composers. Cypres, 2009. Compact disc.

Fauré, Gabriel. *Mélodies, La Bonne Chanson*. Gérard Souzay, vocalist, and various performers. Diapason, 1955 and 2009. Compact disc.

Greaves, John. *Verlaine*. Cristal, 2008–2012. 2 compact discs.

Jaroussky, Philippe, vocalist. *Green: Mélodies françaises sur des poèmes de Verlaine*. Parlophone, 2015. Compact disc.

Lapointe, Jean-François, vocalist, and Louise-Andrée Baril, pianist. *Verlaine: Symbolist Poets and the French Melodie*. Various composers. Analekta, 2007. Compact disc.

Maderna, Bruno, composer. *Liriche su Verlaine*. Stradivarius, 2002. Compact disc.

Poètes et Chansons: Paul Verlaine. Various singers. EPM, 2003. Compact disc.

Sampson, Carolyn, vocalist, and Joseph Middleton, pianist. *A Verlaine Songbook*. Various composers. BIS, 2016. Compact disc.

CRITICAL STUDIES

Adam, Antoine. *The Art of Paul Verlaine*. 1953. English ed. Translated by Carl Morse. New York: New York University Press, 1963.

Bernadet, Arnaud. *"En sourdine, à ma manière": Poétique de Verlaine*. Paris: Classiques Garnier, 2014.

Bivort, Olivier, ed. *Verlaine*. Paris: Presses de l'Université de Paris-Sorbonne, 1997.

Chadwick, Charles. *Verlaine*. London: Athlone Press, 1973.

Cuénot, Claude. *Le Style de Paul Verlaine*. 2 vols. Paris: Centre de Documentation Universitaire, 1963.

Dufetel, Jacques, ed. *Spiritualité verlainienne: Actes du colloque international de Metz (novembre 1996)*. Paris: Klincksieck, 1997.

Dupas, Solenn. *Poétique du second Verlaine: Un art du déconcertement entre continuité et renouvellement*. Paris: Classiques Garnier, 2010.

English, Alan. *Verlaine, poète de l'indécidable: Étude de la versification verlainienne*. Amsterdam: Rodopi, 2005.

Guyaux, André, ed. *Les Premiers Recueils de Verlaine: Poèmes saturniens, Fêtes galantes, Romances sans paroles*. Paris: Presses de l'Université de Paris-Sorbonne, 2008.

Huret, Jules. *Enquête sur l'évolution littéraire*. Paris: Charpentier, 1891.

Morice, Charles. *Paul Verlaine*. Paris: Vanier, 1888.

Nadal, Octave. *Paul Verlaine*. Paris: Mercure de France, 1961.

Porter, Laurence M. *The Crisis of French Symbolism*. Ithaca: Cornell University Press, 1990.

Richard, Jean-Pierre. "Fadeur de Verlaine." In *Poésie et profondeur*, 163–85. Paris: Seuil, 1955.

Richer, Jean. *Paul Verlaine*. 1953. Paris: Seghers, 1975.

Robic, Myriam. *"Femmes damnées": Saphisme et poésie (1846–1889)*. Paris: Classiques Garnier, 2012.

Schultz, Gretchen. *Sapphic Fathers: Discourses of Same-Sex Desire from Nineteenth-Century France*. Toronto: University of Toronto Press, 2015.

Stephan, Philip. *Paul Verlaine and the Decadence, 1882–90*. Manchester: Manchester University Press, 1975.

Symons, Arthur. *The Symbolist Movement in Literature*. 1899. Edited with an introduction by Matthew Creasy. Manchester: Carcanet Press, 2014.

Underwood, Vernon Philip. *Verlaine et l'Angleterre*. Paris: Nizet, 1956.

Whidden, Seth. *Leaving Parnassus: The Lyric Subject in Verlaine and Rimbaud*. Amsterdam: Rodopi, 2007.

———. *La Poésie jubilatoire: Rimbaud, Verlaine et l'Album zutique*. Paris: Classiques Garnier, 2010.

White, Ruth L. *Verlaine et les musiciens: Avec une chronologie des mises en musique et un essai de répertoire biographique des compositeurs*. Paris: Minard, 1992.

Zayed, Georges. *La Formation littéraire de Verlaine*. 1962. Paris: Nizet, 1970.

Zimmermann, Éléonore M. *Magies de Verlaine: Étude de l'évolution poétique de Paul Verlaine*. Paris: Corti, 1967.

JOURNALS

Europe 545–46 (September–October 1974) and 936 (April 2007).

Revue Verlaine 1–10 (1993–2007) and 11–16 (2013–18).

Index of Titles and First Lines

Poem titles are in roman type; first lines and titles of collections are in italics.

Index of Proper Nouns

Ostend (Belgium), 122–23
Ovid (Publius Ovidius Naso), 356–57, 208–9
Oxford, xxiv, 284–85, 286–87, 360, 361

Pablo (Pablo de Herlangnez; pseud. of Verlaine), xxii, 3, 340, 341
Paris
    fin-de-siècle bohemianism, xiv
    Franco-Prussian War and Paris Commune, xi, xxiii, 344, 362
    mentioned, 196–97, 294–95
    in poems: cited as place of composition, 170–71, 244–45; contrasted with
      London, 134–35, 210–11, 284–87, 316–17; other poems about Paris, 324–27, 353,
      364; other poems set in Paris, 80–81, 308–9, 320–21, 327
    Verlaine's life in, xxii–xxiii, 3, 85, 346, 348, 356, 359
Paros, 32, 33, 341
Parsifal, 188, 189, 355, 358
Pauvre Lelian (Poor Lelian; pseud. of Verlaine), ix, xiii, xxiv
Persia, 12, 13
Petits-Carmes (prison), 139, 142–43
Petrarch (Francesco Petrarca)
    and Laura, 180, 181, 354
Pillars of Hercules (colonnes d'Hercule), 184–85
Poe, Edgar Allan, 340
Poictevin, Francis, 290–93, 362
Polyphemus (Polyphème), 306–7, 363
Poor Lelian (Pauvre Lelian; pseud. of Verlaine), ix, xiii, xxiv
Poton de Xaintrailles, Jean (John Poton), 8–9, 338
Poton, John (Jean Poton de Xaintrailles), 8–9, 338

Quixote, Don (Don Quichotte), 6–7, 338

Rachilde (pseud. of Mme Alfred Vallette, *née* Marguerite Eymery), 359
Racine, Jean, 290–91, 361, 362
    "the author of *Esther*," 286–87, 361
Rall, Georges, 349
Revard, 130–31, 350
Ricard, Louis-Xavier de, xi, xxii, 3, 344
Rimbaud, Arthur, viii, ix, xxiii, *82*
    epigraph by, 98–99
    in commentary on individual poems, 339, 346–50, 358
    films based on relationship of Verlaine and Rimbaud, xii
    named as subject of poems, 132–35
    his place in Verlaine's life and work, xi, xii, xv, xvi, 85, 139
Risi, Nelo, xii
Rodo (Auguste de Niederhausern), 240–41, 359
Roland, 62–63